An
Edible Journey

Exploring the islands'
fine food, farms and vineyards

Elizabeth Levinson

TouchWood Editions
VICTORIA • VANCOUVER

TouchWood Editions Ltd.
Victoria, BC, Canada
This book is distributed by The Heritage Group, #108-17665 66A Avenue, Surrey,
BC, Canada, V3S 2A7.

Front-cover painting: Grant Leier. Cover design: Pat McCallum. Book design and
layout: Retta Moorman. Production assistant: Katherine Hale.
This book is set in AGaramond.

TouchWood Editions acknowledges the financial support for its publishing program
from The Canada Council for the Arts, the Government of Canada through the Book
Publishing Industry Development Program (BPIDP) and the Province of British Columbia through the British Columbia Arts Council.

Printed and bound in Canada by Friesens, Altona, Manitoba.

National Library of Canada Cataloguing in Publication Data

Levinson, Elizabeth, 1958-
  An edible journey: exploring the islands' fine food, farms and
vineyards / Elizabeth Levinson.

  ISBN 1-894898-05-2

  1. Natural foods — British Columbia — Vancouver Island. 2. Natural
foods — British Columbia — Gulf Islands. 3. Natural food
restaurants — British Columbia — Vancouver Island — Guidebooks. 4. Natural
food restaurants — British Columbia — Gulf Islands — Guidebooks. 5.
Vancouver Island (B.C.) — Guidebooks. 6. Gulf Islands
(B.C.) — Guidebooks. 7. Cookery (Natural foods). I. Title.
TX369.L47 2003   641.3'02'097112   C2003-910998-4

The Canada Council | Le Conseil des Arts
for the Arts | du Canada

BRITISH
COLUMBIA
ARTS COUNCIL
Supported by the Province of British Columbia

DEDICATION

For my mother, June, who has lovingly shown me the secret of happiness: family and food, preferably together.

ACKNOWLEDGMENTS

Heartfelt thanks to my publisher, Pat Touchie, for supporting this stimulating project; to my editor, Marlyn Horsdal, for her good-natured advice throughout; to Sinclair Philip and Michael Ableman, for their thought-provoking forewords; to Grant Leier, for so vividly reflecting the flavour of my journey in his painting; to Duddy, for reading the manuscript; to Chris Tyrrell, for his expert recipe testing; to Phyllis Remple, for baking up a storm; to Deirdre Campbell of Tartan PR, for taking such an interest; to Tom Ryan of Tourism BC, for sharing his love of Vancouver Island; to Frances Sidhe and Daniel Beiles, for making wine tasting less mysterious and more fun; to Daniela Kraemer, Leyland Cecco and those members of the Macey-Brown-Levinson clan who cheerfully accompanied me on parts of this incredible edible journey.

Special thanks to my dear husband, Clive, for his true love and support.

CAVEAT

The selection of "best food experiences" was made by the author. It was not intended to be exhaustive; rather, the choices were made to introduce readers to a wide variety of organic farmers, artisan food producers and restaurants on Vancouver Island and the Gulf Islands. No financial support was solicited or accepted from any person or business included herein. Every attempt has been made to ensure the accuracy of all data presented. The author and publisher assume no legal responsibility for the completeness or accuracy of the contents of this book.

Contents

Recipes

Starters

Entrées

Forewords

As a farmer and lover of land and good food I always dreamed that there was some place that embodied the right combination of climate, soils and attitudes to establish an agrarian renaissance. California once held that promise for me, with its ideal growing climate, deep alluvial soils and history of progressive thinkers. But after 30 years of farming there, watching populations surge and rich farmland give way to real estate development, I decided to look elsewhere.

While I resigned myself to the fact that apples and pears would have to replace avocados and citrus, Vancouver Island and the Gulf Islands have many of the elements for the revival I have been seeking. Far from ideal, with much of the food still being imported from the mainland, and full-time farmers only a fraction of the population, this region does have a committed group of growers, chefs and activists working hard to create a shift in how fresh food is being valued, produced, prepared and consumed. I have always believed that real change will only take place when media, whether books or articles or film, replace the harangue, the constant drumbeat of all that is wrong, with positive and hopeful models, and focus on placing those models firmly into people's minds.

Elizabeth's book does just that. It introduces us to those individuals who are forging a new way, and provides us with an intimate view into their lives, their land, their kitchens and the food that they so lovingly bring to our tables. It is a celebration of the best culinary experiences that the islands have to offer, without the stuffiness and exclusivity that is too often associated with such works.

This book also accomplishes something else very important to me. It recognizes and honours farmers as highly skilled artisans and craftsmen, and places them at the heart and the centre of a movement that is restoring food as the gathering point for our families and our communities.

Michael Ableman, Madrona Valley Farm, Saltspring Island

If healthy, ethical and pleasurable dining is your focus, Elizabeth Levinson will help make your food purchases and restaurant choices easy and fun. Her book will provide you with a delicious introduction to the foods of our region and also with insights into the worthy people behind this wonderful food. *An Edible Journey* is an excellent guide to one of the world's promising, emerging culinary regions — Vancouver Island and the Canadian Gulf Islands.

The world needs to discover regions such as ours to understand the promise of bringing pleasure and health back into our daily lives. The planet is riddled with increasingly unsafe, unhealthy and unsatisfying food choices and is polluted with globalist food litter that is destroying our health, our environment and the lives of many of the workers who provide us with this so-called food. Through this book, Elizabeth nourishes us all with delicious, satisfying and soul-enriching alternatives. She offers us what the International Slow Food Movement promotes: eco-gastronomic pleasure. She is clearly an authority on the best places to unearth ingredients, where to buy the best regional wines and where to dine on our remote island reaches. Her recommendations are always underscored by an altruistic and generous desire to share ethically produced and natural foods with her readers and friends. Elizabeth has become an important advocate for the natural and organic food movement and is familiar with all of our best markets, food suppliers and restaurants, from the most elegant temples of gastronomy to cafés steeped in counterculture.

If we frequent the restaurants, markets and suppliers recommended in this book, we support small local producers as well as the preservation of agricultural land. Eating local foods will bring more good foods to our area. Through the descriptions of the restaurants in this book and her introductions to their local suppliers, Elizabeth gives us a chance to reconnect with the foods we eat and familiarize ourselves with the stewards of our land and sea.

Over the last few years, *Travel & Leisure* magazine has portrayed Vancouver Island as one of the best tourist destinations in the world. As this book attests, our restaurants, foods and wines have improved tremendously over the past 25 years and Elizabeth's book will lead you to the doorstep of many of our culinary treasures.

Sinclair Philip, Sooke Harbour House, Sooke

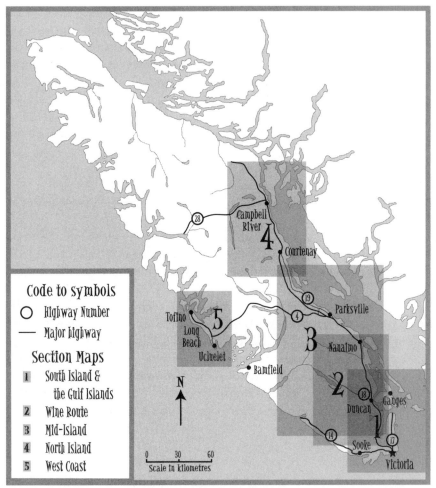

Code to symbols

○ Highway Number

— Major highway

Section Maps

1 South Island &
  the Gulf Islands

2 Wine Route

3 Mid-Island

4 North Island

5 West Coast

N

0   30   60
Scale in kilometres

Campbell River
Courtenay
Parksville
Nanaimo
Ganges
Duncan
Sooke
Victoria
Tofino
Long Beach
Ucluelet
Bamfield

Travel and Leisure *magazine has rated Vancouver Island "the best island destination in the continental United States and Canada" two years in a row. Its natural beauty and outdoor activities offer the ideal backdrop to gastronomic journeys. This book is roughly divided into four geographic areas plus a wine route, but the possibilities for combining them or mapping one's own trail are endless.*

Introduction

The pursuit of good food has become a keen interest (some say an obsession) for me. Even before the food scares — salmonella, E. coli, BSE, listeria et al. — I always wanted to know where my food came from and how fresh it was. Once I began connecting with the local growers and food producers, I discovered an exciting community of people who felt the same way. And these people aren't just consumers like me; they are putting their livelihoods on the line by producing food devotedly, simply and in small batches, to ensure quality and freshness.

The increased availability of fresh, local produce, humanely reared meat, and lovingly crafted cheeses, breads and specialty foods fulfills my desires to eat well and support the local economy. My inherent need to "share" has prompted me to write it all down.

Sorry to ruin anyone's fast-food lunch, but in this globalized society, eating has become a sad state of "garbage in." The homogenization of our city centres, where restaurants and shops are standardized across the country, and the rapid construction of big-box grocery stores, their shelves lined with highly processed, GMO foods, has made it a challenge to find or fix a decent, nutritious meal. Or has it?

From a formaggi in Victoria to a home-based chocolate factory on Denman Island, from an oyster grower in Clayoquot Sound to a beekeeper in Sooke, from a balsamic vinegary in the Cowichan Valley to a nutritional-greens farm in Nanoose Bay and a chèvre maker high in the hills near Ucluelet, come the unmistakable signs of hope. Good food does exist on Vancouver Island. One just has to know where to find it.

Determined to find the best food experiences and then pass them along, I packed up the car in Victoria and headed north. Taking my notebook and only my appetite and curiosity to recommend me, I went in search of the growers, the small, artisanal food producers, the innovative chefs and the grocers who are making a difference and offering an alternative. When I returned home, I couldn't write fast enough to tell you about it.

This is a book about the doors that opened, the food I ate and, most importantly, the passionate people I met — the independents — who are putting fresh, local, seasonal eating back in the centre of our plates.

So, journey forth, and do as I do: enjoy every mouthful.

Elizabeth Levinson, Victoria

South Island

Galiano
Island

Mayne
Island

Ganges

18

Saltspring
Island

Pender
Islands

Saturna
Island

Swartz
Bay

1

17

Sooke

14

Metchosin

Victoria

N

& the Gulf Islands

hen I write about the southern part of Vancouver Island, I am writing about my home turf, which is essentially the urban side of the plate. I emphasize "urban" because my hunting-and-gathering habits in the city are different than they are, say, on a remote Gulf Island. I eat out more, do "the coffee thing" more and do less farmgate shopping because the fresh, local produce is so readily available at my grocer, farmers' market or delivered to my door.

The journey ahead is one I take in whole or in part every week. In Victoria, I make a regular run for just-baked organic whole spelt and fig-anise bread from Wild Fire Bakery's wood-fired oven, French baguette and challah on Fridays from the great Alberto Pozzolo at the Italian Bakery, French and Quebecois cheeses from Ottavio's Gastronomia, Cowichan Bay Farm's pastured chicken from Slater's First Class Meats, and 100% organic produce and all other necessities from Planet Organic.

In summer, I live for the original, organic Moss Street Market on Saturdays and the Metchosin Farmers' Market on Sundays, and make a special trip to Sooke for Tugwell Creek honey, Outer Coast seaweed and a visit with Josephine Hill at her Ragley Farm market. When it's a particularly grey day, I love receiving inspirational produce boxes from Share Organics, or grazing the farmgates on the Saanich Peninsula's country roads. When I've had enough of my own cooking, it's a treat to eat at Brasserie L'École or Zambri's or enjoy the luxury of a take-out from Common Sense Café or a meal cooked in my home by personal chef Jenny Cameron.

Coffee is the pause that restores me: at Chinatown's Cucina where owner Mirjana brews a restorative stovetop black java that I sip from a bowl, at Caffé Fantastico for a straight-up Americano or, when food is also important, at Pure Vanilla Bakery and Café, where coffee and a sweet bun are often all it takes to restore authorial purpose.

VICTORIA

Brasserie L'École

Sean Brennan is contemplating a future herb-and-vegetable garden in the perfect little enclave behind Brasserie L'École. He knows how well suited the hideaway is, because he had a garden there in a previous incarnation: the brasserie moved in where The Met Bistro used to be and Sean did a stint in its kitchen. "Over there," he shows me, "were the tomatoes, and all along the wall here — thyme and arugula." His plan is to restore the garden, both for its bounty and as a backdrop to al fresco dining. It has such appeal, tucked in behind this historic building in Victoria's Chinatown, that I encourage him, and look forward to booking a table in summer.

I've come to the back door because I want to see behind the scenes of what quickly became, and then, more importantly, stayed, the hottest table in town. In 2002, Brasserie L'École was named the third-best new restaurant in Canada by *enRoute* magazine. The magazine's reviewer, Amy Rosen, was looking for restaurants that "had to blow your mind." Says Marc Morrison, Sean's partner and the restaurant's congenial host and sommelier: "The rating came out on a Thursday and after that, every night has been a Saturday night." Sean calls it a "happy craziness."

How do they handle the popularity? As far as I can see, like pros. Both have impressive restaurant backgrounds (Sean cooked at Vancouver's Raintree and Victoria's Vin Santo, among others, before making his mark in Cafe Brio's

"A meal without wine is like a day without sunshine."

— on the chalkboard at Brasserie L'École

3

Chef and co-owner Sean Brennan strikes a pose in the kitchen at Brasserie L'École.

kitchen in Victoria; Marc is a bike racer turned sommelier who also worked at Vin Santo and Cafe Brio). Front and back of house are well choreographed and the wait staff are first class (including the exemplary and charming Lesley Vaughan, formerly of Sooke Harbour House). There's a warm conviviality in the restaurant, and table-hopping is often part of the scene. It's not unusual to go on a Saturday night and have everyone in the place know each other. Even a special cheese and dessert-wine tasting I attended mid-week turned out to be one of the year's best parties.

Like any mind-blowing restaurant, it all starts in the kitchen. Sean has just received a delivery from Josephine Hill of Sooke's Ragley Farm: large buckets of

mesclun — surprisingly prolific for the middle of January — hearty mustard greens and arugula. Earlier, oysters arrived from Cortes Island — large, meaty Stellers Bay oysters and the small, sweet Kusshi variety — and FAS Seafood dropped off sides of high-end sablefish that were processed at sea ("to retain the natural oils," Sean tells me).

I welcome a tour of the walk-in, one of the most immaculate I've ever

seen (the word is local health inspectors show trainees around the place so they can see what restaurant kitchens should look like).

There are inviting stacks of cheese, an increasingly popular course here. Sean buys his cheese from Andrew Moyer

at Ottavio's Gastronomia every Friday. Andrew often calls excitedly during the week to tell him about "something you have to try." The brasserie serves

Rabbit Braised with Picholine Olives

SEAN BRENNAN, BRASSERIE L'ÉCOLE

Serves 9. Mother developed her taste for rabbit during the war when little else was available. Rabbit's mild gaminess takes on a deep Mediterranean flavour in Sean's recipe, which Mother says is the best she's eaten.

2	rabbits, cut into 9 pieces total	2
3	onions, diced	3
5	large tomatoes, seeded, peeled and diced	5
1	small bunch of sage	1
1	small branch of fresh rosemary, chopped	1
5	cloves garlic, crushed	5
1 1/2 c	picholine olives*	360 ml
2	bay leaves	2
3	tbsp flour	45 ml
1 btl	dry white wine	1 btl
	salt and pepper	
	olive oil	

Season the rabbit pieces and brown well in olive oil over medium-high heat. This will need to be done in batches. Remove the rabbit to a plate. In the same pan, add the onions and garlic and cook until translucent. Add the tomatoes, herbs and olives and cook for two minutes. Sprinkle the flour over and stir for three to five minutes to cook the flour. Add the wine, stir to combine, scraping the bottom of the pan to dissolve the brown bits. Add the rabbit pieces, cover and braise in 300°F oven until very tender — 1 1/2 to 2 hours. Season to taste and serve over noodles.
OPTION: add cooked white beans such as Great White Northerns to the sauce.
*Provençal green olives

pasteurized and unpasteurized cheeses from France, Quebec and Saltspring Island. Sean is keen that people order their cheese course before the meal to ensure proper serving temperature, and eventually hopes to have a temperature-controlled display case on the floor. It's all about making sure patrons have the best possible culinary experience.

While Sean begins to prepare a pistou broth with soisson beans for the lamb shank, I ask him about the evening's menu. It is, as always, small and select, with the emphasis on fresh, local ingredients cooked to order. What could be finer? There are half a dozen starters from soupe à l'oignon gratinée to Sean's famous confit of duck leg with braised red cabbage. One of my favourites is the endive salad with mustard wine dressing, apple slices and freshly picked hazelnuts. Mains include the hugely popular steak frites, mountain trout with bacon, chard, dried tomato and mushroom-potato hash and albacore tuna with onion marmalade and Jerusalem artichokes. It's always a stellar night when my husband finds braised buffalo or ostrich on the menu.

Sommelier and co-owner Marc Morrison enjoys a rare relaxed moment at Brasserie L'École on Government Street in Victoria.

As former president of the Island Chefs Collaborative, which promotes local food, Sean says if he can't get something locally, he seriously considers the food miles attached to other products. He's concerned about depletion of the wild fish stocks, and clearly does his bit supporting the local growers and food producers. As he says himself: "I am very comfortable with what I do."

Sean says they want to be known for having "a very good, well-rounded restaurant, with the focus on the food, service, wine and ambiance." I say he can stop wanting; he and Marc have all that and more. Still, Sean tells me he "will like the place even more in a few years. It will look better when it's worn in a bit."

Cafe Brio

If dinner could appropriately begin with dessert, I'd always start with the white chocolate angel food cake topped with mascarpone sorbet, and drizzled with cranberry confit at Cafe Brio. It fits every requirement I have for a great dessert: it's light and therefore couldn't possibly be caloric; it looks pretty on the plate without being fussy; it isn't overly sweet; it includes fruit which must make it healthy; and it fulfils a nostalgic yearning for things my mother used to make as special treats. For this ultimate food-from-the-fifties, I am forever grateful to the café's pastry chef, Adam Jessop.

Of course, there are many more aspects to Cafe Brio that have firmly entrenched it in Victoria's restaurant scene. The dining room itself, with its deep Tuscan yellow and rust walls laden with paintings, its surprisingly wide choice of seating — from private booths, deuces in cosy corners, and see-and-be-seen tables for 12 in the centre of the room to relaxed dining on the patio — and its friendly, central bar, is immediately warm and inviting. The place is

Enjoy the outside patio or enter the warm Tuscan atmosphere of Cafe Brio.

7

family-run, which gives a comfortable sense of dining in someone's home; and, though centrally located, it has an appealing hideaway quality. The food of chef Chris Dignan is the other important part of the equation; it can be sublime.

One is warmly greeted at the door with a "Hi, you two" by owner and bon vivant Greg Hays, a man whose food-industry experience spans the Herald Street Caffé and The Marina restaurant. He and his partner, Sylvia Marcolini, have hit on a concept that combines her Italian heritage with the couple's interest in featuring quality, local ingredients, and the rest, as they say, is a happy culinary history.

I was invited into the kitchen just as service began for dinner one evening. My first impression was how large a space it is, and how well organized (I was reminded of my visit to Rob Feenie's kitchen at Lumière in Vancouver, surely the smallest in the world for so renowned a restaurant). Former chef Sean Brennan (now co-owner of Brasserie L'École) set the high standards, always using the freshest ingredients.

Seasonality is the byword. The restaurant has continued to use many of the suppliers that Sean brought on board, in particular Tina Fraser, who arranges specific plantings for the menus. Lyle Young's pastured chickens and ducks, David Wood's cheese and Hilary Abbott's eggs are some of the many local products used.

The orders start coming in, and the kitchen heats up. Greg is showing a lively party of 12 from Washington's R.H. Phillips winery to their table. Their wines had been delivered earlier in the week to suit a special menu that will be served this evening to some local wine experts. The bartender is uncorking the first bottle of vino. I retreat to a private booth with my friend and fellow foodie, Christopher.

We order tasting menus, which, at Cafe Brio, are well-priced and pleasingly short (the vegetarian tasting menu and chef's tasting menu feature three courses each). As a bit of a wine neophyte, I choose the wine flight because I know each pairing has been carefully selected by an expert (in this case, Greg). My vegetarian menu includes a delicious truffled celeriac soup with red wine and beet glaze; refreshing blood orange and fennel salad; and butternut squash gnocchi in a deeply satisfying porcini mushroom broth served with Swiss chard and a generous dollop of ricotta. Christopher, who goes for the chef's menu, kindly shares bites of his smoked sablefish-potato ravioli with lemon and thyme cream and wild onion oil; chicken liver and apple terrine with raisin toast and cider jelly (a perfect match of flavours and textures); and seared venison loin with caramelized onion and goat cheese tart, grilled radicchio and balsamic reduction.

We eat heartily, we drink wisely and we discuss our common interests for nearly four hours: food and family. When we come near the end of the meal, one of the wine experts at the next table sends over two British Columbia dessert wines for our edification: Pinot Noir Ice Wine 2000 from Domaine Combret and

Enter with an appetite — Cafe Brio.

Heritage Hearth from Alderlea Vineyards. And finally, we can order the angel food, which really takes the cake for me.

Caffé Fantastico

There's no question that Caffé Fantastico is the serious coffee drinkers' haunt. Most people come alone, order their "regular," then sit and savour it. As I sit on the faded couch sipping my own regular (an Americano half-caf) I am always impressed by the characters who drop in, some on foot, some with wheels. One day, a very fancy Mercedes stopped at the curb. A gentleman stepped out, ordered up, and stepped back inside the car. Lovely little vignette there. Who was he? Does he come every day at the same time?

Caffé Fantastico, where the organic coffee is just that — fantastico!

Owner Ryan Taylor is as discreet as they come about his customers, but open and highly knowledgeable about his product. Having spent ten years in the business, he insists on the best beans, properly roasted and freshly prepared for each order.

When he was 18, Ryan set up Espresso Fantastico, a coffee cart in Victoria's Inner Harbour, and began turning locals on to good coffee one cup at a time. A graduate of Camosun College's Entrepreneur Development Program, he has always enjoyed coffee and knew how hard it was to get a good cup locally. He settled into his current "off-Broadway" location five years ago, never advertised and serious coffee drinkers somehow instantly found him. In the last year, he has been joined by Kristy, who tells me: "I was originally a customer who thought Ryan was making those hearts on top of lattes just for me!" In fact, he was making special hearts on her lattes, and the couple married a year ago.

For Ryan, quality is the number-one factor in choosing coffee beans. He is firmly entrenched in the specialty-coffee niche, which represents just 10% of the coffee market (the other 90% is Nescafé, Folger's et al. — not to drop names). So, all the beans he considers are naturally high grade, shade grown and fairly traded. From that coffee niche, he wants the best. And, dealing with a seasonal commodity, he knows that crops will fluctuate, so he has to be very hands-on.

Ryan has a good broker, but he also travels to plantations himself and participates in cuppings (systematic tastings from small-grind samples of beans to evaluate the product). He is a member of the North American Roasters Guild, and subscribes to the recommendations of the international Cup of Excellence, the Brazilian competition that rates coffees and then sends its winners to auction. Ryan has bought a couple of the COE winners for Caffé Fantastico, and is now training to be a judge for that prestigious competition.

Ryan says he is very concerned about the workers on coffee plantations and advocates fair wages and working conditions. He says it's important that these workers, who take great pride in what they're producing, are well treated. He says: "The environment [of the plantations] must be of the best quality for both the coffee and the workers." He agrees with Cup of Excellence quality consultant George Howell, who says the competition is truly "the ladder out of anonymity" for the growers, and is pleased to see their efforts recognized and rewarded.

Caffé Fantastico offers freshly roasted, typically organic, specialty coffee, lovingly prepared by barista Derek Allen. Derek said he came to work at the café because he "had heard they were brewing coffee properly." Others who agree that Ryan and Kristy are getting it very right are the restaurants which serve their coffee: Zambri's, Sooke Harbour House, Wild Fire Bakery, Feys & Hobbs Catering Company, and The Mint and Black Coffee cafés.

Common Sense Café

It was fortuitous that my last interview for this book was at a fully organic, sunny Victoria café. It felt like this was meant to be, that my mission to raise awareness of the important connections between local growers and chefs had been accomplished on the plate before me.

The vegetarian lasagne, salad with beets, carrots and maple balsamic vinaigrette and glass of freshly squeezed grapefruit juice were testament to the possibility of linking organic field with restaurant feast. The restaurant's creators, Jocelyn Therrien and Lisa Pennington, are to be congratulated for getting it right from the start. As Lisa says, they set out to offer "simple, really healthy food," and organic was always part of the equation.

Lisa is an environmental activist who has worked for the Western Canada Wilderness Committee and Greenpeace. Ten years ago, she followed her tree-planting brother to Vancouver Island from Ontario. She inherited a love of cooking from her family that has always been "very festive about eating." Jocelyn worked with special-needs children at the YMCA, and, like Lisa, is pursuing a nutritionist certificate by correspondence through the Edison Institute. The two met through their mutual involvement in the local health-food industry.

They first opened a personal-cheffing business, under the name Common Sense Cookery, and prepared healthy meals for a range of people from busy single women to families, including those with special dietary needs. When their clients, Barbara and Tara Elson, opened the Genesis Centre, an oasis of holistic wellness practitioners in Victoria, they were invited to create an organic, vegetarian café. "It had been our dream to operate in a place like this," says Lisa. The café complements other businesses in the centre, which offer everything from far-infra-red sauna to body-work and metaphysical supplies.

I first dropped in to the Common Sense Café for lunch with caterer Liz Melling. We were immediately taken by the enthusiasm of Lisa and Jocelyn, and their willingness to share information about the food they make and where it comes from. Their goal is to use 100% local organics. Their suppliers include Silk Road Tea Company, Wild Fire Bakery, Caffé Fantastico, Son's

A restored home near Victoria's famous Antique Row houses the Common Sense Café, a respite of healthful eating in the Genesis Centre.

Milling and Health Foods and Lifestyle Markets. In season, their produce comes from Saanich Organics, a local, women-owned farming co-operative. In winter, when it's a bit more difficult to get organic veggies in small quantities, they order British Columbia-grown produce through ProOrganics.

"simple, really healthy food."

— Lisa Pennington, Common Sense Café

Common Sense offers a fresh set menu that includes a daily muffin, soup and entrée. After months of purusing voluminous menus, I am delighted not to be facing a burden of choice. And I'm impressed that I don't have to ask what's organic, because it all is! Lisa says she believes that "people feel the energy you put into what you cook for them," and I must say their energy, commitment to organics and tasty, attractive food make common sense to me.

Cucina

For me, the sun rises and sets on Victoria's tiniest restaurant, Cucina. Located in Chinatown's Dragon Alley, it's right in the city, yet away from the madding crowds; the menu demands nothing of me, i.e., you get what you get; the food is fresh-that-day and expertly prepared; and its dynamic owner lacks every pretense known in the restaurant business.

Mirjana is a hunter-gatherer after my own heart. She tells me that "walking and talking" enable her to familiarize herself with her surroundings, to seek out the best ingredients for her cooking and the freshest blooms for the single, elegant floral arrangement in her restaurant. "The more I walk and talk," she says, "the better gatherer I become." Being located in the heart of Chinatown gives her an endless supply of exotic fruits and vegetables to incorporate in her cooking.

On Valentine's Day, I dined with friends on roasted beet and yam cannelloni in a sauce of ginger, orange, Brie and cream, decorated with pomegranate seeds and red grapes; braised lamb shank finished with quince, shallots, fresh herbs and chocolate (the secret ingredient is out, Mirjana!) on polenta; and a true artist's rendering of chocolate paté with a flourish of cream and glimmer of gold leaf. At the end of that exquisite meal, Mirjana joined us to drink her strong, black stovetop coffee and talk of many things.

Mirjana is an interesting woman: the proud mother of two international, human-rights lawyers (Deborah-Miji works for the UN in Split, Croatia, and Elizabeth works in London); political activist (having lived through war and lost family to war, she often shares her views on Cucina's chalkboard);

The entry to Dragon Alley in Chinatown leads to Victoria's smallest restaurant, Cucina.

and famous cook (her Saltspring Island restaurant, Pomodoro, was widely praised in reviews from *Vancouver Magazine* to *Vanity Fair*). Her progression, from "starving artist" in London to restaurant owner in Victoria, has been filled with great experiences. When she was in London, friends suggested she become a personal chef in order to make ends meet. That turned into "a real upstairs, downstairs position" when Mirjana became the cook in a large household and was sent off to get her Cordon Bleu diploma in Marylebone Lane. "I was the only student who arrived on foot," she tells me. "Everyone else pulled up in Bentleys."

With her certification in hand, Mirjana came to Canada. Here, she decided to take a break from cooking, and became a gatherer of another sort. She worked in food, fashion and interior design styling for the advertising business. Three years later, Mirjana opened the 100-seat Pomodoro, which she operated for four years.

Her new venture, Cucina, finally feels like the right fit for Mirjana. A life-long proponent of fresh, organic food, she always chooses quality over quantity. Her mother told her: "You're not rich enough to buy cheap things," and she carries that

14

adage with her as she gathers superior ingredients for her cooking. Though her roots are in Mediterranean cuisine, Mirjana's style is decidedly fresh and innovative. She tells me: "Food, politics and life are all one thing," and I'm telling you: that heady combination sings on the plates at Cucina.

Fourways Meat Market

The location may be challenging, but Fourways Meat Market has operated from the same spot for 56 years and business is booming. Not only will you get used to turning in there, but you will also find somewhere to park and the best selection of non-medicated meat in the city.

My friend Chris Tyrrell remembers the place in the 1950s when his father worked there. There was sawdust on the floor and a big butcher block in the centre of the shop, and, he tells me: "I was always fascinated with the yards and yards of link sausage being made."

Today, even though new owner Dave Robinson has made a few changes, the look and feel of the shop haven't changed. He wanted to "keep the old style," and give customers the kind of meat he has always "taken home for his own family: free-run, non-medicated, vegetarian fed." He said when he took over the business seven years ago, he lost some customers who were motivated primarily by price, but in the last few years, he's mainly won them back on quality. "Business has grown 100% every year," he tells me, evidence that he's doing things right.

Fourways Meat Market, in its original location since 1947, has a prime selection of non-medicated meats.

Dave was a chef for 20 years, working at local spots like the Oak Bay Beach Hotel as well as in Barbados. He then worked six years as a butcher for Island View Freezers before jumping at the opportunity to have his own shop. His wife, Linda, was raised on a farm in Alberta and they are both adamant about selling humanely raised meat.

With no government-inspected abattoir on the island, he doesn't want to wait for local meat to be shipped to Vancouver and back for inspection. He buys poultry (600 chickens a week!) from the Fraser Valley, beef from Mennonite and Amish breeders in Alberta and Saskatchewan, and pork from Port Alberni. His customers come from all over Vancouver Island. Every two months, a group of people from the west coast comes down to pick up their order, and he has been known to ship hams and salami to Alaska.

A sign of quality assurance at Fourways Meat Market.

Italian Bakery

I really began to understand Italian Bakery owner Alberto Pozzolo when he told me about the cauliflower. He had picked it from his garden and taken it directly to the kitchen, washed and chopped it, leaves, long stalk and all, then steamed it. He set the steamed vegetable outside to cool somewhat, then drizzled olive oil, salt and pepper over it to make a salad. "It was amazing," he tells me. "So fresh and flavourful, even that stalk." Ah, I am thinking. Here is a baker who connects to the earth, to the terroir. He reaps what he grows, and his customers benefit from his own appreciation of food, plain and simple.

Plain and simple may not be the way to describe raspberry chantilly and lemon buttercream cakes, elaborate croquembouche and tiramisu, but these desserts represent only a small part of his, and his wife, Janet Cochrane's, business. The essential products are the breads, among them whole wheat, rye, Italian and French baguettes and the best challah in the world. And those buttery croissants, cinnamon buns and chocolate brioches that my ten-year-old shopping companions, Lizzie and Oliver, proclaim "five star." There is also a range of Italian pastries and cookies including cornetti and ovidi that were created by Alberto's grandfather in the family's original Pasticceria Piana in Turin in 1921.

I drop in on a Friday just as the baker, Marino, takes my challah order out of the oven. That massive oven was brought to Canada 25 years ago by Alberto's father, Michele, and it's still going strong. Alberto and I are kibitzing in the kitchen while his talented team makes magic around us: Jerry, originally from Prague, rolls out the dough for cinnamon buns, Leonardo from Albania is concentrating on chocolate biscotti and Caley, who has worked here for six years, since he was in high school, is gilding a dozen cakes with lemon buttercream. Alberto says he has "spent more time in this bakery than in any house I've lived in," and I can see he is at home here, working diligently to recreate the tastes of his childhood.

Alberto and Janet have recently expanded the business to include a food emporium, next door to the bakery. There, you can stop in for a quick espresso or gelato, or enjoy a leisurely lunch of pizza or pasta. Shopping for everything from housemade lasagne and sauces (pizzaiola, puttanesca and al pomodoro), local fireweed honey and chestnut purée to organic chicken, rabbit, turkey and young goat's meat and Italian cheeses is pure bliss. I can't wait for Alberto to start serving full American and Italian breakfasts as planned: to provide, as he suggests, an opportunity for people to slow down on the weekends and enjoy their food.

The venerable Italian Bakery.

Moss Street Market

Victoria's flagship organic farmers' market has just celebrated 11 years of success. Started by a small group of dedicated organic growers including Mary Alice Johnson of Sooke's ALM Organic Farm, the market offers produce from Umi Nami Farm, Eisenhawer Organic Produce, Rebecca Jehn's Organic Garden, as well as from noted growers Tina Fraser, R.J. Fisher and Robin Tunnicliffe.

Once the bell rings at 10 o'clock (every Saturday, May through October) you can shop for top produce, cheese, flowers, preserves, sausages and delicious, freshly made bite-sized doughnuts.

Victoria's first wholly organic farmers' market, the Moss Street Market.

Ottavio's Gastronomia

I'm not the only hapless hostess who has gone knocking on the door of Ottavio's to find out how to put a cheese tray together, nor the only day-tripper wanting some morsels to pack in the picnic hamper. What surprised me was how un-intimidating it was, how inspiringly and humorously things were explained, and particularly, how much fun I had with owners, Monica Pozzolo and Andrew Moyer.

They certainly have come by their business honestly. Monica's grandparents operated the family bakery in Turin in 1921. When her mother, Ubalda, married her father, Michele Pozzolo, they immigrated to Canada and opened the Italian Bakery, now run by Monica's brother, Alberto, and his wife, Janet Cochrane. Andrew was a soccer buddy of Alberto's. He and Monica opened Ottavio's in 1997 and so the legend continues.

While Ottavio's has many gastronomic offerings, from breads and baked goods to the city's finest range of olive oils, homemade lasagne, soups and pasta, Andrew and Monica have developed a stellar reputation as purveyors of quality cheese.

If you love cheese, it is a treat to spend time in the company of these passionate cheese merchants, to hear them wax poetic about a raw-milk Nectaire they found on a recent journey through the Loire Valley, and to share Andrew's excitement as he demonstrates his new double-handled cheese knife from Dehillerin, the famed cooks' supply shop in Paris. They describe an impromptu feast they had of cheese, half a chicken, some good bread and a bottle of wine from an incredible fromagerie at the side of the road. Ah, the glorious journeys one can have en route to great meals.

Monica and Andrew carry over 150 cheeses in their sunny Oak Bay gastronomia, with at least 100 in stock at any one time. They range from soft to hard types, made from cow's milk to sheep's milk, from French, Italian and Spanish origins to cheeses from Quebec, Ontario and a good showing from Saltspring Island. In short, they have the makings of many delectable cheese courses for both the uninitiated and the educated palate.

Andrew suggests I choose three or four cheeses for a basic cheese course; more, he warns, and "your taste buds might get lost." He says the key is to let texture and flavour guide my selection. As he speaks, he sets out on a thick piece of grey slate the following beauties: Vieille Mimolette, the aged, unpasteurized, hard cheese made from cow's milk, with a deep orange colour, smooth but

firm texture and mild taste; Blossom's Blue, the organic, pasteurized, cow's-milk blue cheese from Saltspring Island's Moonstruck Cheese Company, that is both sweet and has a bite similar to Stilton; St. Albray, the soft, pasteurized cow's-milk Brie that's made at the foot of the Pyrenees; and finally, Valençay, which he describes as "the stinky cheese that's not as scary as it looks." Legend has it that this ash-crusted, unpasteurized, goat's-milk cheese with its meltingly smooth white interior was first served to Napoleon when he returned to France

Monica Pozzolo and Andrew Moyer proudly display their baking at Ottavio's Gastronomia.

from heavy losses in Egypt. The cheese looked too much like
a pyramid for the general's liking, so he lopped off its top.
(By the way, that vegetable ash is a tasteless coating that's
simply used to age the cheese; historically, it kept the bugs off!)

The cheese tray that Andrew has composed seemingly without
effort sits before me as an evocative balance of texture, taste and colour.
Of course, there's nothing effortless about the years he and Monica have spent
researching, tasting and reading about cheese. Their depth of knowledge is a
great resource, not only to customers in the shop, but also to the many local
chefs who buy Ottavio cheeses for their restaurants' cheese courses:
Brasserie L'École, Zambri's, Matisse, Cafe Brio, Suze, The Canoe
Club and The Marina, to name a few.

Back to the tray in front of me: there is soft cheese, hard cheese,
blue cheese and the proverbial stinky or pungent cheese for your more
adventurous guests. The variations and permutations are, of course, endless.
You can focus on a country or a region, or all cow's-milk or all sheep's-milk
cheeses. Monica says her family's cheese course always includes one or two goat
or sheep cheeses for those who are lactose intolerant.

The choice of accompaniments is equally infinite. Andrew suggests steer-
ing clear of acidic condiments like olives at the end of a meal. He and Monica
agree that texture plays a big role in successful accompaniments: roasted or
caramelized hazelnuts or almonds, seasonal berries, dates or figs, a drizzle of
honey, a piece of quince paste or panneforte (that divine concoction of figs,
dates, raisins and toasted nuts), savoury biscotti (particularly good with creamy
chèvre), or sweet biscotti. Monica loves cheese with rusks or plain baguette.
Neither she nor Andrew favours flavoured cheeses or fancy breads, preferring to
let the cheese quality speak for itself.

Presentation is important too and also fun. Monica suggests that this is the
time to show off a special plate, piece of slate, cutting board or small straw mat
(she found hers in Chinatown). Choose a vibrantly coloured surface, as most
cheeses are light in colour. A plainer surface can be decorated with grape or
chestnut leaves or edible flowers before arranging the cheese.

The Personal Chef

You may already have a personal trainer, a house cleaner and someone to
walk your dog, but somehow the idea of a personal chef seems extravagant. If
anyone is going to change your mind, it will probably be Jenny Cameron and
her fresh, wholesome cooking.

Warm, talented and extremely capable in any kitchen, Jenny is also a pleasure to be around. When we met to discuss her profession in detail, it was over latte at her favourite Victoria coffee bar, Caffè Fantastico.

Ever curious, I want to know how she came to be a personal chef, food stylist (for magazines such as *Chatelaine*, *Sunset* and *Boulevard*) and cookbook author (she co-authored *Herbal Celebrations* with her mother, Noël Richardson). It started early, she tells me. By her late teens, she had written to La Varenne,

Spanish Potato Garlic Tortilla

JENNY CAMERON, PERSONAL CHEF

Serves 6 to 8. Jenny learned this dish from a Spanish friend, who made it "very garlicy and with lots of olive oil." Jenny's version uses less fat and more fresh herbs, which vary with the seasons. It's a brunch or lunch dish to make again and again, and serve with a big, mixed-greens salad.

3 or 4	medium potatoes, peeled and thinly sliced	3 or 4
3 or 4	cloves garlic, finely chopped	3 or 4
4	large brown eggs, beaten well in a large bowl	4
1 c	of mixed, coarsely chopped greens (arugula, mustard greens, spinach leaves, watercress, cilantro, basil — any combination is fine) olive oil salt and freshly ground pepper to taste	240 ml

Heat a large, well-seasoned, oven-proof frying pan over medium heat for 3-4 minutes. Add 2-3 tablespoons (30-45 ml) olive oil and the sliced potatoes. After about five minutes add the garlic, and sauté until crispy golden, a little soft, and almost cooked, about ten minutes. Transfer the potatoes to the bowl of eggs and combine well, add the mixed greens, and season. Transfer back to the frying pan, and evenly distribute the potatoes. Cook over medium-low heat until three-quarters cooked (the top should be a little wet). Transfer to the broiler, and briefly cook the top to a light golden brown. (Note: you may add grated cheese to the top before putting it under the broiler.) Transfer to a serving plate, golden side up, and cut into pie-like wedges. Serve warm, or room temperature for a picnic, brunch or supper. It is also delicious with aïoli or pesto on the side.

Personal Chef Jenny Cameron prepares her winning Spanish Potato Garlic Tortilla.

the famed cooking school, to seek a place in their program. They very kindly suggested that she first improve her French.

She decided "it would make more sense" to travel around Europe, cooking as she went, and then attend Dubrulle cooking school in Vancouver. She worked for catering companies in London, and then returned to Vancouver to teach in the Granville Island Market kitchen where she became known for her theme demonstrations: from northern Italian and Asian fusion to basics and grilling. After a stint at the Deep Cove Chalet near Victoria, she took the plunge into her own personal cheffing business.

Jenny has always enjoyed taking on the full responsibility of organizing and cooking for dinners and cocktail parties. Through word of mouth, she has built up a base of clients who rely on her good taste and efficiency, and she loves the challenge of putting it all together.

"There's no set arrangement," she tells me. Sometimes, her clients ask her to plan, shop, cook and serve a meal from soup to nuts. Other times, they may have something particular in mind to serve, or "the husband may have just caught a fish, and they want it incorporated into the menu."

As a hostess, I know that the best arrangement is when Jenny arrives around lunchtime with all the groceries and her Swiss Victoranox knives, and takes over the kitchen. By four o'clock, a helper arrives and by seven o'clock, they're passing around the hors d'oeuvres and the hostess can enjoy her own party.

Jenny says hosts and guests often ask questions about the food. More and more, people are interested in where she buys her ingredients. Fresh is most important to her, and she is a big supporter of local growers, particularly her family's legendary Ravenhill Herb Farm where she lives with her mother and stepfather (master gardener Andrew Yeoman), husband and young daughter. She cooks for all special dietary requests, from low-fat to vegan.

Jenny has cooked everything from an extravagant New Year's Eve dinner for two (vol-au-vents with shrimp, orange-tarragon soup, roast Cornish game hens and Pouilly-Fuissé), to an outdoor, waterfront luncheon for 200 (she had to have the host's kitchen re-wired to accommodate a second fridge that day) and just about everything in between. Generally, she likes to serve up to 60 for a drinks party; up to 40 for a buffet dinner; and up to 20 for a sit-down dinner.

Planet Organic

My mother and I shop at Planet Organic grocery store every Tuesday morning, and may it always be so. We love that when we walk in the door, the floor gleams, the 100% organic produce looks and feels like it has just been picked,

The fruits of the season are all organic at Planet Organic.

Maple Pecan Cookies

DIANE SHASKIN, PLANET ORGANIC

Makes 24 to 32 cookies, depending on desired size. Mother and I agree: this is the perfect cookie to serve with morning coffee.

1 c	pecans	240 ml
1 1/4 c	rolled oats	300 ml
1 c	whole-grain cake and pastry flour	240 ml
1 tsp	aluminum-free baking powder	5 ml
1/4 tsp	salt	1.2 ml
1/2 c	butter	120 ml
1/2 c	honey	120 ml
3 tbsp	maple syrup	45 ml
12-16	whole pecans, split in two (for cookie topping)	12-16

Preheat the oven to 350°F.

Pulverize the pecans in a blender or food processor. Blend the nuts until some of them are flour-like and some are still chunky. Reserve them. Then grind the oats until they are like flour. Combine the blended pecans, blended oats, pastry flour, baking powder and salt in a mixing bowl. In another bowl, cream the butter. When it's smooth, cream in the honey and maple syrup. Add the dry ingredients to the creamed butter mixture; it will be sticky. Spoon the cookie dough onto ungreased cookie sheets with a teaspoon (use a larger spoon if you prefer larger cookies). Use a small glass to press the cookies into uniform size. Use your fingers to form into a uniform shape. Place half a pecan atop each cookie. Bake 16 to 20 minutes. Let cool several minutes on the cookie sheet before removing to a cooling rack.

and the staff responds to our food queries with genuine interest and knowledge. We appreciate that the store supports many local growers and producers. We enjoy the homey atmosphere combined with good service and efficiency.

When I meet the new owner, Diane Shaskin, I can see why Planet Organic is in a galaxy all its own. Above all, she is passionate about food. She and her husband, Mark Craft, are experienced grocers. She is committed to — no, adamant about — stocking only organic produce. She listens to her customers.

In the early 1990s in Edmonton, Diane was a producer for CBC Television; Mark built energy-efficient homes. She knew she wanted to be involved with food, so, when a natural-foods store came up for sale, the couple bought

it. At that time, they had no experience with food or retail, but they welcomed the learning curve. Within a year, they had transformed the business. Terra Natural Food Market, with its distinctive Italian-country-grocer look and feel, took off running.

Says Diane: "Initially, we offered organic and some conventional foods, but quickly found that organics outsold conventional even when the price was higher." She made the decision early on to focus on organics. A slow-food proponent, she "doesn't like the idea of doing what's convenient." Even though "only 15% of the population shops at health-food stores," she is fully committed to her market.

Diane and Mark ran Terra for seven years, then looked at expansion options. With help from Darren Krissie, they went public. In the style of the U.S. company Wild Oats, which owns Capers, they are looking to "consolidate the health-food industry" in Canada. The company now owns four stores (Edmonton, Calgary, Lower Mainland and Victoria), with others planned. While the structure is corporate, the real mission, says Diane, is "to provide the highest quality organic and natural foods while emphasizing customer service, employee satisfaction and community involvement."

It's evident to me that supporting local food producers is the foundation of their business. I often run into growers I know dropping off their wares, and one day, I picked out my produce with *E.A.T. Magazine*'s Gary Hynes merrily snapping photos in the aisle. Planet Organic veggies were about to make the magazine's list of 50 Great Things to Eat in 2003.

Pure Vanilla Bakery and Café

The ultimate urban bakery café does exist this side of Manhattan — a perfect perch for the café-society set. Pure Vanilla opened on a busy Oak Bay thoroughfare with no time for fanfare. The staff has been too busy selling out of organic artisan bread by 11 o'clock in the morning and producing delectable lunch specials like the mushroom, arugula and asiago panini with lentil soup that I recently enjoyed.

What's not to love here? The interior is bright and welcoming ("the colour of golden pastry," my husband says); the staff, under the direction of front-end manager Shoshannah Buck, are young and blond and charming; the vast picture windows provide a continuous spectacle of people to watch and the food is pure ReBar, owner Audrey Alsterberg's long-time successful modern-food restaurant in Victoria's Bastion Square.

You can drop by for Torrefazione coffee and a sticky bun, have a full lunch or just stock up on six kinds of bread (from whole wheat-walnut to fig-anise), buns and beautiful cookies (chocolate cherry crackles, shortbread and white-iced fleurs-de-lys), fresh fruit galettes, the café's signature Chocolate Swoop cakes, tiramisu cakes and luscious lemon tarts that will take you back to the 1950s. I love that the cakes and tarts come in three sizes to fit every celebration.

Being the nosy foodie that I am, I went snooping behind the scenes where the gleaming new bakery was in full production: half a dozen female bakers were mixing, rolling, and lifting trays into ovens and Audrey was making a huge vat of pesto. Audrey has quietly fashioned a large segment of Victoria's modern, good-food culture: ReBar has had a loyal following for its wholesome, predominantly meat-free home cooking since 1988 and Cascadia, her flagship downtown bakery, has an equally appreciative audience for its hearty baking and café fare.

The neighbourhood coffee shop with an uptown feel — Pure Vanilla Bakery and Café.

Shady Creek Ice Cream Company

I'm with my young writer friend, Leyland Cecco, when we are greeted at the door to the Shady Creek Ice Cream Company by office manager Elisha Rothfels and asked to don hairnets. Having spent a great deal of time researching this book clad in some form of protective clothing, I give full marks to the island's small food producers for the care they take with regard to sanitation, often beyond the governmental Food Safe requirements. And, of course, I'm impressed by any 14-year-old guy who doesn't blink at wearing a net.

Inside, the rap music and inviting aroma of vanilla beans draws us to the cooking area where ice-cream maker Ben Lyon is busy slicing vanilla beans and dropping them into a large vat of simmering cream. He is preparing both the company's best-selling vanilla bean ice cream and the seasonal cinnamon ice cream.

Shady Creek Ice Cream began in 1997 when former police department employee (she looked after women prisoners) Christie Eng started experimenting in her kitchen. She missed the excellent ice cream she and her family had been able to buy in Calgary, and was looking to change careers. The company has evolved slowly, gradually taking over the first floor of the Engs' home in Saanich. Today, Christie produces over $100,000 worth of ice cream annually.

She is associated with the Social Ventures Network, an international organization of socially responsible entrepreneurs. I first heard of this group at Hollyhock, on Cortes Island, which hosts a meeting of its members every September. Members include people like Judy Wicks of Philadelphia's White Dog Café Foundation known for its success in linking local farmers and chefs; Ben Cohen of Ben & Jerry's Homemade Ice Cream whose business embraces both a social and a financial mission; and Happy Planet Foods which makes those great smoothies and donates 10% of profits to environmental and humanitarian organizations. Says Christie: "It enhances the quality of the food we produce that we care about the quality of our environment and the world we live in."

The ingredients are all high quality, many organic: Callebaut chocolate, Dutch cocoa, Australian ginger, maple sugar from Quebec, local blackberries and raspberries, lavender from Happy Valley Lavender and Herb Farm, Santa Cruz lemons, coffee from the Saltspring Roasting Company and many gallons of Avalon Dairy's pure whipping cream. Cardamom, cloves and cinnamon are ground for the chai tea flavoured ice cream (Christie credits Victoria chef John Hall with educating her palate in the development of this flavour). The blackberries are cooked, then strained through a chinois to remove seeds before

Christie and Marvin Eng proffer tuiles with roasted banana ice cream at the Harvest Bounty Festival.

Blackberry Lavender Trifle

CHRISTIE ENG, SHADY CREEK ICE CREAM COMPANY

 Makes 8 generous portions. I was honoured when Christie created this recipe especially for this book. It's the ultimate modern take on the English classic, and I love that it incorporates local wild blackberries and Cherry Point Vineyard's excellent blackberry port.

	sponge cake torn up into roughly 2" pieces	
2 c	Shady Creek Lavender Ice Cream	480 ml
1/3 c	Cherry Point Vineyard's Cowichan blackberry	80 ml
	port (may substitute rum or sherry)	
1 c	whipping cream, whipped	240 ml
1 c	fresh seasonal berries soaked in	240 ml
1/6 c	more blackberry port	40 ml

Remove the ice cream from the freezer. In a glass bowl or four individual goblets spread a thin layer of the whipped cream — about one-fifth of it. Randomly set pieces of sponge cake into the cream. Sprinkle with the blackberry port. Dab in another one-fifth of the whipped cream to support the next layer. Drop dollops of slightly softened lavender ice cream somewhat evenly over the whipped cream. Add a few of the berries. Cover with the remaining whipped cream. Top with the remaining berries soaked in port.

♟

being made into sorbet. Star anise is roasted, ground, then steeped in cream to make the popular licorice ice cream.

Ben refers to "the science of ice cream," and shows me the amazing computer-generated recipes he works from. It is Christie's husband, Marvin, who inputs the number of tubs of each ice cream flavour required for a particular day's order. The computer program then determines the quantities that will be needed for each recipe to meet the order. Generally, Christie and Ben make ice cream Monday through Wednesday, and freeze it on Thursday and Friday. Often they produce 200 tubs a day. It gets so cold in the freezing area that Ben wears a scarf.

Christie and her son, University of Victoria student Erin Eng, personally deliver the ice cream up and down Vancouver Island. They load up to 1,600 tubs into her refrigerated truck and drive to Parksville and points north. Chefs call Christie all the time for special orders (killer bee honey and lime sorbet being one of the more interesting). Shady Creek is often on the menus at The Fairmont Empress Hotel, Butchart Gardens, Government House (ginger ice cream was available to Queen Elizabeth II and Prince Philip during the 2002 Golden Jubilee visit), The Med Grill, Malahat Mountain Inn, Truffles Catering Group and The Canoe Club. Buy it from the island's best grocers and you can eat it straight from the tub the way Leyland and I did on our way home.

Share Organics

Susan Tychie dropped by my house herself with a hamper brimming with fruit and veg. The produce is normally delivered by one of her five helpers on Tuesday or Wednesday by bicycle or car share (Susan books a vehicle through the fuel-efficient Victoria Car Share).

She has just returned from a "once-in-a-lifetime holiday" with her children in Spain, yet her jet lag is not noticeable, particularly when she starts to tell me about the produce she's brought. The winter months are, not surprisingly, her busiest. The farmers' markets have closed up and gardens are less productive, so she gets a lot of calls on grey days from folks like me seeking some inspiration in the kitchen.

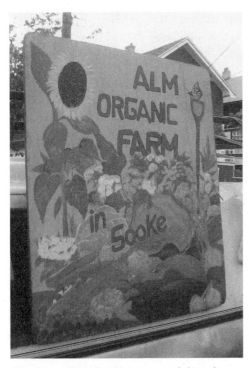

Share Organics' brown-box delivery service includes produce from Sooke's exemplary ALM Organic Farm.

Susan supports farmers who use organic growing methods, and maintains a "local first" policy. She imports from the British Columbia mainland or California when she has to. Today, she's brought me white Kennebec potatoes, Macintosh apples, oranges, lemons, kiwis, Bosc pears and a big bunch of bananas, hearty Lacinato kale, beets, onions, romaine lettuce and a bag of oyster mushrooms.

I follow her suggestions of sautéing the onions until caramelized, then laying the kale over top to wilt and finally drizzling with a little balsamic vinegar; sautéing the oyster mushrooms and mashing the potatoes with a whole head of roasted garlic. Finally, I grill some sole, cut up the fruit for an easy dessert, and presto — a healthy dinner is on the table.

It's always fun to create meals from the brown-box delivery programs. I'm a big fan of Susan's Share Organics because the produce is fresh and mainly local, she offers a good range of add-on products (from Cowichan Bay Farm chicken and Wild Fire breads to Silk Road teas and Nature's Path cereals) and her heart is in the right place.

A former employee of Victoria's Nature's Fare health-food store, she began her own business as a food co-operative among a handful of families. It evolved from there into a weekly box program for 140 singles and families throughout Victoria. Susan says she caters mainly to young families and university students.

Her produce comes from well-regarded local organic growers such as Mary Alice Johnson of Sooke's ALM Farm, Heather and Lemont of Saanichton's Northbrook Farm, Brian Hughes of Deep Cove's Kildarra Farm and Violet Leclair of Metchosin's Bentback Farms. Susan says she enjoys "connecting with the farmers." She loves it when the veggies arrive at her own door to be sorted into the boxes. She tells me: "Often I'll get lettuce bouquets so beautiful you could walk down the aisle with them!" The romaine she's brought me is just such a bouquet.

With her commitment to "be as green as possible and sell as reasonably as possible," Susan is making a big impact on the health of many local families.

Spinnakers Brewpub

I slipped into Spinnakers Brewpub early one Monday morning for a tour and chat with beer maker Lon Ladell. The pub's recently launched organic brews, Honey Pale Ale and Nut Brown Ale, were receiving rave reviews and I wanted to know more about them.

It seems that, in addition to being organic, these are Victoria's only aquifer ales. The brewpub has dug its own well, from which water is pumped through a light filtration system. Lon says that "incredibly good water" is one of four essential ingredients in the Spinnakers beers. The other essentials are malted barley, hops and yeast. Says Lon: "Knowing what you want to make and how you want it to taste can only be accomplished by starting with good ingredients."

Spinnakers gets its malted barley from an organic barley farm in Saskatchewan. Lon takes me upstairs to see part of his annual order of six to eight tons.

Spinnakers Brewpub, located on Victoria's scenic Inner Harbour, with an adjacent bed-and-breakfast and restaurant.

We nibble on some nutty crystal malt kernels and he tells me how he got into the business. After working at Royal Oak Dairy in Victoria, where he made cottage cheese and other dairy products, he began at Spinnakers as an apprentice. After a couple of years, he was offered the opportunity to set up a brewery in Bourges in France's Loire Valley. Spinnakers' owner Paul Hadfield encouraged him to go, and later welcomed him back.

The Loire brewery gave Lon great experience in his own craft, but also gave him an insight into slow food. "There was a fromagerie down the road owned by an old woman. I'd stop for cheese, and a little farther on, pick up a baguette." When the French brewery was up and running, he came back to Spinnakers as planned.

He loves what he does, and delights in the creative aspect of his work: "I can taste a beer in Belgium, as I have done, and know how to make it." Lon and his fellow beer makers at Spinnakers produce 132,000 litres of beer each year, and the demand is increasing.

Lon first creates a mash of malted barley and hot water, and lets it steep for an hour or so at 64.5° to 65°F. The starch in the barley is converted to sugar water, called "wort," which is then transferred into a large kettle and boiled for one to three hours, depending on the type of beer being made.

a fine stop for an organic cool one on a hot day ...

Whole-leaf hops (specifically, the female flower of the hop vine) are added, and then the mixture is cooled down to provide a perfect environment for the yeast. The beer is then transferred either to an English-style open fermenting vat or to a closed, German-style vat — again, depending on the beer. Because the beer mixture is not filtered or pasteurized, there is always some risk of spoilage, so the beer makers have to keep a close eye on this stage of the process. In the fermenting process, Lon says the yeast basically "eats the sugar [the wort] and creates alcohol and carbon dioxide." I ask about the nutritional value of beer, and he points out that a glass of beer gives more than the daily requirement of vitamin B.

Following fermentation, the beer is stored in large cooling vats. Light ales are kept at 3°C in one cooling room. The traditional English beers, which tend to be less bubbly and are served warmer, are stored in another room at 8° to 13°C.

Lon and his friends are big proponents of local, organic slow food. He says he would like to see organic barley grown on the island. This year, the yields were not good on the prairies, and he "can't support the fossil fuel it would take to bring supplies from farther afield."

Spinnakers, with its prime location on Victoria's Inner Harbour, charming adjacent bed-and-breakfast accommodation and restaurant now in the very capable hands of former Oak Bay Marina chef Mel O'Brien, makes a fine stop for an organic cool one on a hot day. The beers are also available at local liquor stores, and on tap at top bars like the one at Brasserie L'École.

Travel with Taste Tours

One day, when Kathy McAree was in her teens, she asked her grandmother: "How do I know how to make all these things?" Said her grandmother: "When you were younger, you watched your mother in the kitchen like a hawk." Kathy's grandparents owned a restaurant in her native Winnipeg, giving her early exposure to the foodie life.

Kathy was working as an account representative for Kelloggs Canada when she decided to take a break and do some travelling. Her wanderings took her to

Eggplant Parmigiana

KATHY MCAREE, TRAVEL WITH TASTE TOURS

Makes 8 to 10 servings. Chef Francesco Palumbo of Masseria Salamina taught Kathy to make this dish during a culinary holiday in Pezze di Greco, Italy. "Many have been transformed into eggplant lovers with this dish," she tells me. I know; I'm one of them!

2	medium eggplants	2
	tomato sauce	
1	egg	1
4	slices mortadella,	4
	sausage meat removed from casing	
1 c	grated Swiss Gruyere cheese	240 ml
1 c	grated Parmigiano Reggiano cheese	240 ml
1	bunch fresh basil, roughly chopped	1
	breadcrumbs	
	olive oil as needed	

Cube eggplant and fry until soft using lots of olive oil. If the eggplant sticks to the pan, keep adding more oil. Mix together the egg, ground mortadella, grated Swiss cheese, chopped basil and a bit of tomato sauce. Combine with the cooked eggplant mixture. In the bottom of a shallow, 9" by 13" casserole dish, spread a very thin layer of tomato sauce. Add the eggplant mixture. Cover completely with another thin layer of tomato sauce, then lots of grated Parmigiano Reggiano cheese and breadcrumbs. Bake at 400°F for 15 to 20 minutes or until top is golden brown.

Ecuador, Las Vegas and Vail, but it was a hands-on cooking vacation on the Amalfi Coast that ended up changing her career. She knew then and there that she wanted to offer her own culinary tours.

A keen gastronome, Kathy is now sharing her love of good food and wine with locals and tourists through her Travel with Taste Tours of the island. The tours range from a four-hour wine tasting in the Cowichan Valley to seven-day itineraries that include private meetings with chefs, six-course meals in Relais & Châteaux dining rooms, hands-on cooking classes and visits to interesting farms, cheesemaking operations and bakeries. (Relais & Châteaux is an association of luxurious, privately owned hotels and restaurants in 51 countries around the world.) Says Kathy: "I want my clients to leave thinking Vancouver Island is an amazing place for culinary delights."

It's not difficult to be impressed on one of Kathy's intimate tours. Taking only six participants at a time, she does all the driving and organizing. Her clients can literally sit back and enjoy themselves, without having to worry about how many glasses of wine they sample or where the next meal is coming from. Working closely with Cowichan Valley's Engeler Farm, Cherry Point, Glenterra and Venturi Schulze vineyards and Vinoteca restaurant, Sooke Harbour House, Victoria's Café Brio and Ottavio's Gastronomia — to name only a few — Kathy has created the kinds of itineraries that foodies from across the planet are lining up to indulge in.

Wild Fire Bakery

One might expect the owner of Victoria's hip, happening, wildly successful, only fully organic bakery to be a more imposing figure. The fact is that Cliff Lier is a genuinely unassuming guy who rides his bike over to the bakery to meet me, breaks bread with me and answers my questions thoughtfully. One of his bakers had been off the day before, so Cliff pulled two shifts back to back. A strong cup of coffee revives him as we sit chatting in a window seat. He tells me that the three years since he and partner Erica Heyerman started Wild Fire have been "overwhelming and wonderful."

Cliff Lier and Erica Heyerman, organic bakers extrordinaire at their Wild Fire Bakery.

I find Cliff to be both modest and happy. He is pleased with the bread he produces and the crew he has working for him, whose praises he sings several times during our meeting. The bakery is now at a stage where Cliff and his bakers "are all learning from each other," and what they're producing reflects that collaboration.

The ingredients are all organic, from the flour and butter to the olive oil and sea salt. Says Cliff: "The highest quality ingredients emphasize the best flavours." Most of the flour comes from Anita's Flour in Chilliwack. Anita's white whole-wheat flour is the basis of all Wild Fire's whole-grain breads. It's golden in colour, sweeter and nuttier in taste than regular whole-wheat flours. The spelt comes from an organic spelt pool on the prairies. Cliff started his magic wild yeast four years ago with wheat flour and artesian water from Cobble Hill. As is the practice in developing levain, he made a stiff ball, added more flour and water, then waited for the fermentation. He feeds his yeast four times a day with more flour and water. For him, the process worked perfectly from the start. Even the great Jeffrey Steingarten (*The Man Who Ate Everything*, Vintage Books, 1997) had to make many attempts over many months to cultivate an active culture. Obviously, you either have it or you don't.

Cliff travelled to Italy last summer to participate in the Slow Food Conference, and was thrilled to meet "people so passionate about food." He connected with a number of bakers, "people on the other side of the world who are doing what I'm doing." They talked bread — grains used, shapes made — and sampled each other's products.

Cliff is hooked on the history of bread, "this basic, nourishing food that can bring people together." He is concerned that organic foods are often seen as economically exclusive, and so he supports eating locally and seasonally to stimulate the local economy and help people connect to their food and community.

As we chat, an old friend of Cliff's drops by to say hello and buy his daily bread. Cliff cuts thick slices of a newly launched onion and rosemary ciabatta and we all get lost in its crispy, flavourful crust and moist, soft interior. He talks about bread pairings: like wine, different loaves can be served at different stages of the meal. A crusty fougasse, for

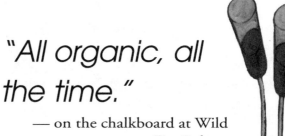

"All organic, all the time."

— on the chalkboard at Wild Fire Bakery

example, pairs perfectly with salad or soup; plain baguette is the best foil for the cheese course.

Cliff is moving toward pairing breads to sandwich fillings in the bakery's funky café. Today, there's a cold frittata with mayonnaise on focaccia; nourishing tomato-lentil soup is bubbling in the crockpot and there are several personal-sized thin-crust pizzas on offer. Stopping in every week for my whole spelt loaves, I find it impossible to leave without trying something from the pâtisserie selection: fudge cookies, meringues shaped like mushrooms, vegan carrot muffins, lemon soufflé tarts, for heaven's sake. And the greatest indulgence: florentines. Okay, so now I'm not just running in for bread; I've settled in to the café where that great Caffé Fantastico coffee, chai and apple cider are always on tap and there's lots of New Age reading material.

Future plans for Wild Fire Bakery include a roof garden with herbs, fruits and edible flowers that will be used in the breads and pastries. While Cliff and Erica believe in staying small, they want to make a visible statement with the garden: using compost from the bakery, they will show that even the tiniest urban bakery can produce some of its own ingredients. That garden will perhaps inspire other downtown dwellers and businesses to develop edible green areas.

Zambri's

It's four o'clock and Zambri's restaurant is between sets. Lunch has concluded and dinner is on the horizon. The owners, siblings Peter and Jo Zambri and their staff, have a short intermission, but nobody's sipping champagne. In that time, the restaurant is fully cleaned, dinner is prepped, candles are set out on the tables, flowers and fruits are arranged. Before the curtain goes up, Peter Zambri pours two glasses of Venezia Guilia, hands me one, and invites me into the kitchen.

It is always an honour to be taken behind the scenes. As I follow Peter, his phone rings. Without missing a step, he banters a little with Chef Edward Tuson of Sooke Harbour House while he leads me to a section devoted to the evening's antipasti. In immaculate stainless steel containers are roasted red peppers; mushrooms marinated in olive oil, balsamic vinegar, carrots and basil; marinated kalamata olives; red Italian onions roasted cut-side down in balsamic vinegar, olive oil, salt and pepper; celery sticks with Gorgonzola and mascarpone. These will be added to house-made meats and wonderful cheeses from Ottavio's Gastronomia to comprise the antipasti platters for which Zambri's is known.

The previous Sunday, Peter took delivery of a 200-pound pig from Andrei Fedorov of Mon Plaisir Farm in Sooke. He'd spent the day preparing pancetta from the belly, coppa from the neck, even fromage de tête. A highly regarded chef who is also a talented butcher, Peter takes pride in using every part of the

Jo and Peter Zambri on the line at Zambri's.

animal. He bemoans the absence of traditional salami making here, and is determined to keep making his own and challenging himself to "always learn."

Peter's been cooking all his life. He effectively started his professional career as a teenager when, with his buddy Rob, he operated a catering business out of his mother's basement in Toronto. It's a career that has taken him from stints of cooking in Italy, to Toronto's Windsor Arms Hotel, Vancouver's Wedgewood Hotel, Château Whistler and Sooke Harbour House (it was Peter who hired Edward Tuson and the two are good friends). At Sooke Harbour House, Peter was the chef, but he also gardened and developed the inn's highly efficient organic composting system. When the concept for Zambri's restaurant came together in 2000, it was the culmination of Peter's, and his partner and sister, Jo's, life-long commitment to serving good food, simply prepared.

Peter is a great supporter of local organic vegetable producers including Mary Alice Johnson of ALM Farm, Dave Wiebe of Cowichan Valley Organic Farm, Michael Ableman of Madrona Valley Farm and Candace Thompson of Eagle Paws Organics. He tells me he particularly loves the summertime, when he can buy everything locally. This summer, he will also cook with the herbs grown by his girlfriend, Suzanne Reimer, in their backyard garden. Several island vineyards are represented on the select wine list: Blue Grouse, Alderlea and Venturi Schulze. I'm impressed that Peter sees the restaurant as a place not only to feed people, but also to educate them in the benefits of local, seasonal and, as much as possible, organic cooking. This is a man whose food ethic I have always admired. Though many will not know this, he cooks a free lunch on Saturdays for the Moss Street Market vendors from their leftover produce.

The night before I visited Peter in his kitchen, I attended a general meeting and special dinner for Vancouver Island's Slow Food convivium held at Zambri's. The dinner began with lasagne made with local organic winter broccoli, then Cowichan Bay Farm chicken involtini with Saltspring Island Cheese Company's truffled goat's cheese fonduta, and finished with Poplar Grove blue cheese semifreddo with an Alderlea Hearth (port) glaze and an Italian anise cookie. The organic onion-sourdough bread had been baked by Cliff Lier from Wild Fire Bakery. The convivium's membership includes some of the most gifted island chefs, and it is a mark of Peter's own ability and his complete lack of pretension that he not only pleases the palates of so auspicious a group, but also has fun with it. Says Peter: "I love to cook, especially for people who are happy and enjoying themselves." With his cooking, what's not to enjoy?

METCHOSIN

Happy Valley Lavender and Herb Farm

Lynda Dowling always knew she would farm on Happy Valley Road: her property originally belonged to her grandmother and she used to spend summers there. When Lynda was very young, her grandmother had told her: "There will be a piece of land here for you."

Lynda, her husband, Michael, and their children moved onto the property in 1986 and turned it into a little corner of Provence. On one acre, there are five sections with 800 to 1,000 *Lavandula angustisolia* plants each. The overall effect is purple-luscious, and I love the little eccentricities scattered about: the canopy bed in the middle of one block, the mannequin dressed in lavender finery. Lynda says the farm is so much work that they like to have a little fun decorating the gardens. Behind the lavender are lovely ornamental beds and greenhouses.

The road to bountiful — bountiful lavender, that is, at Happy Valley Lavender and Herb Farm.

All the lavender is organically grown. As Lynda says: "We eat it, so there is no other way to grow it." The local chefs adore her lavender. You'll find lavender shortbread on The Fairmont Empress' tea menu in Victoria, and now you know where Shady Creek Ice Cream Company gets its blooms.

In lavender season, the Dowlings open the place for visitors to enjoy the harvest in many ways: there are tours, as well as lavender sachets, lavender lemonade and lavender shortbread, lavender soaps and lavender plants and seeds for sale. Lynda composes a new lavender recipe every year to encourage her customers to cook with the ancient plant.

Lavender Lemonade

LYNDA DOWLING, HAPPY VALLEY LAVENDER AND HERB FARM

Makes 6 cups (1.4 L). It took me a while to get my taste buds around lavender as food, but Shady Creek Ice Cream Company's lavender ice cream, Madrona Valley Farm's lavender yogurt and Lynda Dowling's lavender lemonade easily converted me. This drink is not only refreshing; it's very pretty.

1 c	sugar	240 ml
1/4 c	(a generous handful) fresh OR	60 ml
1 tbsp	dried lavender blooms stripped from stems	15 ml
1 c	freshly squeezed lemon juice, strained	240 ml
	ice cubes	
	lavender sprigs for garnish	

Combine sugar with 2 1/2 cups (600 ml) water in a medium pan. Bring to a boil over medium heat, stirring to dissolve the sugar. Add the lavender blooms to the sugar water, cover and remove from heat. Let stand at least 20 minutes (and up to several hours). Strain mixture and discard lavender. Pour infusion into a glass pitcher. Add lemon juice and another 2 1/2 cups water. Stir well and watch lemonade change colour. Pour into tall glasses half-filled with ice or refrigerate until ready to use.

For that extra touch, garnish lemonade with the fresh lavender sprigs.

NOTE: *Lavandula angustisolia hidcote,* an English variety, is a sweet lavender that turns the lemonade a beautiful rosy pink. Other varieties turn it a paler colour. Avoid piney-smelling lavenders, such as spike.

Owner Lynda Dowling crouches in a field of lavender at Happy Valley Lavender and Herb Farm.

How did she choose lavender in the first place? "I didn't," she tells me. "It chose me." Lynda had regularly visited an elderly lady to pick lavender until one January, the lady arrived on Lynda's doorstep with a huge plant. She had decided to move to a smaller home, and wanted Lynda to have her lavender. From that plant, Lynda took 500 cuttings and started her first garden.

Metchosin Farmers' Market

The Metchosin market is a favourite of mine because it is so naturally presented. It's held on Sundays, outdoors, just behind the fire hall, and never fails to impart that lovely sense of being in the country. The pace is slow, the vendors are friendly and the produce always looks and tastes like it has been picked only minutes before you arrive.

You'll find organic farmer extraordinaire Dieter Eisenhawer with his tiny, perfect fingerling potatoes, arugula, beans and tomatoes; Yoshiko Unno and Tsutomu Suganami of Umi Nami Farm with their exquisite Oriental vegetables; Gini and Peter Walsh of Swallow Hill Farm with apples, Asian pears, blueberries and rhubarb; and Bernie and Marti Martin-Wood of Two Wings Farm with the most amazing salad mix, heirloom tomatoes and organic seeds.

43

There are 15 to 20 stalls at every market. Call ahead for the date of the Harvest Festival in the fall, when local musicians, clowns and a rooster-crowing contest add to the fun.

SOOKE

Ragley Farm

Josephine Hill left her job as a systems manager with a wholesale food company in Victoria to become a working farmer on 30 acres in East Sooke. Her husband, Rob, was a key grip in the Vancouver film industry and now works on the farm and on his cars. They've never looked back.

Saturdays (and Sundays in season), Josephine opens up part of her barn to sell the fruits of her labour. Customers can take a wicker basket, then fill it with tomatoes, collard greens, chard, baby radish, spring onions, squash, arugula, mesclun, jalapenos, and many more veggies. The large baking rack holds still-warm loaves of whole wheat, sourdough, fruit and olive breads, and blueberry and cranberry apple muffins. Josephine grinds all her own flour. One morning when I visited, she was a little low on bread because the power had been out for five hours the night before.

Near Christmas, Josephine takes orders for her boxes of exquisite holiday cookies. She often has samples of her baking, not that the palate needs to be tempted first. I am particularly fond of her spekulatius cookies, which she kindly delivered just before the big day. She makes a wonderful range of organic jams such as black currant, cascade berry and apple-ginger. Farm-fresh eggs are always available.

The atmosphere in the barn is warm and friendly, with a steady stream of regular, mainly local, customers dropping by. They buy and they catch up on the week. Even their dogs catch up with each other. I was amused by one car that drove up with its owner's dog hanging out the window to announce his arrival to the Hills' dogs.

Josephine says it was Rob who first spotted the farm, and knew she would love it; when it finally came on the market in 1995, they made the move. They had a lot of work to clear the place up, but now thrive in their rural lifestyle. The farm has an interesting past, having been settled by Reverend and Lady Walker. Lady Walker, daughter of Lord Seymour, Marquess of Hertford, was also related to Lady Jane Seymour. She was a noted agricultural pioneer, setting up the East Sooke Farmers' Institute around 1927 and hosting many of its meetings at Ragley Farm.

The Seaweed Lady

In some ways, Diane Bernard has naturally progressed to her nickname: The Seaweed Lady. She was born to Acadians and lived half her life in the Maritimes. She has a strong background in coastal communities and a passion for the ocean, so, as she says: "I came by my new profession honestly."

That new profession — gatherer and purveyor of west coast seaweed under the Outer Coast Seaweeds banner — has local chefs and gastronomes buzzing. At the 2002 Feast of Fields, Diane teamed up with Chef Edward Tuson of Sooke Harbour House to serve a raw seaweed salad to the 600 participants. It was a huge hit. In the lineup was Lisa Ahier, then chef at Long Beach Lodge in Tofino, who encouraged Diane to "walk into restaurant kitchens with your bucket and show chefs what they can do with seaweed."

Diane credits Lisa, and her friends, Sinclair and Frédérique Philip of Sooke Harbour House, for mentoring her in her new venture. Sinclair encouraged her to begin working with the chefs, so she spent a season taking them out to see

The Seaweed Lady, Diane Bernard, gathers seaweed near Port Renfrew.

Seaweed Salad with Tahini Soy Dressing

LISA BARBER-AHIER FOR OUTER COAST SEAWEEDS

Serves 6 to 10, depending on size of portions.
A great Asian creation using seaweed — a healthful and
delicious natural Vancouver Island ingredient.

Seaweed Salad

2 c	Egregia seaweed	480 ml
2 c	Alaria seaweed	480 ml

Rinse, then blanch the seaweeds in boiling salted water for 2 to 3 minutes. Rinse again and de-rib.
Use the Egregia in its natural shape after the ribs are removed. Cut Alaria into thin strips. Add the
seaweeds to the following thinly sliced or julienned vegetables:

1 1/2 c	leeks	360 ml
1 1/2 c	carrots	360 ml
1 1/2 c	cucumbers	360 ml
1 1/2 c	red peppers	360 ml

Toss with the Tahini Soy Dressing to taste; sprinkle with toasted black sesame seeds and serve.

Tahini Soy Dressing

6 oz	tamari soy sauce	180 ml
4	limes, juiced	4
4 oz	sherry vinegar	120 ml
6	minced shallots	6
4 tbsp	molasses	60 ml
1 1/2 tsp	light brown sugar	7.5 ml
3	chipotle peppers (in adobo)	3
1 1/2 c	olive oil	360 ml
8 tbsp	sesame oil	120 ml
1 1/2 tbsp	minced ginger	22.5 ml
1 c	tahini paste	240 ml

Combine all ingredients and purée very well in a blender. Store chilled for up to one week.

the seaweed and introducing them to their "good, healthy, distinctive yet sub-tle" properties. At first, she found it was the "progressive, more avant garde" chefs who took an interest, but now she is inundated with enquiries. Once people see and taste the possibilities, they're hooked.

The nutritional value of seaweed is extremely high. As Diane points out, seaweed has no root system. It attaches itself by its stipe to a rock, a log or to other seaweed, and so "the nutrients taken in directly from the ocean" are all available to the eater. Seaweeds are "nutritionally dynamic. They're high fibre, low fat and have no cholesterol."

Diane collects her seaweeds west of Sooke, often hiking out great distances along the Juan de Fuca Strait where "no industry or big ships" interfere with the environment. She harvests eight to ten different types. Her personal favourite is Alaria or winged kelp, a versatile variety with a very rich, sweet-pea taste and rhubarb smell. Her family goes through about a pound of seaweed a week and, as she says: "I've got teenagers!" I'm reminded of the tofu-eating teens on Saltspring Island (see: Soya Nova Tofu), and start to have hope for the next generation.

In addition to her online wholesale business, Diane is now supplying the retail market through Lifestyles and Planet Organic markets in Victoria, and will soon be selling through a couple of local brown-box programs.

Sooke Harbour House

It's fair to say that Vancouver Island gastronomy started with Sinclair and Frédérique Philip. From their "romantic little white inn by the sea," they have heightened our awareness and raised our expectations of food in general, and reawakened our taste buds specifically to the pleasure and purpose of eating fresh, local, seasonal ingredients.

There is a reason why Sooke Harbour House has been a veritable training ground for the best local chefs, including Bill Jones, David Feys and Peter Zambri, and a Mecca for gardeners wanting to learn and apply organic methods to the cultivation of over 400 edible flowers and herbs. It has played a huge role in the revival of market gardening. Many Vancouver Island farmers regard Sinclair as a mentor because of the interest he takes in their operations and the knowledge he so generously shares. Tugwell Creek Honey Farm is one beneficiary of his tutelage: Sinclair encouraged Bob Liptrot and Dana Le Comte to produce honey

Chef Edward Tuson adds love and humour to the pot at Sooke Harbour House.

and mead at their nearby apiary, and they now have a thriving business that includes the production of linden honey, so prized by the European guests at Sooke Harbour House. The Philips persuaded Diane Bernard to start up Outer Coast Seaweeds, now another successful local food business. Mary Alice Johnson of ALM Organic Farm and Ernie Knott are part of the inn's family of suppliers. Mara Jernigan of Cowichan Bay's Engeler Farm says: "What Sinclair and Frédérique have achieved at Sooke Harbour House is really a remarkable piece of Canadian culinary history."

The reason for their far-reaching impact is not only that they care; they have a long-held conscience about sustainable farming and land preservation which extends beyond their own business. They want to ensure that agricultural land is used for farming, not development, and they want to see other people succeed in the food business: growers, grocers and chefs.

In some ways, the couple's position in the local food chain was inevitable. They have plowed a lifetime of knowledge and enthusiasm into making their inn the "Sixth Best Small Hotel in the World" (*Travel and Leisure*, 2002). Its authentic

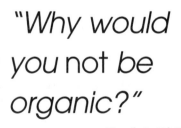

"Why would you not be organic?"

— Sinclair Philip, Sooke Harbour House

local cuisine was voted first in the world by *Gourmet* magazine in 1997 and it won a Pinnacle Award for best independent restaurant in Canada in 2002. For three consecutive years, the inn has been awarded the *Wine Spectator's* rare Grand Award for having one of the world's 95 best wine lists, and this year, Frédérique was named Woman of Distinction for business and entrepreneurship in Victoria.

Frédérique tells me their story really began in France, when Sinclair was taking a Ph.D. in political science and international economics and Frédérique was studying economics at Grenoble. Ten years later, they went to Toronto to be with Sinclair's mother who had fallen ill. When his mother passed away, they headed west because "Sinclair had always wanted to be by the ocean." They drove around and ended up at Whiffen Spit in Sooke, a far less populated area 25 years ago.

There, at the water's edge, was the 1929 clapboard house that would be improved incrementally, as the Philips could afford it, to become what it is today. They moved into the basement with their three children (the fourth, Rissa, was born in Sooke) and began to convert the house into an inn. They had no experience as innkeepers, but Frédérique remembers thinking: "It shouldn't be that complicated." The Philips' children grew as the inn grew, and all have worked in various capacities. Nishka tends the gardens, Benjamin is a sommelier and waiter in the dining room and Jasmine is the ever-gracious hostess. Rissa, who is currently in Europe, has bussed in the dining room.

What impresses me, as I have coffee by the fire with Sinclair one crisp autumn day, is how uncomplicated it all appears and how immensely relaxed both he and the inn make me feel. Intellectual, food activist, gastronome and oenophile, he is, most importantly, a very decent guy who treats his own success as a gift to give back — to his guests and to others in the local food and farming industry.

I ask about organics and Sinclair says it's the only ethical choice. He is proud to have influenced many local growers and

Co-owner Frédérique Philip lights the candles before dinner at Sooke Harbour House.

Roasted Pumpkin Soup with Apple Pear Compote*

EDWARD TUSON, SOOKE HARBOUR HOUSE

Serves 10 to 12.
Edward's autumnal soup is an artful explosion of taste and colour.

Roasted Pumpkin Soup

1	pumpkin, 2 - 3 lbs (1910 g - 1.3 kg)	1
1	large onion, chopped coarsely	1
1	large carrot, peeled and sliced into 1/4" pieces	1
4	cloves garlic, sliced thinly	4
1/4 c	butter	60 ml
1/4 c	safflower oil	60 ml
2 tbsp	finely chopped fresh sage	30 ml
6 c	chicken or vegetable stock	1.4 L
	pinch of salt	
	pinch of pepper	

Preheat the oven to 350°F.

Cut the pumpkin in half and remove the seeds with a large spoon. Place the pumpkin cut-side down on an oiled baking sheet and bake for 40 to 50 minutes, or until the flesh is very soft. Remove from oven and let cool for 20 minutes in the fridge. Once it is cool, scrape the flesh from the skin and place it in a bowl. Discard the skin. Put the butter and the oil in a four-quart pot over medium heat. Add the onions and the carrots; sauté for eight to ten minutes. Add garlic and cook for another two minutes, stirring constantly. Add the stock and roasted pumpkin. Simmer for 35 to 40 minutes. Remove from heat and let cool for 15 minutes. Purée on high speed in a blender in small batches, until all of the soup is blended and smooth. Reheat the soup with the fresh sage and serve with apple and pear compote.

Apple Pear Compote

2	Braeburn, Granny Smith or Royal Gala apples	2
2	Bosc, Bartlett or Anjou pears	2
1 c	apple juice	240 ml
1/4 c	white wine vinegar	60 ml
1/4 c	honey	60 ml
1 tsp	mustard seed	5 ml
2 tbsp	unsalted butter	30 ml
1/4 c	safflower oil	60 ml
2 tbsp	minced ginger	30 ml

Peel and dice the apples and pears into half-inch cubes. In large sauté pan, place the oil and butter over medium-high heat. Once the butter has melted, add the pear and apple cubes. Sauté for eight to ten minutes, or until the fruit starts to soften. Add all remaining ingredients and reduce, (i.e., simmer on low), until the liquid is barely visible. Remove from heat and place one heaping tablespoon in the middle of each serving of roasted pumpkin soup.

Chef's Notes:

Pears should be firm and not overripe. Whipped cream makes a nice garnish for this dish. When reheating the compote, add a little butter and apple juice. Substitute squash for the pumpkin or replace the honey with maple syrup and the result is equally delicious.

*Reprinted with permission from *The Art of Sooke Harbour House* (Sooke Harbour House, 2003).

producers to transition to organic. And he is pleased to have popularized formerly unpopular ingredients and created great interest in growing and foraging for indigenous ingredients. Those include many First Nations foods, from uncommon

The white clapboard house on the water's edge in Sooke has become an internationally acclaimed inn and restaurant — Sooke Harbour House.

fish to berries, prolific local mushrooms (when we later meet up with Chef Edward Tuson, Sinclair excitedly tells him about the Slippery Jack boletes he found on his morning forage), and bitter winter greens, which people used to regard as inedible. Sinclair had a pretty good idea what would grow in Sooke because it has a climate similar to where he lived in France.

I ask about Slow Food — Sinclair is head of the Vancouver Island convivium of this international organization — and he tells me that he and Frédérique have "always lived by Slow Food values, as we understand them." He says it's all about using and promoting "foods in their regional, seasonal and historic context," and preserving traditional foods such as First Nations dishes. He allows that Slow Food is also about "reintroducing foods," such as the importation of Italian ingredients, in recognition of the needs of our multicultural society.

I'm anxious to see how philosophy translates into cuisine, so Frédérique offers to take me into the kitchen. En route, she shows me some images for the

Une table à deux *in the alcove at Sooke Harbour House.*

first of three books she is producing, *The Art of Sooke Harbour House*. These are photographs of some of the inn's food-themed art collection. Each image has inspired Chef Tuson to create a special recipe that will be included in the book. Proceeds will go toward the development of the art department at the local high school.

A great inn being the sum of its parts, it would be remiss of me to not mention the menu of spa treatments designed by Frédérique. At Sooke Harbour House, the treatments actually come to the guests, in their rooms (or, if preferred, they are given in the exotic Potlatch Room where one can have a massage behind the curtains of a marquee straight out of the Arabian Nights). Frédérique recognized something that we spa aficionados have long decried: after a relaxing treatment, one is

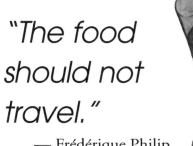

"The food should not travel."

— Frédérique Philip, Sooke Harbour House

forced to get dressed and leave the sanctuary. The answer is in-room everything, from sea salt scrub to Swedish massage.

Before leaving me and my thousand hungry questions with Chef Tuson, Frédérique tells me: "Following the seasons is everything to good cooking." She finds it strange that chefs are making a big story about going to the markets. "We've always done that," she says, "and we didn't do it to be trendy."

Edward Tuson has a ten-year history at Sooke Harbour House where he loves that "every day is different." I love the fact that he is different from what one might expect of a chef with so stellar a reputation. I'm not referring to the nose ring or the tattoo; I'm impressed that he's like the boy next door, a genuinely humble guy who takes a lot of time showing and explaining things.

He says he's "a farmer at heart," and he lived a few other lives before coming to cooking. He delivered furniture for Sears Roebuck in Los Angeles and worked on an oil rig in the Beaufort Sea before enrolling in the chef-training program at Vancouver Community College. That was the year he'd hurt his back and figured construction jobs were out of the question. Besides, cooking had always been part of his repertoire from an early age. His mother was a hairdresser who worked at home, and he would often "try to cook her dinner."

While cheffing at places like Vancouver's Pan Pacific Hotel, Edward used to come to Sooke to snorkel for abalone. That's how he met fellow diver Sinclair.

He signed on at Sooke Harbour House for five years, then took off in 1995 on an adventure across Asia (the Bangkok portion of that journey was spent with Peter Zambri of Victoria's Zambri's restaurant). Gathering culinary knowledge wherever he went, Edward finally returned to Vancouver Island in 1999, working briefly at The Aerie, Micheline's and the Malahat Mountain Inn, before settling back into the kitchen at Sooke Harbour House.

"It should be required that every young chef studying in Canada eat here at least once!"

— Mara Jernigan, Engeler Farm

As we chat, his highly qualified staff work around us: Riley is tying fresh scallops with spaghetti-thin strands of rutabaga before searing them with smoked bacon from Andrei Fedorov's nearby farm; Marc-Andrei is changing from metal cookie sheet to Silpat in order to perfect his chocolate wafers; and Tim is preparing a winter chanterelle cream sauce that will be served with duck raised exclusively for the inn by Cackleberry Farm.

There is a great deal of creativity in the kitchen, and a lot of room for individuality. Edward lets his staff know what's come in fresh that day, then leaves each person to write his or her own portion of the evening's menu. The results are electrifying: spicy albacore tuna served rare on a buckwheat-noodle, root-vegetable and cilantro salad with fennel-seed duck sausage, a clam parsnip fritter and a tamari, red wine vinegar and ox-eye daisy vinaigrette. As we contemplate the dish, Edward cuts me a thick slice of that albacore tuna and I'm lost for several minutes. Or: caramelized apple and dried cranberry terrine in a calendula-petal-and-apple glaze with lavender marshmallows, frozen sour cream jellies, pumpkin seed wafers and nasturtium leaf juice.

Edward is "Entrée Dude" to his staff; he handles the creation of the main offerings and fine-tunes the rest. He also visits the local farms and markets, takes early-morning calls from fishers on their boats, manages the supplies, writes recipes and gives interviews to the likes of *The New York Times, Bon*

Appétit and *Canadian Living* (not to mention demanding book authors!). And yet, this is an executive chef who is always on the line during service. He tells me it's all made worthwhile "when someone tells me I've cooked them the best meal they've ever eaten in their life."

I move from back of house to the oceanside dining room to eat the best meal of my life with Toronto chef and sommelier, Daniel Beiles. It is a graciously served and elegantly presented six-course dinner. The kitchen's attention to detail and relentless pursuit of excellence is evident, from the scrumptious warm albacore tuna, apple, red onion, sourdough tartlet with chickweed–ox-eye daisy salad, Korean mint, cilantro yogurt and pickled ruby beet to the roasted Pekin duck breast with a buttermilk and grand fir glaze, lapin cherry-fennel sauce and split-pea tortilla torte. Daniel appreciates the opportunity to sample a flight of British Columbia wines with his meal, and is overwhelmed by his tour of the cellars.

Tugwell Creek Honey Farm

Dana Le Comte trained as a fashion designer at Ryerson College and worked as a merchandiser in Vancouver, so I'm not surprised that she manages to look fabulous in protective clothing. We're talking full beekeeper regalia: head-to-toe canvas suit, gloves and large straw hat with netting. She and her husband, Bob Liptrot, have invited me to visit them and the three million bees that

Life in a beehive at Tugwell Creek Honey Farm.

reside at Tugwell Creek Honey Farm in Sooke. No worries, I say, and pull on my own space suit.

Bob has been fascinated with bees since he was seven. He used to help an elderly neighbour with his hives, and always received a chunk of sweet honeycomb in return. He went on to earn a Master's degree in entomology, then took apiculture (beekeeping) at Simon Fraser University. He has more knowledge about his charges than most people, but I can instantly see an intuitive asset: he is completely in tune with the bees and is able to work with them without protective clothing (don't try this at home).

It's one thing to see bees in a museum setting; it's something else to stand with beekeepers as they dismantle a hive, and introduce you to the clan. Each of the couple's 90 hives contains some 40,000 to 60,000 Carniolan bees. The proletariat includes 13,000 to 20,000 foraging workers and at least 26,000 workers that stay in the hive to contend with brood rearing, comb construction, housecleaning, defense and temperature regulation. The brood consists of thousands of eggs, pupae in sealed cells and larvae being fed. Significant family members are the drones, of which there are 100 to 300, and the queen.

As I hover over the hive, Dana points out the queen (she is larger than the others and marked with a little dot of blue nail polish), and I'm fascinated by her obvious coterie of attendants. These bees are assigned to stay with her at all times to groom, feed and protect her. She's the J-Lo of the insect world, and I learn that these queens are in big demand. A good breeder can fetch as much as $150, and it is not unusual for queens to be delivered from one beekeeper to another via the postal service.

The queens breed after completing their mating flight with five drones, whom Shakespeare aptly described as "the idle bachelors." Yet there are no winners here: the drones die in the process (suffice to say, the penis snaps off), and the queens go on to lay some 2,000 eggs per day for the rest of their lives.

The workers have finely honed phonetic and kinetic forms of communication. The "dance of the honeybee" is a much-studied ritual, whereby the foragers return to the hive and, through sound, taste and smell, "provide information regarding the location of a particular source of forage." The recipients of that information can then head out on their own to collect pollen.

The ultimate winners, of course, are you and I, and a visit to Tugwell Creek Honey Farm can only heighten our appreciation of one of nature's perfect foods. Dana and Bob chose their ten-acre farm for its proximity to Survey Mountain. Located 25 kilometres inland, it provides an ideal warm, dry climate

Honey Spice Cake with Mascarpone and Honey Icing

DANA LE COMTE, TUGWELL CREEK HONEY FARM

Dana originally created this recipe for my column in *Focus on Women* magazine. It's light and not overly sweet, and the icing is gorgeous. When my baking partner, Phyll Remple, and I made it, it attracted a swarm of happy tasters.

Honey Spice Cake

1/2 c	40% bran cereal flakes or bran buds	120 ml
1/2 c	water	120 ml
1/2 c	butter	120 ml
1/2 c	sugar	120 ml
1/2 c	honey	120 ml
1	egg	1
1 tsp	vanilla	5 ml
1 3/4 c	sifted all-purpose flour	420 ml
1 tsp	baking powder	5 ml
1/4 tsp	each soda, salt, cinnamon, cloves and ginger	1.2 ml
1/2 c	finely chopped walnuts (optional)	120 ml

Heat oven to 350°F.

Combine bran flakes or buds and water. Set aside until most of water is absorbed. Cream butter and sugar until light and fluffy. Continue creaming while adding honey in a fine stream. Add egg and vanilla. Beat well. Sift together the dry ingredients. Add alternately to creamed mixture with the bran mixture. Fold in the walnuts. Spread batter in a greased, lightly floured 9" by 2" round baking pan. Bake about 30 minutes or until cake tests done in centre. Cool on wire rack five minutes. Remove cake from pan. Finish cooling on rack.

Mascarpone and Honey Icing

1 lb	mascarpone	454 g
2 1/2 tbsp	honey (or more to taste)	37.5 ml

To make icing, mix room-temperature mascarpone and honey together and beat for three minutes until smooth. Ice cake, then drizzle an additional tablespoon of honey on top.

and a proliferation of hawksbeard, fireweed and salal for foraging. The couple transports their hives to the mountain, as well as to nearby Muir Creek, where the bees collect nectar from linden tree blooms, and the Sooke River Potholes, where they feast on blackberry flowers.

I first sampled Tugwell Creek Honey at Feast of Fields three years ago, and it has become a firm favourite. New this spring is Dana and Bob's meadery, a first for the island, where you will be able to buy Vintage, Melomel and Sack meads. Mead was traditionally drunk in the "honey month." The father of the bride would supply his son-in-law with all the mead he could drink during what is now known as the honeymoon.

A whole lot of buzzing going on at Tugwell Creek Honey Farm.

Dana says they are delighted to have control of the whole process, from hive to honey and honey wine. She is happy that their business has become a family affair: her sister and mother come from Vancouver to help during the harvest and another assistant recently arrived — daughter Teagan was born just as we went to press.

In the meantime, if you're tired of trawling superstore aisles in the city, get thee to the meadery. Dana and Bob offer a delicious and educational respite down on the honey farm.

SALTSPRING ISLAND

Happily, Saltspring Island has not come a long way since I used to go over with my middle-class hippie friends in the 1970s. The counter-culture is alive and well, and the various nouveaux who have built expensive summer homes have come for the peace, not to create any new scene. Sure, it can get pretty busy in the summer. You wait longer for the ferries. You probably have to queue for your latte at the Saltspring Roasting Company or Morningside Organic Bakery and Café. The Bread Lady may be sold out of your favourite loaf if you don't get to the Saturday market early enough, but switching over to island time tends to keep all of this in perspective.

Saltspring really is the organic capital of British Columbia, and the many growers are refreshingly vocal about food supply and sustainable agriculture.

The Bread Lady

Heather Campbell's mother always said: "It doesn't matter about your china; it's sharing the food you have with other people that counts." She would divide whatever she had for supper by the number of people at her table, and Heather does the same today. On Friday nights, before she bakes 400 to 500 loaves of bread, she cooks and leaves her porch door open. Neighbours and friends know they can just drop by. Some eat, some drink; all contribute to the lovely sense of joie de vivre that Heather exudes.

When I arrive on a Saturday afternoon, the week's work is done. Heather has just returned from the Market-in-the-Park, where she regularly sells every loaf she bakes. She and her architect husband, Phillip van Horn, are looking forward to a sunset picnic with friends that evening. There's a beautiful salmon lying on the butcher block, about to be cooked. Phillip has gone off for a swim. Heather and I sink into a couch and talk baking.

Unlike many people I've met who have changed careers to become food producers, Heather always sought an alternative lifestyle and always baked bread. It was a natural evolution for her to turn a passion into a business. She says she likes doing hands-on things, loves "making something that I really like and passing it on to others. It's a way to pass your energy around."

For 15 years, she and Phillip lived "in the bush" on 25 acres in the Ottawa Valley. There was no power or running water, and no phone. When they came to Saltspring in 1991, the locals warned them that the lifestyle was quite rustic. To them, it was practically luxurious.

A friend of Heather's had heard Alan Scott, author of *The Bread Builders*, speak at a conference and Heather liked the sound of his wood-fired bread ovens. She bought plans from Scott (which Phillip revised somewhat to make the oven stronger) and had a local mason build her a 4- by 6-foot oven. The oven holds 35 loaves at a time, and she bakes up to 700 loaves of bread a week. She mixes and hand-shapes every loaf, but has help loading the oven — from Phillip, and from Mark Stevens, who grows seeds for Dan Jason of Saltspring Seeds at his own farm down the road. People are very much connected on the island. Heather says it's one of the most caring places she's ever lived.

Heather's bread is sold at the seasonal Saturday market, and year-round at Admiral's Sushi Bar and NatureWorks in Ganges. One morning a week, she and Charlie Eagle of Bright Farm sell at a small organic market in Ganges (Tuesdays, 10 A.M. to 2 P.M., 112 Hereford Avenue). People who know her phone ahead to place their orders.

The bread is made with certified organic flour, and mainly organic ingredients. I find it impossible to choose from 95% rye, 100% spelt, whole wheat levain — plain, or with walnuts, raisins, apricot/hazelnuts, dates/ginger or rosemary. Heather is always experimenting, and one week, produced cranberry with white and dark chocolate. Her customers couldn't get enough.

When I finally get up to leave, Heather invites me to come back for dinner "any Friday evening." I'm truly touched, and reminded of something Mara Jernigan once said: "You can go to Italy and eat in all the best places, but if an Italian family invites you into their home, you'll remember it forever."

Bright Farm

I'm sitting on the back porch of Charlie Eagle and Judy Horvath's farmhouse, sampling juicy Italian plums straight off their trees and then chewing on the dried version — prunes that Judy proffers from one of her collection of big kitchen jars. Hastings House chef Thomas Render and I are spending a Sunday touring farms and food producers on the island, and this is our first stop.

Charlie and Judy came up from the Bay Area in the early 1990s, and bought their ten-acre farm in about two hours, en route to the ferry. It was a fortuitous move. They had been homesteading on a remote property in California since 1980, but, with their daughter, Bree, ready to begin school, they felt they wanted somewhere more community oriented. Saltspring was the answer, and Judy found the house and property so idyllic that she cried the first time she walked through the door.

I find it idyllic as well, and Charlie tells me most visitors feel a sense of wonder here. The property was originally 153 acres, bought for $153 by Thomas and Jane Mouat in 1890. It has a creek running through it that drains St. Mary's Lake and runs through to the Vesuvius estuary. It is something of a bird

Braids of Bright Farm's Korean garlic for sale at the Saltspring Island Garlic Festival.

sanctuary. As we wander about the farm, we stop to watch a turkey vulture, a hawk and then a great blue heron soar above us.

Charlie's main crop is garlic: Chinese, Spanish, Early Red Portuguese and Korean, some of which I'd bought at the Saltspring Garlic Festival in August. He sells it in big fat braids. This was a good year — 560 braids! Other crops include potatoes, beans, corn, carrots, leeks, lettuce, chard, zucchini, broccoli, winter squash and celery. There is a vast greenhouse of tomatoes, tomatillos, hot peppers and cucumbers. There are watermelons and cantaloupes and gorgeous Concord grapes (Charlie and Judy make Concord jelly together).

And then there's the orchard, an amazing planting of 200 varieties. The trees were moved to Bright Farm as a complete collection in 1993. They were just "little two-foot whips when I planted them," says Charlie. They'd been amassed by a woman from Sloan River who collected heritage apple varieties. Charlie and Judy press some 40 to 50 varieties into juice and also make cider. People buy caseloads of the farm's 20 varieties of crabapples to make jelly. Because the nights have been cold this summer, Charlie is anticipating a good, sweet apple harvest this year.

As we wander through the orchard, Thomas spots a hawthorn bush. He's just found a recipe for hawthorn jelly and a discussion ensues, mainly around how long it would take to pick enough of those tiny berries to make a batch of jelly. We pass the chicken coop, a field of sheep (Charlie counts on the neighbour's ram busting through the fence every year to propagate his herd) and a couple of hives (the bees are mainly kept to pollinate his crops, but he also harvests as much as 40 pounds of honey annually).

The orchard is watered directly from a large pond on the property. Gravity draws the water from Jane's Spring (named for original owner Jane Mouat) into a storage tank for the drip-irrigation system that waters the rest of the farm's plantings. Charlie has help in the form of a dozen WWOOFers (Willing Workers on Organic Farms) throughout each year. Some of them stay on the property in a sweet little cabin behind the house. They all sit down to Judy's hearty dinners after their working day.

Charlie is clearly proud of his daughter, who loves the farming life (yes, these young people do exist!). Bree is taking a degree in environmental studies in Santa Cruz, but can't wait to move back to Bright Farm when she graduates. She worked in the gardens of Hastings House as a teenager and, like her mother, she enjoys selling at the local markets.

Back on the porch, Charlie and Judy are singing the praises of their dinner in the kitchen at Hastings House four days earlier. It seems the experience of dining stove-side was "incredible," and Charlie rushes off to get some of his homemade cider to send back with Thomas for the kitchen brigade. I make a mental note to book a seat at that particular kitchen table as soon as possible.

Hastings House

The winding drive to Relais & Châteaux's Hastings House takes us past fields of sheep before arriving at a charming cluster of buildings, all facing Ganges Harbour. There's a converted barn, an authentic Hudson's Bay Company post (now The Post House, a honeymooners' delight) and a stately replica of a 16th-century Sussex manor house built with locally quarried stone.

Received as if we've come home, my little group of foodies is invited to join the manager, Shirley McLaughlin, in the front parlour of The Manor House for morning coffee, or "elevenses" as the English affectionately call the respite. Meandering along the garden path, we are inspected by one of two resident cats, the indomitable Mr. Hastings. Some years back, word got out that Chef Marcel Kauer was leaving bowls of fresh cream and tidbits of fish at the kitchen door. Mr. Hastings and Squeaky were first in line, and soon took up permanent, luxurious residence here.

Inside, the perfect welcome awaits. A fire roars in the open hearth and organic coffee from the Saltspring Roasting Company is set out in Minton china cups. There are freshly baked strawberry muffins and a selection of jams made from the inn's own heritage fruit trees. The *Gulf Islands Driftwood*, Saltspring's leading (and only) newspaper, is at hand. We sink into chintz and happily give ourselves over to our edible journey's most relaxing stop.

Diners enjoy a special evening at Hastings House.

The Manor House at Hastings House.

Poppyseed Crusted Pacific Halibut, Beetroot Risotto and Lemon Thyme Beurre Blanc

THOMAS RENDER, HASTINGS HOUSE

Serves 4. A creative contrast of colour, texture and flavour: firm, black-crusted fish married with creamy, maroon risotto. Plated on white china, it's a work of art!

Beetroot Risotto

1 c	arborio rice	240 ml
2	shallots finely diced	2
1	fresh bay leaf	1
1 1/2 c	beet juice	360ml
1/2 c	white wine and	120ml
1 1/2 c	chicken stock	360 ml
4 tbsp	butter	60 ml
2 tbsp	grated Parmesan cheese	30 ml

Sweat the minced shallot in 1 tbsp (30 ml) of butter until translucent. Add arborio rice and stir to coat evenly with butter. Add bay leaf. Add 1 c (240 ml) of liquid and stir gently until most of the liquid has evaporated. Continue this process until all the liquid is used and the rice is creamy but still firm. Fold in remaining butter and Parmesan. Season with salt to taste.

Halibut

4	5-oz (150g) portions halibut	4
	Dijon mustard	
	poppy seeds	

In a hot fry pan, brown the halibut on the outside and remove to a baking tray. Brush lightly with mustard and sprinkle on some poppy seeds, pressing gently so they adhere.

Beurre Blanc

3	sprigs lemon thyme	3
1/2 c	white wine	120 ml
1	lemon, juiced	1
1	shallot, minced	1
1/2 lb	cold unsalted butter, cut into cubes	227 g

In a saucepan reduce the wine, lemon thyme, lemon juice and minced shallot until 2 tbsp (30 ml) remain. Strain out the solids. Return liquid to saucepan and warm. Add cold butter to the sauce a few cubes at a time, whisking vigorously. Continue adding all the butter, taking care not to heat the sauce too much as it will split. NOTE: Adding 1 tbsp (15 ml) of whipping cream will stabilize the emulsion. Season with salt to taste. Just before serving, place halibut in a preheated oven at 425°F and cook until firm to the touch. (Be careful not to overcook it!) Place risotto in the centre of the plate. Place the halibut on top. Spoon the sauce around. Garnish with fresh lemon thyme sprigs.

Hastings House is located on the site of an old working farm of 25 acres. The Manor House was built in 1940 for Warren Hastings to replicate a home he had owned in Sussex. Features like the large inglenook fireplace in the lounge are typical of those found in Tudor homes in Sussex. When Donald Cross bought the property from Hastings in 1980, he brought in a local architect, Jonathan Yardley, to develop it into a country resort.

It faces south across Ganges Harbour, which provides a continuous show of boating activity, particularly in summer. The lush, rolling lawn, with its immaculate flower beds, is dotted with Adirondack chairs just calling guests to curl up with a book, or sit, as I did, with a glass of port after dinner and watch the sun set.

Pastry chef Carley Makela with bread just baked for the evening meal; Chef de Cuisine Thomas Render checks the evening's menu at Hastings House; private fireside dining.

65

On one visit, I enjoyed a room upstairs in The Manor House, which reminded me of a cosy hotel I'd stayed in near Salisbury Cathedral many years before. The suite's living room faces the harbour, and you can read before a wood-burning fire (remember those?). It's private and cosy with thoughtful appointments throughout. Your name is on the door and a stuffed toy cat can be hung out to alert the housekeeper that the room can be cleaned (its other side is a dog that appears to have bitten off part of the housekeeper's uniform, a sign that privacy is desired).

Of course the highlight for any gourmet trailblazer is dinner, and Hastings House doesn't disappoint. Many celebrities have dined here, although the inn

Fine dining at Hastings House on Saltspring Island.

is discreet enough to divulge only names of those whose presence was already known, including Johnny Carson, Martin Short, Goldie Hawn and Kurt Russell.

There are several choices for dinner: the Verandah dining room where no jackets are required, which is often booked for weddings and special parties; the Snug dining room next to the cellar, for private parties; the main dining room; and, in summer, the porch, where a lucky party of four can dine privately. Foodie fanatics can have it all by dining at a special table right in the kitchen (this experience books up fast, so do call well in advance). It all adds up to a true English country-house feeling, where someone like me imagines intrigue in every corner.

Executive Chef Marcel Kauer is Swiss born and trained. At the age of 16, he did his apprenticeship in his uncle's restaurant in Germany, then went into the army. When his parents were travelling in Vancouver, they ate at La Raclette, and his father asked if the restaurant would employ Marcel. They agreed, and Chef Kauer came to Canada. He worked both at La Raclette and at the Galiano Lodge, spending half of the week in each kitchen. He said it was a busy time for him, and challenging because he "had no English." He loved it when the lodge was quiet and he could go fishing.

Kauer came to Hastings House 13 years ago, and is now both chef and co-manager. He believes in cooking with the seasons, from what's available. "Wait until the food comes to you," says Kauer. What doesn't come from the Hastings House gardens, he buys from local growers, going off the island only for things like bulk potatoes and flour.

Chef de Cuisine Thomas Render joins us at the kitchen door, and we all inspect the day's produce delivery. There are slender eggplants, several varieties of tomatoes and peppers, green beans, portobellini mushrooms, pattypan squashes, greenflash cantaloupes, leeks, yams and a large tray of fragrant basil. As various members of the kitchen brigade pass by, they touch and comment, all impressed and excited by the quality. Most of it comes from Charlie Eagle's Bright Farm on the island. Sweet little strawberries arrive from Rosalie Beach's Wave Hill Farm, and saddles of venison from Broken Briar

Fallow Deer Farm near Chemainus. Michael Ableman's Madrona Valley Farm supplies the golden and red plums, as well as green, and prized white, asparagus. Blueberries come from Cathy Bull's Bluebeary Hill Farm in Victoria. Kauer says they also buy 300 to 400

pounds of blackberries from local pickers who come to the kitchen door every summer. Many of those berries find their way into Hastings House jams and jellies, which guests can buy to take home.

Earlier in the day, sockeye salmon and snapper came in for the evening's menu. Typically, they get calls from the boats of local fishers like Don Bemi with the day's catch. They meet the boats at the dock in Ganges, and it's seriously fresh fish for supper. Lamb, which is featured on the Hastings House menu every night by popular demand, comes from Mike Byron's neighbouring farm.

Tofu comes from Soya Nova Tofu on the island. Chef Render loves the smoked tofu and includes it in delicate strudel as well as vegetable sautés. Tempeh, the cultured soy curd that is mixed with barley and allowed to ferment, is now being made on the island, and used by Hastings House.

Chef Render apprenticed in the Okanagan, then worked in restaurants in Vernon and Kelowna. He's worked four seasons at Hastings House, alternating with stints at The Raintree in Whistler and other restaurants in the off-season.

Pastry chef Carley Makela is pulling loaves of whole-wheat bread out of the oven. A graduate of the Pacific Institute of Culinary Arts in Vancouver, she originally learned how to bake from her grandmother. Following stints at Cin Cin and other Vancouver restaurants, she is now responsible for the tea trolley, breakfast and all pastries at Hastings House. Her desserts — like the Dark Belgian Chocolate Brownie Torte with Blackberry Ice Cream which I enjoyed — are fresh and creative without being overly fussy or loaded with unnecessary ingredients. Carley recently won a top award with her Simply Grand Chèvre Cheesecake at the Grand Marnier Dessert Challenge in Victoria.

The Garden at Hastings House

I venture into the herb garden, where Shelley Kobylka and her friendly dog, Tessa, are tending to plants in one of the greenhouses. Shelley had been working as a landscape gardener in Duncan when an interesting ad appeared in the local paper. The rest is happy history. From March to November, she grows all the flowers for the dining rooms and the 18 guest suites. She works closely with the housekeeping staff, ensuring that flower colours complement the furnishings and that fragrances are never overpowering.

As well as the ornamental flowers, there are many grown for the kitchen, including nasturtiums, calendula, roses, day lilies and scented geraniums. Shelley regularly picks a selection of flowers and takes them to the chefs, so they can see what's available for cooking. She is gradually converting the flower garden over to perennials, but it's a big job as there have been as many as 5,000 annuals planted each year.

The flower beds around The Manor House and guest suites are changed regularly and instantly. Shelley has developed a system of growing plantings in pots that can quickly be moved to a bed with a wheelbarrow, unpotted and, presto — winter pansies where summer's petunias once bloomed.

Herbs and veggies are prolific in the 70-square-foot kitchen garden, which has been designed in the European wheel shape. There's a bay leaf tree in the centre, and each section of the wheel holds something different: herbs, salad greens, Oriental mix, snow and snap peas, cabbage, rhubarb, artichokes, arugula, sorrel (we nibble the lemony leaves as we talk), green beans, cantaloupe, beets, peas and Swiss chard. Before new plantings go in, Shelley, Chef Render, Michael Ableman and Charlie Eagle sit down to plan what will be grown for the Hastings House menu.

It's a popular garden where guests are often seen strolling around. Shelley says people come out to the gardens because "they like to see where their food comes from." She enjoys conversations with guests, and is flattered when they photograph or sketch the garden with a view to recreating aspects of it. "One couple from Minnesota actually paced it out, and planned to copy it in detail back home," she tells me.

Like all gardens on the Gulf Islands, these are surrounded by tall fences to keep out the bold local deer who also appreciate fresh veggies. Shelley tells me that the fawns, who "don't know what they like yet, eat everything." She sprays rotten eggs around the fences to further deter the deer. Shelley maintains organic-growing methods in the gardens, even treating the slugs to repellants such as piles of eggshells and inorganic strips surrounding plants, but she says it's an ongoing battle.

The heritage orchard has crabapple, apple, plum and pear trees from which come the delectable jams and jellies served for breakfast and tea.

The sheep grazing on the property are delightful, and you could, as I did, spend hours just watching them. Spring is of course the most fun, with the newborn lambs frolicking about. There's an admirable orphan project in operation, managed by the local 4-H club that cares for lambs which have become separated from their mothers.

House Piccolo

Saltspring Island never fails to amaze me. You can literally cross the street from farmers' market to fine dining without changing your blue jeans. Even though the attire is casual everywhere, the attention to food is generally high-

Chef Piccolo and Kirsi Lyytikainen in the kitchen of House Piccolo.

class all the way. Such was my first experience at House Piccolo. I arrived for dinner in jeans, and was treated as if I were in head-to-toe couture.

The 36-seat restaurant (which expands to 56 seats with outside seating in summer) is in a cute little blue house right in the village of Ganges. Inside, it has a homey feel, with the paintings by owner's aunt and various European knick-knacks on the walls. There is a whole display of Russian dolls that were originally owned by a Finnish prime minister interspersed with copper pots and awards, including a prestigious award of excellence from *Wine Spectator* in 2000.

The meal is one of the best I've ever eaten, from the complementary salad and warmed house-made bread to start, to the meltingly rich, yet surprisingly light gorgonzola tart with port wine, toasted cumin seed and Bosc pear chutney and the Saltspring Island lamb chops with a hearty aïoli, designer vegetables

Warm Gorgonzola Tart

 Serves 6 to 8. Rich and deeply satisfying; a little slice goes a long way. It took some cajoling on my part to get the recipe from Chef Lyytikainen and understandably so, as it's one of his most popular appetizers at House Piccolo.

Seaweed Salad

7 oz	Gorgonzola cheese	200 g
4	egg yolks	4
1 3/4 c	heavy cream	420 ml
1 tbsp	flour	15 ml
	9" pre-baked, unsweetened tart shell	

In a mixer or blender, mix the cheese, egg yolks and flour well. Once consistency is smooth, blend in all the cream at once. Do not whip the cream. Pour the mixture into the tart shell and bake at 350°F for about 40 minutes. Let the tart rest for 20 minutes before cutting it into slices. Delicious served with a fresh green salad and vinaigrette.

♟

and scalloped potatoes. Sticking to one glass of wine, as is my custom, I enjoyed the fruity Bacchus from Cowichan Valley's Alderlea Vineyards (Piccolo's wine list is an extensive, much lauded collection of over 250 selections). I'm often asked where I put all the food I eat, but I had no trouble finishing my meal with the unique lingonberry crêpes with vanilla ice cream and a bottomless cup of Saltspring Island Roasting Company coffee. Everything was excellent and the service was friendly, but not intrusive.

Besides the local coffee, the restaurant uses Saltspring Island ingredients as much as possible. The lamb is always local; Moonstruck and Saltspring Island cheese companies supply the cheese; vegetables come from Bon Acres and lettuce comes year-round from Living Lettuce, an organic hydroponic farm nearby. Saltspring Island Sea Products smokes the salmon. Even the beer is island-made, from the Gulf Island Brewery in the Fulford Valley.

In 1989, Piccolo Lyytikainen and his girlfriend, Kirsi, were ready to move away from the big city — in their case, Helsinki. They had no preconceived ideas but, as an avid boater, Piccolo knew that he wanted to live by the sea. They came to Saltspring Island at the invitation of his uncle who lived here. It was Christmastime, and they liked the place very much. They returned in the summer to really check it out, and ended up deciding to get married and make a permanent move in January 1991. Whatever happened, Piccolo tells me, there would be boating 12 months of the year! Piccolo brought a wealth of cooking experience and Kirsi, bookkeeping and self-taught pastry-making, from their Finnish homeland.

He credits his mother with his life-long interest in good food. "She actually had more than salt and pepper in her spice cabinet, so our food had different flavours," he tells me. Her good cooking gave him "a little kick," and he began his career driving for a catering company, then working in restaurants in Helsinki "from the very bottom to becoming a schnitzel cook."

Somewhere in between, he worked in the boat electronics industry. His boss owned a small island, and Piccolo ended up becoming a cook on the island for guests of the company. He loved that "summer gig," because he could take his own boat to work and was able to cook with great, local ingredients. Back in Helsinki, he decided to get some proper training under a Swiss chef at the restaurant Bellman. And then came the trip to Canada, and Piccolo and Kirsi's love affair with Saltspring Island.

They found the little house on Hereford Avenue right away. It had been a Mexican café, then a restaurant called Carol Feeds the Planet (only on Saltspring!), and the décor needed a lot of work. They weren't sure they could afford it, but decided to do it anyway. The couple worked together and with friends to renovate the place, and opened in October 1992. They originally served breakfast, lunch and dinner on blue and white checked tablecloths, but gradually honed their style to dinners-only on white linen.

When I ask Piccolo where he wants to be in five years, he tells me, "Right here. We have the one thing that everyone wants — to live on Saltspring."

Madrona Valley Farm

Jeanne-Marie Ableman and I are sitting on a chaise longue under a heritage apple tree, one of the farm's cats stretched in the sunshine at our feet. Before us are fields of strawberries, basil, chard, many lettuces and herbs. Jeanne-Marie is peacefully feeding her son, five-month-old Benjamin, and telling me about her journey from California's Goleta Valley to Saltspring's Madrona Valley.

She is originally from San Francisco. Her husband, organic-farming pioneer and activist Michael Ableman, is also American, but spent time herding sheep and working on farms near Nelson, B.C. They came together at Fairview Gardens in Goleta, the farm that Michael is credited with saving in the early 1980s.

It's a compelling story, and one I've enjoyed reading about in one of Michael's books, *On Good Land*. When he arrived at Fairview Gardens in 1981, the area was still largely agricultural, but over the years, development encroached until it became the only surviving farm property. In 1995, Michael and a group of local activists formed a non-profit society and raised money to buy the land, ensuring that it would remain a working organic farm in perpetuity.

That same year, Michael, Jeanne-Marie and Michael's son, Aaron, took a biking holiday on Vancouver Island and the Gulf Islands, staying in B & Bs and, as Jeanne-Marie tells me, "meeting great people with connections to farming," including Dan

"How was this grown? What materials were used in its production? How far did it travel?"

— Michael Abelman, speaking to the 2002 International Federation of Organic Agriculture Movements (IFOAM) conference, Victoria

Jason and Mara Jernigan. The decision to look for a place of their own on Saltspring evolved naturally and, after looking for a couple of years, they bought a unique Victorian farmhouse on five acres.

"Even though it's bottom land that floods in winter," says Jeanne-Marie, "we're fortunate to have Cowichan soil and one of the most fertile areas on Saltspring." The previous owner was a hobby organic farmer, so the foundation was there for their vegetable beds. Michael did some intensive planting and established an irrigation system off the property's two ponds. He follows organic-gardening practices, including the use of cover crops so the soil is held intact in winter; drip tape on the vegetable and herb beds to ensure low water use; companion planting (for example, seed garlic shades the lettuce)

Corn Pancakes with Maple Blackberries and Lavender Yogurt

REBECCA TESKEY, MADRONA VALLEY FARM

 Makes 4 servings. Every time I make these pancakes, I mentally connect to Madrona Valley Farm, where Michael and Jeanne-Marie Ableman's hard work and commitment to sustainable, organic agriculture gives me a whole new appreciation for the ingredients.

1 1/2 c	ripe blackberries	360 ml
3/4 c	pure maple syrup	180 ml
	(Canadian dark is preferable to light or amber)	

In a small saucepan, bring the maple syrup and 1/2 c (120 ml) of the berries to a bare simmer. Gently mash these berries. Put the remaining fruit in a bowl and pour the maple/berry mixture over. Let stand while you make the pancakes.

Lavender Yogurt

1 c	natural 3 percent or whole milk yogurt*	240 ml
1 tsp	chopped fresh lavender leaves	5 ml
	the purple flowers from one sprig of lavender	

*organic yogurt will drain much faster than regular yogurt because it almost never contains stabilizers like gelatin or guar gum. Place a layer of cheesecloth or a clean dishcloth in a fine mesh sieve. Put this over a bowl to catch drips and empty the yogurt into the sieve. Stir in the lavender leaves and flowers. Let drain one to one and a half hours.

Corn Pancakes

1 1/3 c + 2 tbsp	cornmeal or a coarsely ground cornflour	320 ml + 30 ml
	(not masa harina)	
1 3/4 tsp	baking powder	8.75 mL
	pinch of salt	
2	eggs, separated	2
1/4 c	unsalted butter	60 ml
1 tbsp	brown sugar	15 ml
1 c	buttermilk or milk, or 1/2 c (120 ml) of each	240 ml
1 c	corn kernels, freshly cut**	240 ml

** Michael Ableman grows a bi-colour, hybrid variety of corn that is so sweet and juicy you can eat it raw. It is important to choose a local organic corn because the sugar in corn starts to turn into starch as soon as it is picked. Chances are that your local corn will have spent less time off the stalk.

In a large bowl, whisk together the first three ingredients. In a small saucepan, melt the butter with the sugar. Place the buttermilk in a glass measuring cup and whisk in the egg yolks and the butter/sugar mixture. Make a well in the centre of the dry ingredients, add the milk mixture and blend until just combined. Fold in the corn kernels. Beat the egg whites in a clean, dry bowl with a small pinch of salt until soft peaks are formed. Fold the egg whites into the batter. Drop batter to form 2" to 3" rounds on a lightly oiled griddle or non-stick pan, and cook the corn cakes until they are well browned on both sides. To serve, make a semi-circle of three or four cakes on one side of a plate. Using a slotted spoon, place a mound of the blackberries in the center of this. Top with a dollop of the lavender yogurt. Serve the remaining berry syrup on the side, warmed if you like. Garnish with a sprig of lavender.

and protective tenting to keep veggies warmer and hold the moisture that naturally evaporates off the plants.

Jeanne-Marie redecorated the house to provide bed-and-breakfast accommodation, which *Gourmet* magazine described as, "traditional but unfussy, as relaxed as the hosts themselves." There is a self-contained cottage next to the raspberry patch that's perfect for families. Guests can buy eggs and produce from the farm and make their own meals. I think of all the city families I know whose children would benefit from this simple experience.

I'm delighted that the food is organic, that I can see most of it growing before it appears on my plate, that the sheets and towels are air-dried and smell divine and that all the cleaning products are natural. Guests are treated to superb organic breakfasts. I devour tiny strawberries and custard enhanced by the stimulating conversation in the dining room. It's all about the food and the issues surrounding the food, and it's presented in such a natural, easy way that one learns willingly. For me, the essence of the Madrona Valley Farm experience is the hosts themselves and their interest in sustainable agriculture.

It's hard to believe that, on top of the farm and B & B operations, Michael still works part-time at Fairview Gardens, and Jeanne-Marie takes their abundant produce to the island's Market-in-the-Park every Saturday morning. They do it all with minimal help. Horticultural students come to learn about organic gardening, and guests are welcome to pick up a hoe. Michael says: "If people leave here without gaining some new understanding of food and how it comes to them, we haven't done what we set out to do."

Rebecca Teskey is a self-taught chef who came to Saltspring from Winnipeg with her mother to "look around," and ended up staying when she was offered work at both The Currant Café and Madrona Valley Farm. She respects the "integrity of the food" that she works with at the farm. "There's a big difference when you are cooking French beans that you've spent three back-breaking hours picking. You want to do the best job of cooking and presenting them that you can."

Market-in-the-Park

Nothing takes me back to the 1970s more than the Saltspring Island market, held on Saturdays from May to October. Market-in-the-Park, as it is now known, is a testament to community pride and unwavering commitment to sell only items made, grown or baked on the island. With over 120 vendors at the height of the summer, the market has become a top-billed event. It makes a wonderful day-trip for non-residents. In addition to produce from familiar growers and food producers including Michael and Jeanne-Marie Ableman of Madrona Valley Farm, David Wood of the Saltspring Island Cheese Company,

Wave Hill Farm's Rosalie Beach at her flower stall at Market-in-the-Park.

Heather Campbell, The Bread Lady, Rosalie Beach of Wave Hill Farm and Chintan and Satva Hall of Monsoon Coast Exotic World Spices, there is a plethora of handcrafted items from charming gumboots "planted" with flowers to natural soaps and hemp clothing. Many non-profit groups — from The Land Conservancy to the Raging Grannies — raise awareness at the market.

Monsoon Coast Exotic World Spices

Nobody is more hospitable than Satva Hall, a warm and dynamic American whose career has taken him from the clothing and jewellery businesses to his real passion: creating exotic spice blends. He spent his early 20s travelling through Pakistan, and when the war ended in 1973, he walked into India. At a train station, there was the "Vegetarian Eating Room," and the "Non-Vegetarian Eating Room." As a lifelong vegetarian, he decided he had found his country. Then he found his future wife, Swiss-born Chintan, whom he met at an ashram in northern India. He says "the whole India thing touched him deeply" when he was young, and it has stayed with him.

In true Indian fashion, he first invites me for a cup of chai — in this case, his Railway Chai, "spicy and warm with ginger and pepper, fragrant with cinnamon, cardamom and cloves." We sit on the couple's sun-drenched porch, drinking the tea and nibbling papaya, avocado and pear slices that have been sprinkled with chat masala, which is based on garam masala, but goes best with fruits, and his divine Monsoon Balti Spread on crackers. Hall's spices are incredibly flavourful, complex and fresh tasting, but not over-the-top hot. He says he is mainly catering to North American tastebuds, many of which are just waking up, but can also satisfy his "macho customers," who want seriously hot flavour.

Satva imports spices from India and develops his own spice combinations. Traditionally added at the end of cooking, his concoctions give it those unmistakable exotic flavours. The room he does his mixing in has a deeply intoxicating aroma of cardamom, coriander, chilies and star anise, to name but a few of the dozens of individual spices he employs.

It's both a simple and a complex process. Satva says there's a lot of experimentation, but he is gifted with a taste for layering flavours, so he doesn't make too many mistakes. He says: "It's great when the wow factor happens, when it all comes together like one of Chintan's mixed-media artworks." At the moment, he

Satva Hall and friend examine the distinctive jars of Monsoon Coast Exotic World Spices.

is on a mission to create totally organic mixtures. He has been sent some organic spices from Orissa that he's experimenting with, and is also working with Saltspring Island seed guru Dan Jason to see what spices might be grown on the island.

Tempeh in Peanut Sauce with Bengali Panch Phoron and Kerala Chaunk

SATVA HALL, MONSOON COAST EXOTIC WORLD SPICES

Serves 4. A tasty vegetarian curry that packs a big nutritional punch.

2 tsp	oil	10 ml
2 tsp	minced ginger	10 ml
1 1/2 tsp	Monsoon Coast Bengali Panch Phoron	7.5 ml
1 1/2 tsp	Monsoon Coast Kerala Chaunk	7.5 ml
4	cloves minced garlic	4
1	medium onion, chopped	1
1	sweet red pepper, chopped	1
8 oz	package tempeh, cut into 1/2" cubes	227 g
2-3 heaping tbsp	peanut butter	30-45 ml
1 tbsp	miso	15 ml
1 c	boiling water	240 ml
	dash of soy sauce	
1 c	coconut milk (optional)	240 ml
	small bunch of chopped cilantro	
1 c	fresh or frozen peas	240 ml
	salt to taste	

Sauté the Bengali Panch Phoron and the Kerala Chaunk, along with the ginger, in the hot oil until the seeds begin to darken. Add the onion, pepper and garlic and continue cooking until the onion begins to soften and become translucent. Stir in the tempeh, with a dash of soy sauce and cook until it begins to brown. In the meantime add the peanut butter and miso to the cup of boiling water and stir while it dissolves and then pour it into the pan along with the coconut milk if desired. Turn the heat to low and simmer the ingredients together for about 20 minutes, adding more water if the sauce gets too thick. Five minutes before serving add the peas and cilantro. Serve over rice or Chinese noodles.

NOTE: You can substitute tofu or chicken for the tempeh if you wish. For a hotter sauce, increase the amount of Kerala Chaunk.

Monsoon Coast is receiving a lot of attention — B.C.'s *E.A.T. Magazine* recently rated it "one of the best 100 food experiences in the province" — but for now, it is strictly a small, family-operated concern. Satva develops the spice blends; Chintan leaves her artwork to help with packaging. When they're in full production, Chintan's mother comes over to help. Chintan says it's nice to have her mother involved; they can work and have a good chat at the same time.

Morningside Organic Bakery and Café

Alan Golding and Manon Darrette have created a café that not only serves "everything organic, all the time," but provides a comfortable venue for good conversation, an outlet to talk things over. Says Alan, "There are a lot of scary things happening in the world. We've been disconnected. We need to be bold, to reconnect with each other." Those reconnections are regularly made over cups of excellent coffee, house-made muffins and pizza.

Alan is a gentle man, with a lifetime of mindful thinking and responsible action, who has created a mod-ern-day salon in a little adobe building at Fulford Harbour. The café came about at the right time, after he had looked for the ideal situation on some of the other Gulf Islands.

Alan and Manon had been living in Victoria, and came to Saltspring in 2002 to take in the Market-in-the-Park. Getting off the ferry at Fulford Harbour, Alan had an instant, wonderful feeling about the place and said to Manon, "We're not going to the market. We're staying here." They looked around, discovered that the little café on Morningside Road was vacant, and signed the lease that day.

The café menu is focused on nutritious, organic fare

Looking for Morningside Organic Bakery and Café? Just turn right at the breadbasket in Fulford Harbour, Saltspring Island.

made from mostly local ingredients. The Caffé Fantastico coffees and Wild Fire breads and pastries, delivered daily from Victoria, are exclusive on Saltspring to Morningside Café. There is a wide range of organic fine foods available for purchase, including olive oils, balsamic vinegars and teas. In spring and summer, local organic produce is sold in the café's courtyard. Alan has also been working with island farmers to grow some special vegetables for the café menu. Eventually, they hope to grow herbs on the roof of the building, an urban-gardening concept that would be well suited to this little place.

Alan's aim to provide "food for the stomach and food for the mind" has already been more than fulfilled here. I find myself returning not only for the good eats, but also for the inspiring conversation.

The Personal Chefs

A few of us are lucky to have in our memories meals enjoyed at The Currant Café on Saltspring Island. Though relatively short-lived, it was one of those restaurants that seemed to get everything right: the food was fresh, seasonal, modern; the owners, with their California-style cooking, introduced a certain sophistication to island dining; and their commitment to using local foods was exceptional. Ingredients came from island farmers and food producers — David Wood (cheese), Soya Nova Tofu, Heather Campbell (bread), Jeanne-Marie Ableman (eggs), Charlie Eagle, Lisa and Jennifer Lloyd (produce) — as well as some other favourites of mine: Victoria's Silk Road Tea Company, Wild Fire Bakery and Millstream Flour, and the Okanagan's Zebroff family (organic jams sweetened with honey).

On my first visit, the waitress, having heard I was organically inclined, told me: "You'll love the food. They really walk the talk here." I enjoyed everything I ate, in particular the farmhouse torte, a delicate, individually baked ricotta-and-egg torte served with organic greens, sprouts, carrots, tomatoes, cucumbers and Saltspring Island goat cheese. Another favourite was the local tofu served with soba noodles, organic vegetables and almonds, which I enjoyed with a glass of Chapoutier's La Ciboise. On that occasion, wanting neither to miss the ferry back to Victoria nor to forego a Currant Café dessert, I left with ginger cake, just-picked organic strawberries and cream and later enjoyed them on the boat.

At The Currant Café, Jacqueline Gengé and Brian Perry had taken a wealth of talent into a very small space. She is a self-taught chef; he was an engineer and landscape architect before training in New York at Peter Kump's. She describes her own style as intuitive, while his is linear. They make a dynamite team. In California, they worked as private chefs in the film business. Brian also cooked at Chez Panisse, and both call Alice Waters their mentor.

Jacqueline has always gardened, and was raised on the concept of eating what's in season. Living in Santa Monica, she was a regular customer of the farmers' market there. She believes that eating anything other than organic foods, "takes away from health and the excitement of life."

Ginger Cake

JACQUELINE GENGÉ, PERSONAL CHEF

I know several people who have patiently waited for this book to be published just so they could get their hands on Jacqueline's ginger cake recipe. Made famous at The Currant Café, the cake is not sweet and has a deep ginger flavour that marries well with fresh fruit and whipped cream or crème anglaise.

1/2 c	water	120 ml
1/4 lb	unsalted butter	114 g
1/2 c	dark brown sugar	120 ml
1/4 c	maple syrup	60 ml
1/4 c	molasses	60 ml
1	4" piece fresh ginger, peeled and grated	1
1	egg	1
1 1/2 c	unbleached white wheat flour OR	360 ml
1 3/4 c	white spelt flour	420 ml
1/4 tsp	salt	1.2 ml
1 tsp	baking soda	5 ml
	icing sugar to finish	

Preheat oven to 350°F. Butter and flour the sides of a round 8" by 2" cake pan. Place an 8" circle of parchment paper on the bottom. Melt the butter in the water, then pour into a mixing bowl. Add all the sugars, grated ginger and then the egg. Mix well. Add the dry ingredients and beat until smooth and light. Pour into the prepared cake pan and bake 35 to 40 minutes. Cool for 5 to 10 minutes and then turn the cake on to a wire rack face up. When cool, dust with icing sugar.

When they closed the café this year to pursue other interests, Jacqueline and Brian took a short break to "visit friends and eat yummy food at Chez Panisse, Roxanne's and Terra in the Napa Valley." Buoyed by their experiences there, they have returned to Saltspring to finally offer cooking classes and fulfill the many requests for personal cheffing that came while they were running the café. "Now we can do a lot more things," Jacqueline tells me. Their ultimate fantasy is to introduce off-island people to the island's bounty through farm visits and meals made exclusively from Saltspring ingredients.

Salt Spring Flour Mill

What must be the world's smallest flour mill is located on north Saltspring Island. As I approached the architecturally designed home of Pat Reichert, I found myself looking in vain for a water wheel. The actual mill is in a tiny yellow room in the back of the house. Its main feature is a wood-framed stone mill that's beautiful enough to be a piece of furniture.

Pat greets me at the door of the mill and asks if I'd like a demonstration. Once the mill starts grinding the grain, which she brings in from her partner's family-owned, certified organic farm in Saskatchewan, I can see her passion for milling. This is a second career for Pat and one she hadn't exactly planned, but which seemed like the right thing to do at the time.

She's always baked. When she was working as a social researcher, she travelled a lot, and found herself coming home and baking bread "to ground myself." A few years ago, she saw a photograph of a stone mill, and felt herself connecting to it. It wasn't long before she started looking for her own mill, which turned out to be more difficult than she had imagined.

Her research finally led her to the only person who still makes mills in Canada, and he agreed to make hers. It's constructed of untreated solid pine whose natural resin prevents bugs from developing in the flour. Pat tells me that grain and flour should never be milled against metal as it destroys nutrients. Inside the mill are two specially tumbled granite stones from the Tyrol that work together to grind the grain.

Pat produces only about 15 to 20 pounds of flour at a time, using a cool-milling process in which the stones turn very slowly; fast action creates heat and heat reduces nutrition. She estimates she has personally ground 12,000 to 15,000 pounds of flour in the last three years.

Orange Honey Muffins

Makes 10 to 12 muffins.

Pat is a wonderful creator of recipes and an excellent baker. These muffins are light, with a serious orange flavour.

Preheat the oven to 400°F. Place a paper muffin cup in each of the cups in a 12-muffin tin. Place in a food processor or blender and blend until smooth:

1	whole, unpeeled orange, washed and cut into 8 sections	1
1/2 c	orange juice	120 ml
1	egg	1
1/4 c	vegetable oil	60 ml
1/4 c	liquid honey	60 ml

Combine in a small bowl, mixing together with a fork:

1 3/4 c	multi-grain bread and muffin flour	420 ml
1/2 c	brown sugar	120 ml
1 tsp	baking powder	5 ml
	pinch of salt	
1 tsp	baking soda	5 ml

Add the dry mixture to the liquid mixture in the food processor/blender. Blend until just combined. Don't overmix. Chop 1/2 cup (120 ml) of dates (or other dried fruit such as raisins or dried cranberries). Add to the mixture in the food processor/blender and blend about 30 seconds. Spoon the mixture into the muffin cups. Bake at 400°F for about 15 to 20 minutes until the top springs back when lightly pressed with finger. Cool in the tin about 5 minutes before lifting out and placing on a cooling rack.

Most of her flour and cereal products are distributed through the local Market-in-the-Park, at NatureWorks health-foods store and through the Growing Circle Co-op, on whose board she sits. Local restaurants such as Hastings House use her flours.

Pat says she is pleased to be doing something useful for the community. In the old days, people would take their grains to the local mill to have them turned into flour. She says she would love to "bring that quality back to Saltspring." She is proud to be offering fully certified products that are distinguished in the marketplace.

Not only does Pat produce flours, she has some delicious cereal combinations, as well as quick bread, muffin and pancake mixes. When I visited her at her home, she was working on her new line of cake mixes, which includes a tempting double chocolate cake. Later in the year, I ran into Pat at Saltspring's Seedy Saturday event, where she was launching Hearty Seed, Lemongrass and Cilantro and Mediterranean bread mixes. For those wanting organic baked goods without having to start from scratch, these products are a godsend.

Saltspring Island Cheese Company

I was introduced to David Wood's famous goat and sheep cheeses in Victoria at Ottavio's Gastronomia, and found them not only delicious, but beautiful. Each perfect mound of cheese is decorated and flavoured with different edible flowers (from Rosalie Beach at Wave Hill Farm), peppercorns (David recommends the peppercorn cheese with a nice scotch: "There's something so right about that combination."), white truffles and roasted garlic. They make a notable addition to the cheese tray. There's a marcella (dried-out soft goat cheese) and a croutin chevignon, which holds its shape when baked. There are creamy camemberts including a delicious blue camembert, some aged sheep-milk cheeses, and a hearty feta. The thing about sheep, though, is they take the winter off, so the goat cheese is really the Woods' bread and butter.

Before visiting the fromagerie and meeting the cheese-maker himself, I have been invited to picnic atop the island's 1975-foot Mount Maxwell. At its lookout, we open the lovely, wicker picnic hamper to reveal a cornucopia of delights packed this morning by Chef Render at Hastings House. There are a tasty chicken salad, fresh fruits, bread, a root-vegetable terrine with onion confit and an assortment of David Wood's cheeses, some freshly baked gingersnaps, chocolate cookies and almond shortbread. The wine is the popular Millefiori 2000 produced by Venturi Schulze Vineyards of Vancouver Island. I couldn't wait to see how this diverse range of cheeses was produced.

David's story is not untypical of the kinds of people who settle on Saltspring. He paid his dues in Toronto with the highly successful David Wood's Fine Foods in trendy Yorkville, wrote a couple of cookbooks, then, 12 years ago, picked up the family and bought a peaceful sheep farm on Saltspring. He says the change in lifestyle has been good for family life: "You get to do things with your kids like milking the sheep." It's hard work, but they are making a living and loving their new life. A few seasonal milkers are hired, but otherwise this is a family-run operation.

David considers himself a "gumbooter," one of the hardy and hearty south Saltspring Island residents, whose outdoor lifestyle requires them to keep gumboots at the ready. (There is also an implication that these are the real Saltspringers who collect oysters, clams and seaweed.) As I tour the fromagerie with him, I sense a quiet pride of accomplishment. The goat cheeses are made from milk brought in from "goat people" in Abbotsford on the mainland, and from Mill Bay on Vancouver Island. They're mostly fresh cheeses; because of the smaller fat globules in the milk, they have a great

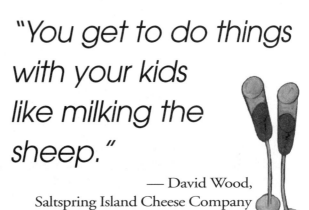

"*You get to do things with your kids like milking the sheep.*"

— David Wood,
Saltspring Island Cheese Company

silky texture — not gritty or grainy in the mouth. I happily learned from David that the higher the moisture content, the lower the fat. His soft goat cheeses have only 19% fat content — what a pleasure!

The milk is pasteurized (heated to 145°F for half an hour, then cooled), then a culture is added and it's left to ripen. This, says David, is the curds and whey or "Miss Muffet" stage. The whey or water is drained off, leaving the curds — the fat and protein. "Differences in time, temperature and acidity make a huge difference to the finished product," says David, so these aspects are closely monitored. His soft goat cheeses age for four days; the camemberts take 25 days. He makes 280 soft cheeses per day and 120 camemberts.

We gathered around the Sweet Heart stove in David's kitchen and sampled his beautiful cheese. It's a food memory I recall each time I buy Saltspring Island Cheese in Victoria — another rewarding link from field to feast.

Saltspring Island Garlic Festival

Garlic ice cream, anyone?

From early August until the end of September, that distinctive waft is in the air at the many garlic festivals across North America. West coasters can celebrate on Saltspring Island, where the island's garlic growers come together

Saltspring Island grower John Wilcox displays his abundance of garlic at the Saltspring Island Garlic Festival.

for a real love-in on the first August weekend. There's the odd off-island grower like the exuberant Ken Stefanson of Gabriola Island, who brings his Russian Hard Neck, Porcelain and Purplestripe varieties — fresh, pickled or made into chutney and potent chocolate bars. Dozens of vendors set up tents at the Farmers' Institute Grounds on Rainbow Road in Ganges, and people come from as far away as the mainland to stock up on the season's first juicy harvest.

Yes, there is lots of garlic ice cream on offer, but it's a bit too early in the day for that, so I buy a braid of Korean garlic from Charlie Eagle's Bright Farm, and wander from stall to stall absorbing the festivities. Garlic has come along way, baby, since its odour offended those unaccustomed to Mediterranean flavours and it's now firmly embedded in the North American culinary lexicon.

87

Soya Nova Tofu

I consider a visit to Soya Nova Tofu a quintessentially Saltspring Island experience. There's something wonderfully communal about the operation, which is also home to owner Deborah Lauzon. Located in one of the island's old orchard areas, Soya Nova Tofu has been in production for 20 years.

Deborah invites Thomas Render and me to join her in her "office." She sets out real sofas and tables on her patio in summer and receives her visitors in the sunshine. All around her, her employees are coming and going. They're just finishing off a long day of production and the place is really buzzing. All her employees are young, many sport interesting dyed hair and tattoos. All seem wildly passionate; Deborah calls it "energized enthusiasm."

When there's work to do, she has a policy of "hiring whoever walks through the door," and she is proud that all three of her children — Zoltan, Nova and John — are tofu makers.

What, I ask, is her secret? I mean, how is it that these young people are so obviously turned on to tofu? She laughs. When her own kids had parties, she always cooked something for them. Being a vegetarian for 30 years, she often made tofu burgers and they loved them. She says the kids of Saltspring eat tofu: burgers, soy-sausage rolls and her famous Zed Spread. Now, her grandchildren are enjoying the benefits of tofu. When they are "strung out on candy from a birthday party," she feeds them tofu with nutritional yeast and tamari, and watches them "mellow right out."

Deborah gives the okara (the pulp by-product of tofu production) to local farmers to feed their animals. She would like to see more farmers using this high-protein organic feed.

Wave Hill Farm

Those are Rosalie Beach's rosemary sprigs and edible flowers atop the artisan chèvre made by the Saltspring Island Cheese Company, and her jewel-like strawberries and figs are on the menu at Hastings House, yet this enterprising woman is actually best known for her flowers.

Today, I have a bouquet of Rosalie's dahlias on my desk, globes of deep fuchsia, purple and pink that take me back to the tranquillity of her flower garden every time I look at them. The garden itself is overwhelming, both in colour and in variety: dahlias, tiger lilies, casa blanca lilies (Rosalie's favourite) and daisies. Giant purple and golden cardoons have also found their way into the flower bed. The day I visit, Rosalie is about to make up a special order for the IFOAM conference in Victoria: 200 hand-made bouquets that she will deliver herself.

She takes me on a rambling tour of her orchard, greenhouses and market garden. I soon see that not only did she and husband Mark Whitear save this property, but she is deeply passionate about growing and wholly committed to their new life in Canada. The couple spent 25 years in England where they raised three children and Rosalie lectured on holistic health care.

Forty years ago, Rosalie's parents bought a 575-acre property on Saltspring Island. Twelve years ago, when they were forced to sell off a few acres to pay the enormous taxes, Rosalie and Mark decided to try to keep the place. The couple moved to Saltspring, converted some of the land to organic farming, started a natural-selection timber business, and felt they were finally home.

The flower garden meets up with the vegetable and fruit gardens, where Brussels sprouts and broccoli are underplanted with mizuna, and companion planting is used extensively. There are strawberries, cascade berries (a cross between a wild trailing blackberry and a loganberry), figs, asparagus, grapes,

Apple Pudding

ROSALIE BEACH, WAVE HILL FARM

Serves 8. This is an easy, all-in-one-pan pudding that tastes yummy straight from the oven, or even a day or two later. Rosalie makes it with her heritage apples (Wolf River, Warner Kings or Bramley), but it is also well suited to a tart Granny Smith.

6 c	chopped apple	1.4 L
5	eggs, beaten	5
1 1/2 c	turbinado or raw sugar	360 ml
2 c	whole-wheat pastry flour	480 ml
4 tsp	baking powder	20 ml
1/4 tsp	salt	1.2 ml
3/4 c	toasted walnuts, chopped	180 ml
2 tsp	vanilla	10 ml

Place the chopped apples in a 13" by 9" buttered baking dish. Mix all the other ingredients together and pour evenly over the apples. Bake in a 350°F oven for 30 to 35 minutes.

Rosalie Beach of Wave Hill Farm with her flower garden's bounty.

watermelons, Ogen melons, St. Nick melons (they keep until Christmas), plums, potatoes and herbs. There are greenhouses for tomatoes, cucumbers, peppers and aubergines.

Theirs is the oldest orchard on the island, planted in 1855 by pioneers Trage and Spikerman. It originally had 1,600 trees. Rosalie loves the Braeburn apples for their taste. Her Wolf River variety is well-known for its flavour and for the size of its fruit ("One apple, one pie," says Rosalie). She also grows the King of Tompkins County, Baldwin, Wadhurst Pippins, Gravenstein, Mann and Fallow Water varieties. As we wander through the orchard, "the slug patrol" marches by: a family of Rouen ducks. The sheep regard us from a distance. Rosalie and Mark press and sell apple and grape juices in the fall.

As many as 20 WWOOFers (Willing Workers on Organic Farms) work on Wave Hill Farm every year. Once, one of them asked Rosalie why they never eat citrus fruits. She replied that, with so many fruits and vegetables in season on the farm, they had no reason to buy oranges from some place else. One night, she and Mark counted 23 vegetables,

"The slug patrol" at Wave Hill Farm.

herbs and fruits on their dinner plates. To me, theirs is an enviable, self-sustained existence.

Rosalie and I walk back to her barn (actually, it's underneath her house), past the fence lined with grapevines, lavender and rosemary. She tells me how those plantings remind her of holidays in Provence. She loves gardening and loves Saltspring Island, and, gazing at the dahlia bouquet on my desk in Victoria, I reflect on her enviable state of contentment.

PENDER ISLAND

Iona Farm

As I attempt to stroll casually by Ellen Willingham's vegetable stall at the Pender Island Farmers' Market, apparently I'm not casual enough. "Taking notes this morning?" is her friendly enquiry. The old notepad has blown my cover, and we have a great chat over samples of her divine goat cheese with fresh herbs and garlic.

A queue begins to form at her stall, including popular chef and cookbook author James Barber and a host of locals and weekenders who buy her tubs of cheese two at a time. It's a very social market, and I enjoy the banter and friendliness around me. The news à la minute is that Canadian singer Mae Moore has bought the Barbers' house, and they're moving to Cowichan Bay.

Ellen and Rob Willingham are both Anglican priests and crisis counsellors who came to Pender Island seeking a healthier lifestyle. They had been practising in separate parishes in Winnipeg, their youngest daughter had been diagnosed with leukemia and they felt they had a lot of stress to deal with. On a visit to the west coast, the family visited a cousin on Pender Island. Amazingly, after having coffee with his cousin, Rob bought her house and the Willinghams went back to Winnipeg to sell their home there.

Ellen says they have never regretted the move. Eventually, they were told about the Iona property by Tekla Deverell, and they decided to farm in earnest. The 20-acre farm is mainly forested, but they have five large vegetable gardens and pens for their goats, sheep and chickens. They began farming to feed themselves, and later started selling at the Saturday Market. They've been certified organic since 1995.

Ellen tells me they are essentially "boat people," who used to enjoy sailing on Lake of the Woods in western Ontario. The Gulf Islands reminded them of

The organic beans went fast at this farmgate on Pender Island.

that. "We feel like seals, torn between wanting to be on land or water," she jokes. She and Rob are always on the water on Sundays, heading out on their diesel-powered boat, although they spend the day apart. One of them gets off on Mayne Island, to conduct the Sunday service there; the other carries on to Galiano Island to lead that congregation. When they're not leading services, farming or at the market, the Willinghams provide crisis-counselling services on the island.

I buy a big tub of chèvre and some of Ellen's green peppers, and then move on to speak to her tablemate. Tekla Deverell, formerly a psychologist living in Vancouver, is the island's undisputed doyenne of organic gardening and wife of the famous crime writer Bill Deverell, who, she tells me, is in New York promoting the paperback version of *Laughing Falcon*.

From Tekla, I buy the freshest walnuts and I ask her what brought her to Pender. She smiles and tells me: "I followed Bill." Now, Tekla owns one of the island's most beautiful and prolific organic gardens, and she loves bringing her produce to market.

Pacific Shoreline

One of the ironies of living on a Gulf Island, surrounded by water and fish, is that it is not easy to buy fish. It has to do with the whole licensing and regulatory system of the fishery and the fact that shellfish must go to Nanaimo to be inspected and then Vancouver to be cleaned before being sold just metres from where it was first gathered.

Between them, Bonnie and Cal have been involved in the area's fishery for over 60 years. Bonnie grew up in a fishing family on Long Beach on Vancouver Island's wild west coast. She and Cal, a fellow fisher, met in Victoria one night after she and her mother dropped into a pub after bingo.

Several years back, the couple recognized a need for fresh fish among all the Gulf Islanders, and began mooring their boat for a few hours each week at

Cal and Bonnie of Pacific Shoreline selling the day's catch from their boat on Pender Island.

The sign says it all: Cal and Bonnie of Pacific Shoreline will be back at the dock at 2:00 p.m. — with a lineup!

docks on Mayne, Galiano and Pender islands. Naturally, they have a loyal following on each island, with many people appreciating their fresh-from-the-boat deliveries. When they're not delivering, they run a fish-export business from their home on Pender Island.

My sister and I met this industrious couple at 2 P.M. precisely on a Thursday afternoon at the Hope Bay dock on North Pender. A sign had been hung there earlier in the day: "Salmon today 2 PM" I saw a similar sign when I was on Saturna Island the following week. Cal was happy to remove head, tail and fins from the fine spring salmon we selected for dinner. We took it back to the cottage, stuffed it with sliced onions and lemons and rosemary, and threw it on the barbie. With some fine fresh corn from the island's mainly organic Southridge Farms Country Store, carrots bought on Mayne Island the previous afternoon, and a blackberry crumble made from the berries I'd picked at the side of the road, we feasted like queens. We had foraged for the freshest local ingredients, supported local producers and were now revelling in our bounty. What better island foodie experience?

Pender Island Bakery Café

Dorothy Murdoch is a long way from hotel management in Vancouver, and she's a lot happier. "I'd had my eye on this bakery for a couple of years," she tells me, "and when it came up for sale, I was ready to buy."

She is delighted to finally be working for herself and providing employment for eight islanders. She operates as a bakery by day and pizzeria by night, when creations like The Gulf Islander (smoked oysters, anchovy, tomato sauce, spinach and three cheeses) and The Spicy Thai (breast of chicken with sweet Thai chili sauce, peanut sauce, lime juice, cilantro, mozzarella and peanuts) get rave reviews.

Dorothy is not a baker, and many people thought she was crazy to operate in the same plaza as the island's main grocery store with its in-house bakeshop. It seems she saw something they didn't: a craving for back-to-basics, made-from-scratch baking. She hired the shop's original master baker, Dorian Wilde, and took on a pastry baker and several assistants. From the day she opened, Dorothy has put the Pender Island Bakery Café on the map. Her impressive range of breads and buns — many organic — walk out the door. We took Cornish pasties (a nod to Dorothy's English roots), spanakopita and the biggest cinnamon buns ever back to the cottage for lunch, and it was thumbs up all around the table.

Dorothy is very attuned to the baby boomers' desire for organics and interest in knowing what's in their food. She serves only organic coffees from Reingold, a German roaster in Vancouver, and uses organic ingredients in baking whenever possible. Sitting at the window on a sunny Sunday morning, my niece and I enjoyed our Americanos, and yes, just one more of those sinful cinnamon buns.

Pender Island Bakery, run by Dorothy Murdoch, is a bakery by day and a pizzeria by night.

Saturna Island

The southernmost Gulf Island has only 320 permanent residents, a population that Michael Vautour of Saturna Island Vineyards describes as one big family. Certainly, after taking a walk on the island's foodie side, I felt I'd made new friends.

Haggis Farm Bakery

I follow Priscilla Ewbank by car to Haggis Farm Bakery, which she co-owns with her husband, Jon Guy. Part way there, an oncoming car stops in the middle of the road, and Dottie, Priscilla's dog, is transferred to her car. Seems Dottie has been out for a walk with another dog, and her play date is now over.

The bakery is a clapboard building a kilometre or so from the Saturna General Store, which is also owned by Priscilla and Jon in partnership with Hubertus Surm. As we walk in, we enjoy the residual aroma of the 600 loaves that were baked the day before. Priscilla shows me the walk-in cooler ("refrigeration is very important here"), the stacks of grains that are milled on site, the big mixer, oven and cooling racks. Behind the bakery is a greenhouse where tomatoes, basil and peppers are grown for the store's café.

Besides the bread, cookies and cereal baked twice a week for customers all over the Gulf Islands, Victoria and Vancouver, the bakery produces pasta and some special-order cakes. Priscilla attributes the success of the bakery to Jon: "He's an excellent baker — he's a Virgo. It's really his heart and head in the whole operation."

My conclusion is that both Priscilla and Jon, together with their dynamic, extended family, are all responsible for the success of Haggis Farm Bakery and the Saturna General Store and Café. And their success is a reflection of their commitment to the land and to each other.

Saturna General Store and Café

The hub of the island's food and social scene has to be the big ol' general store, which offers everything from a post office to groceries and video rentals. There's also an excellent selection of B.C. wines, and a café where I could happily eat every meal.

Co-owner Priscilla Ewbank takes me to an outside table, telling me she needs some air after packaging a bread order for Vancouver and Victoria until 4 o'clock that morning. Her husband, Jon Guy, is now making the off-island deliveries in their new refrigerated truck. Bread deliveries have come a long way since Jon started baking a decade ago, and their two eldest daughters took the loaves door-to-door by horseback.

Today, they appear to have it all — a thriving store, bakery and café that together employ 23 islanders — but, understandably, it's been a long journey. They met as students at Berkeley during the heady 1970s, and came to Canada when Priscilla decided she "didn't want Jon to be cannon fodder in Vietnam." She tells me that the suburban values she was raised with, but never embraced, collided with the activist scene at Berkeley. She and Jon then attended Simon Fraser University, but Priscilla thought it restricting, and found herself looking across the pond to Saturna Island.

When they first arrived on the island, they lived and worked at Jim Campbell's farm. They milked cows and helped with the haying, and Priscilla spun and wove wool from the sheep. Today she says she is "so grateful to have experienced that way of life, and realize how it informs my own."

As we chat, a young woman comes out with Priscilla's breakfast — a beautiful, fat omelette with ricotta and spinach, and a side of bacon. The plate is decorated with nasturtium flowers. Priscilla introduces her youngest daughter, 20-year-old Jessie.

That Jessie is the café's head chef this summer is no surprise: she began cooking her famous pizzas at the age of 12, and worked for Hubertus Surm at the Saturna Lodge & Restaurant as a teenager. She now cooks at the café in the summers and lives in Mexico and other warm climes every winter. She says, "Cooking makes sense to me," and it's obvious that she has a gift for bringing out the best in her ingredients, and a refreshingly un-fussy sense of presentation.

The evening's dinner menu reads like a gastronome's dream: Organic Mayne Island Greens with Buttermilk Feta Dressing and Summer Vegetables; 40-clove Roasted Chicken Breast with Roasted Vegetables; Haggis Farm Pasta with Basil Pesto and Parmesan;

Owner Priscilla Ewbank takes a break for breakfast at the Saturna General Store.

Tagliatelle with Roasted Eggplant, and for dessert, the blueberry tart, cheese-cake or their specialty: big, luscious fruit pies.

One by one, the café staff drop by our table, each one hugging Priscilla, and introducing themselves to me. I find myself in the centre of a warm and loving extended family. Katie often stays with Priscilla when she works evenings, as her family lives on the other side of the island. Amy divides her time between the café and Saturna Lodge & Restaurant. Kolton is working in the kitchen before heading off to university on the mainland in September. Priscilla says she believes in "teaching the kids well" and giving them something meaningful to do. I think of how a lot of city teenagers I know would turn around in this hugely nurturing environment.

Priscilla says their philosophy includes "organic wherever we can," "feed people well," and "keep bread affordable." She is proud to be a significant employer on the island, and enjoys buying organic products from many on- and off-island growers. Ron Pither of Mayne Island supplies vegetables and Flora House of Saturna Herbs supplies herbs. Four local wine connoisseurs advise on the store's selection.

There's an impressive symbiosis between the store, the bakery and the café. The café produces pesto and other things for the store's deli. Priscilla says when the café recently had a corned beef sandwich on the menu, the bakery produced "really big rye bread." Left-over crumbs from the bakery go into Hubertus' famed Go-Nut Burgers that are sold in the store.

I stock up on spelt bread, whole-wheat croissants, giant Loon cookies and Date Crunch Cereal, before following Priscilla by car to the bakery. Those exceptional Loon cookies and many of the Haggis Farm Bakery breads are available in Victoria at Seed of Life, Lifestyles Markets and Planet Organic.

Saturna Herbs

The 25-acre Breezy Bay Farm is located in a sheltered valley, just across the road from the Saturna Lodge & Restaurant. The property is mainly in forest with about ten acres of pasture for sheep, together with greenhouses and an acre under cultivation. There's also a bed and breakfast, where guests stay in the pretty 1892 farmhouse, surrounded by orchards and scented lindens. I learn that the farmhouse was built by Gerald Fitzroy Payne, the grandfather of Noël Richardson of Victoria's Ravenhill Herb Farm.

 It's a co-operative farm, owned by members of the Saturna Freeschool Community Projects (SFCP). The SFCP was named for a freeschool that operated on the property in the early 1970s. Member Flora House says: "Since then the farm has been run by members and a number of 'newcomers' — that is, you've only been on Saturna for 20 years or so!"

Flora and some of the others grow culinary herbs including thyme, sage, oregano and basil. The basil greenhouse is a beautiful thing to look at, and I stand inside a long time just inhaling. All drying and packaging of the herbs is done on site, and they're sold through the farm's website, and at the Saturna General Store. You'll also find them on the menus at the Saturna Lodge & Restaurant and the Saturna Café.

Flora says the SFCP members have farmed organically for over 25 years, feeling "it's better to feed the land to feed ourselves." They have recently also become organically certified.

Saturna Island Vineyards

A relative newcomer to Saturna Island, the vineyards have made a big impact on 60 acres of south-facing waterfront, and their wines made quite an impact both regionally and nationally. At the 2000 Northwest Wine Summit winemaker Eric von Krosigk won a Crystal Rose award for the 1997 Vancouver Island Riesling Brut and a silver award for both the 1998 Gewürztraminer Rebecca Vineyard and the 1997 Okanagan Valley Riesling Brut. At the 2001 All-Canadian Wine Championships, the vineyard won "Best Dry Riesling" for its 1999 vintage.

In some ways, it's all happened very quickly for the Page family of Vancouver. Larry and Robyn Page had been looking for a retirement property on Saturna when this spectacular property became available. They bought it and, with encouragement from their friend and viticulturist, Jean-Luc Bertrand, decided to grow grapes in 1995.

Daughter Rebecca is the general manager, and I chat with her between tastings in the winery. She loves Saturna and is used to a small community, having lived in Pemberton, B.C., where she ran the gas station and deli. She is delighted to have her young son in the local school. She tells me the vines have been planted to take advantage of sun trapped on the property by vast sandstone cliffs. The cliffs act as a sort of heat radiator that "keeps the soil warm — several degrees warmer than the rest of the island." The land slopes, so it's ideal for drainage, and the soil is well fertilized "from nearly a century of sheep farming."

Michael Vautour is the cellar master who runs the convivial wine tastings and tours of the vineyards. It's a fairly hot day, so he suggests a tour by air-conditioned van. A former Vancouverite himself, he tells me how much he enjoys living in a small community now: "I feel everyone is family on Saturna."

The vineyards are magnificent. The Rebecca Vineyard produces the award-winning gewürztraminer, as well as pinot gris, pinot noir and merlot. The two Robyn Vineyards produce chardonnay and pinot noir. The Long Field Vineyard also produces pinot gris, and in the Falcon Ridge Vineyards, 14 experimental varieties include muscat, cabernet sauvignon and syrah. Because of its age, the vineyard has been using some grapes from the Okanagan, but it will eventually be self-sufficient. Eric, "the flying winemaker," actually lives in the Okanagan, so he is able to make the grape selections personally.

I stand in the Rebecca Vineyard and catch my breath. The sun beats down. The grapes hang heavy with mellow fruitfulness on the vines. At the end of each row there is a pretty rose bush that "attracts aphids and provides early warning signs of any mould or mildew." Eventually, the Pages will plant olives and produce oil, but for now, their days are full with the vineyard, the winery and the casual bistro.

I enjoy a nice antipasto plate and glass of riesling on the patio and take my time leaving.

MAYNE ISLAND

Deacon Vale Farm

Shanti McDougall asks: "Have you ever had the divine pleasure of eating a sun-warmed tomato fresh off the vine?" and picks me a handful of her best cherry tomatoes. We're touring her greenhouse, and she's pointing out some of the special varieties that she grows for her famous (but still only in small production) tomato sauce: San Marzanos (she brought the seeds back from Italy); Alicante (considered the best tomato by the British Horticultural Association); and the heritage variety, Brandy Wine.

Shanti will harvest as many as 3,500 pounds of tomatoes, and then go into serious sauce production in her commercial kitchen. Her tomato sauce is in hot demand, mainly from private customers in Vancouver who buy it by the caseload. Local Mayne Islanders can buy it, and her jams, chutneys and relishes, at the

Saturday Farmers' Market and Tru-Value store; in Victoria, they're available at the Market on Yates and Planet Organic. Shanti says she will move beyond direct marketing once her production levels are higher. Eventually, she would like to be able to hire local residents because she believes the island needs more small-scale industry.

When the McDougalls started out, tomatoes were their main crop, but they now produce more of a variety. They grow 800 pounds of Spanish Roja garlic, pinot noir grapes, raspberries, artichokes and greens. There are Damson plums and yellow plums, from which Shanti makes jam. They harvest 500 chickens a year, and sell 20 to 24 sides of beef. Shanti says some people buy a whole year's supply of chicken from her and freeze it.

Deacon Vale is a magical, certified organic farm of 95 acres, co-owned by the McDougalls and the Abbotts (Shanti's brother is Vancouver doctor Bill Abbott). About half of the land is in hay or pasture, and another large section is in woodlot. There's a large, 20-foot-deep pond in the centre of the property, surrounded by fruit trees. Closer to the McDougalls' house is a one-acre market garden, and another half acre of new plantings, including the grapes. Shanti is thinking about putting in some hazelnut trees because organic nuts are hard to find. Saltspring Island bread-maker Heather Campbell had told me that she couldn't find organic hazelnuts for her bread, so I introduce them — the grower and the baker — and, perhaps, organic hazelnut bread will one day be coming out of Heather's oven.

The farm operates on a closed-cycle system, producing what it needs to operate. To keep the soil viable, the McDougalls maintain a hot compost which measures about 25' by 8' by 6', and is turned four times a year. The soil gets a good dose of micronutrients from local seaweed which is collected by the Village Bay Improvement Association and scattered over their plantings.

Mayne Island Farmers' Market

Shanti and Don McDougall were instrumental in starting the farmers' market on Mayne Island "to forge a closer bond between people and the food they eat." It's held at the "Ag Hall," built around 1900, the place where things happen on the island. The hall and grounds offer an ideal setting. In the middle of the grounds, the McDougalls have built a quaint pole structure, used as a stage for local performers.

The market offers a stunning array of the island's bounty: goat cheese, produce, sauces and chutneys, jams and jellies, pies, soft lamb pelts and yarn made from mohair goats. Deacon Vale Farm cooks up a delicious lunch (homemade sausages, hot beef sandwiches, salmon burgers, etc.), so many people spend the morning shopping, eating and chatting with their neighbours. The lunches are delicious, not surprising when one discovers they are prepared by a chef trained at London's Dorchester Hotel — that's Don McDougall! Market organizers hope to develop a complete food court in future.

Shanti says she values the quiet and privacy of her farm, but also enjoys the social aspect of the market. There are usually ten vendors, and this increases to 20 stalls for the annual Fall Fair. The market runs from the Victoria Day long weekend in May to Thanksgiving.

Oceanwood Country Inn

Romance and food are always a good combination, and English country house gentility provides a relaxed setting. I arrive alone to find a lovely, rambling home set in the caress of the aptly named Dinner Bay, and ring the doorbell. Jonathan Chilvers, looking dapper in khaki shorts, greets me with: "Are you planning to come in, or have you just missed the bus?"

Jonathan is a long way from his birthplace "in the shadow of Wandsworth," but his dry, particularly English humour is fully intact. An ex-pat myself, I take an instant liking to my host, and ask him how he happens to own this charming place.

He and his late wife, Marilyn, were living in Vancouver, working in advertising and public rela-
tions respectively, when the idea emerged to have a weekend place in the Gulf Islands. The couple bought a low-maintenance cottage on Mayne Island, and escaped for long, Friday-to-Monday weekends as often as they could.

"The best food is pulled out of the ground."

— Chef Steve Kruse,
Oceanwood Country Inn

In 1989, a realtor friend suggested they look at a property that had just become available, and Jonathan agreed on the understanding that he and Marilyn were only looking. When they returned to see it a second time, they took friends. Their friends said: "All you could do with this property is open a B & B," so they did.

Sorrel and Spinach Soup

Steve Kruse, Oceanwood Country Inn

 Serves 4. "The green leaves of sorrel give a lemony zing to this spring soup. Though not usually found in the regular supermarkets, sorrel is easy to grow from seed. In early spring, the tender young leaves are delicious in a salad or can be cooked like spinach as a vegetable. The secret to success with sorrel is not to cook it too much or it becomes brown and unattractive — although it will still taste delicious." — *Chef Kruse*

2 tbsp	unsalted butter	30 ml
1/2	medium yellow onion, thinly sliced	1/2
2	carrots, peeled and thinly sliced	2
2	stalks of celery, thinly sliced	2
1 c	white wine	240 ml
4 c	chicken or vegetable broth	1 L
2 c	spinach leaves, washed	480 ml
2 c	sorrel leaves, washed	480 ml
2 tsp	finely chopped fresh thyme leaves	10 ml
	salt and pepper to taste	

Sweat the onion, carrot and celery in the melted butter for 3 minutes over medium heat. Add the white wine and allow to reduce for a further 3 minutes. Add the chicken or vegetable broth and the spinach and bring it to a boil. Turn the heat down to a low simmer and let cook for 40 minutes. Turn the heat off. Add the sorrel, stir it in, then immediately purée well in a blender in small batches. Return the purée to the pot and reheat but do not boil. Serve in warm bowls. Garnish with a drizzle of cream that has been steeped with roast garlic and some finely chopped lemon zest.

♟

While Jonathan excuses himself to change for dinner, I take a leisurely tour of the grounds. There's a prolific vegetable-and-herb garden overlooking the bay, and comfortable nooks and seating areas, all situated to take in the view. An impressive flagstaff sports the British Columbian, Canadian, American and British flags. Through an open window, I can see the kitchen in the full flutter of preparations for dinner.

As I wander around the side of the inn, I chance upon Chef Steve Kruse taking a brief coffee break before service. He worked extensively in restaurants as both waiter and dishwasher before "getting serious and going to school in

1994." A graduate of the Stratford Cooking School, he worked at Sooke Harbour House and owned his own bistro, the Miner's Bay Café on Mayne Island, before landing the big job at Oceanwood.

He loves living and working on the island, and appreciates the opportunity to use high quality, refined ingredients in the Oceanwood kitchen. He says he tries to keep his cooking "straightforward and honest," and says the best food is "pulled out of the ground."

He relies on the inn's own gardens for much of the spring and summer, but also buys from some of the local cottage growers including Helen O'Brien and Naralaya Farm's Ron Pither. While the menu is planned a week in advance and posted on the inn's website, it can change daily, such as last Thursday when no fisher had caught the anticipated skate that day. For chefs working on these somewhat remote islands, menu planning is both a challenge and a joy (the joy is when something fresh and inspiring arrives unexpectedly at the kitchen door).

Jonathan greets me again in the library with: "Would you like a beautiful martini or a nice, delicate sherry?" As I settle onto chintz with a glass of Harvey's Bristol Cream, Tony Bennett croons in the background and a kitchen helper passes by the window with a bowl of fresh-picked salad greens from the garden. An American couple joins us for a drink while their teenage daughter "completes her makeup" in their room upstairs. Returning guests, they ask Jonathan to recommend a local chardonnay, "something we haven't tried before."

Jonathan later tells me that the British Columbia wines are in great demand, and he is pleased to be supporting the local economy. I enjoy his comments on the restaurant's wine list, such as that against the popular Venturi Schulze Millefiori: "Enjoy it here because it is unique and you won't find it back in Kansas, Dorothy."

We all head downstairs to the oceanside restaurant for dinner, where a window seat has been reserved for me, although I can see that every table in this dining room commands a sea view. There is a rather large yacht in the bay tonight, the owners of which are dining at the table next to mine. When I mention that I will be overnighting on Pender Island, they point to it across the bay and we contemplate whether or not it's within swimming distance.

When the *prix fixe* menu is presented, I drift away into foodie heaven. One can choose from two appetizers and two mains, and the rest of the menu involves no effort on the part of the diner, other than emitting a few ooohs and ahhhs when the food arrives.

This evening's *amuse bouche* is a simple (or "honest," as Chef Kruse would say) cucumber slice topped with Smoked Sooke Trout Mousse. What follows is an amazingly good soup: Mayne Island Lamb Broth with White Beans, Zucchini and Tomatoes. A fresh sage leaf from the garden adds to the delicious, earthy taste. The lamb was delivered from the island's Iredale Farm. The accompanying breads, Calendua (edible marigold) and Whole Wheat Walnut, are both excellent.

I have chosen the Pacific Octopus in Carrot Broth with Thai Basil, Daikon and Nasturtiums, a brilliantly coloured presentation that reminds me of a Chagall painting. I ask for a soup spoon to finish every last drop of the broth. A raspberry and fennel sorbet cleans the palate, and then I move on to Albacore Tuna Loin seared rare served on Lemon Couscous with Rosemary-Caper Butter Sauce. Jonathan has paired this with a Tinhorn Creek merlot.

My waitress, Candida, is a charming woman who also looks after the inn's gardens and paints and decorates in the off-season. Like many Gulf Islanders, she has embraced the necessity of employment diversity. Working two or three different jobs is the way many are able to sustain life on the islands.

Alas, the ferry calls, and I take my leave. Jonathan opens the big gates and waves me off into a dark night. I foolishly tell him I know the way. With no sense of direction and only the moon to guide me, I somehow avoid all three deer that leap across the road en route, and find myself the only passenger boarding the 9:10 P.M. ferry from Mayne Island.

GALIANO ISLAND

Atrevida in the Galiano Inn

With my great love of "the hunt," part of a good foodie experience is getting there. I am relaxing on the deck of a friend's cottage on the south end of South Pender, chatting with Chef Frank Pabst of Galiano's Atrevida restaurant on the phone, when he happens to mention the water taxi service from Mayne and Pender islands to the Galiano Inn on Wednesday and Friday evenings. Never mind that it is now 4:40 P.M. on a Wednesday, and the taxi leaves from the north end of North Pender Island at 5:00 P.M.; we both have the same idea.

Pabst radios ahead to Mike, the skipper, and I hit the road. Twenty minutes later, I arrive dockside at Port Washington to find Mike and two American couples waiting for me to board the Zodiac. We zip through Active Pass to Galiano's vibrant harbour in Sturdies Bay, disembark, and stroll over to the inn for dinner.

I am greeted on arrival by Kelley Pabst, Frank's wife and the inn's co-manager, who shows me around. Each of the ten rooms is oceanfront, and the décor is lemony-Mediterranean. I am already sorry that they are fully booked that night, and that I am expected elsewhere.

There is a lovely spa and warm, yet professional, meeting facilities. The Labatts' brewery directors, gathered in the boardroom when I peek in, must feel they are meeting in a Tuscan villa, so charming is the conference room.

The restaurant commands a stunning view of the harbour, with small craft and giant ferries passing by the window. I find it so engaging that only Chef Pabst's food can divert my attention. And the cooking is some of the best I've had, not surprising when one considers that Pabst was formerly at the famed Lumière restaurant and later owned and cooked at Pastis in Vancouver.

His credentials certainly raise my expectations. Born in Aachen, Germany, he grew up in Belgium and then apprenticed at a French restaurant in Germany for three years. He went on to cook at the Negresco, Nice's serious celebrity hotel, and later took positions in Cannes and St. Jean-Cap-Ferrat. Ultimately, Pabst says, his cooking shows that his "heart is in the south of France." Light fare, good olive oil, fresh vegetables: bringing the ingredients up to their full potential is his aim.

I'm enjoying the live, classical guitar music in the dining room. It's a full house here tonight, lots of chat and joie de vivre, but still the room has a homey, comfortable feel. I'm joined by Chef Pabst, who tells me it's a challenge to secure the ingredients he wants when he wants them. His contacts in Vancouver are making that easier, and the inn arranges a couple of runs across for specialized foods twice a week, but that will change as he gets to know the local growers and food producers.

When Pabst heads back to the line, waitress Nahanni tells me to sit back and relax, with the music-to-my-ears line: "The chef is choosing your menu." First up is a snow-crab mousse on crostini with a fresh tomato salsa and pea shoots, followed by Chilled Summer Corn Soup with Crab Meat and White Truffle Oil. There are generous pieces of crab in a puréed corn broth — so tasty that I would happily have ordered a second bowl.

The chef's special Citrus and Herb Cured Gravlax with Yellow and Green Beans on a Tomato Concassé with Crème Fraîche and Shallot Vinaigrette made my list of top ten best appetizers ever. The ingredients were startlingly fresh and clean; the presentation, exquisite. This was the essence of summer on a plate.

Next came Pan Fried Rock Sole with Ratatouille on Spinach and Mashed Potatoes with a Roasted Red Pepper Sauce, accompanied by a glass of Dr. Loosen's riesling. An appropriate break, before Roast Duck in a Black Currant Jus with Asparagus, Baby Beetroot and Roast Potatoes, served with a Mondavi pinot noir. The black currants had come from a grower on Mayne Island. The explosion of tastes on this last plate was fabulous, and here I am, not even a fan of duck. Chef Pabst's bird was fat-free, and perfectly medium-rare. As with venison I have eaten at The Aerie, I was here converted to something that I had previously ignored on menus.

Dessert and the cheese course beckoned, but unfortunately, so did the last water taxi back to Pender. We set sail, so to speak, under a full and luminous moon.

WINE ROUTE

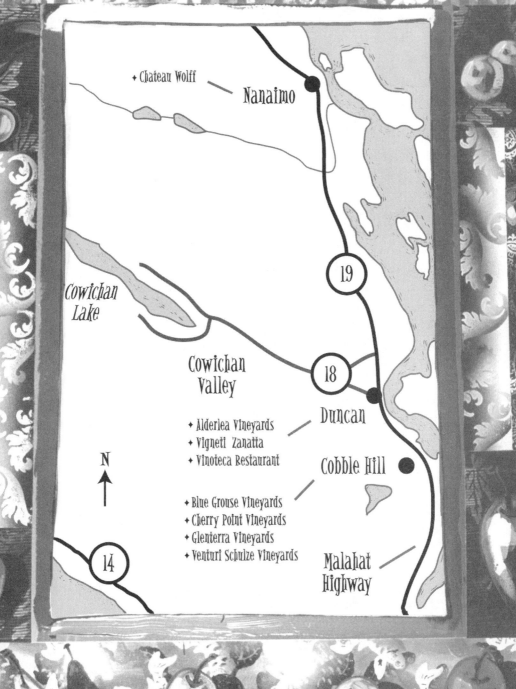

Chateau Wolff

Nanaimo

19

Cowichan
Lake

Cowichan
Valley

18

Duncan

✦ Alderlea Vineyards
✦ Vigneti Zanatta
✦ Vinoteca Restaurant

Cobble Hill

N

✦ Blue Grouse Vineyards
✦ Cherry Point Vineyards
✦ Glenterra Vineyards
✦ Venturi Schulze Vineyards

14

Malahat
Highway

omewhere along the way, I knew I would have to admit a weakness; it's about wine. I love the stuff and drink a glass of vin rouge every day. I know exactly what I like, but I'm no expert. So it seemed appropriate (and also turned out to be fun) to invite not just oenophiles, but professional sommeliers, to accompany me on the wine route. That route loosely includes vineyards in the Cowichan Valley and Cobble Hill area, a destination that might not yet be Napa North, but, as vintner Roger Dosman says is "something like Mendocino."

My experts of choice are Daniel Beiles, sommelier and wine importer with Vinifera Wine Services based in Toronto, and Frances Sidhe, sommelier at Zambri's restaurant in Victoria. Both are not only knowledgeable, they're patient with me!

Daniel was certified as a sommelier by the International Sommeliers Guild in Toronto. He first trained as a chef, working at The Royal York Hotel and Scaramouche in Toronto, followed by a stint at The Wickaninnish Inn. With both family and business on Vancouver Island, he maintains a bi-coastal existence, and I was delighted to meet up with him for visits to Blue Grouse and Vigneti Zanatta vineyards, as well as Sooke Harbour House. Daniel's unpretentious enthusiasm for his craft make him an ideal wine-tasting companion.

Frances achieved her certification from the International Sommelier Guild in Vancouver. She now designs the Zambri's wine list, which is 90 percent Italian. Both intellectual and gracious, Frances is a pleasure to learn from. She tells me she "has a problem with big descriptions of wine," and tends to comment more on weight and sensation than aroma.

Frances says she is interested in adding some Vancouver Island picks to Zambri's offerings. So, if we had a mission at all, it was to discover what was on offer at some of the local wineries, and possibly find out what Vancouver Island wine really is. So, we set out early one morning to visit Alderlea, Cherry Point and Glenterra vineyards with a road-trip picnic of Wild Fire Bakery's walnut and raisin loaf, chèvre and a couple of bottles of water, and the great anticipation of finding some winning "weights and sensations."

Alderlea Vineyards

Frances and I find vintner Roger Dosman pruning the canopy ("the curtain of leaves and shoots that is formed by the grapevines," Frances tells me). He agrees to give me a lesson. As it's January, he first removes the clips that attach the vertical shoots to the wire fencing — there are some 100,000 clips among his eight acres of vines. Then, aiming to keep the shoots separate so that when the clusters of grapes appear, they won't touch each other and create rot, he choses two or three of the shoots to salvage, and clips the rest. The tiers will come along after him and tie the shoots down. Ideally, one wants to leave two vertical shoots from the previous year for renewal (Roger sometimes leaves a third as the shoots are susceptible to breakage when they are tied down).

He explains that it's all about allowing sunlight and air to get to the fruit. Mid-June to the end of July is the heavy-labour period when he and his workers will be "deleafing in the fruit zone" of each vine. Roger is a lot like the Venturi Schulze clan: he does everything the hard way, beginning with propagating his own plants. Says Roger: "Higher quality canopy management gets a better fruit."

Roger had an automotive shop in Vancouver, but didn't want to live in a big city any more. He took note when the provincial government passed legislation in 1989 to allow small farm wineries. Frances jokes about how to make a small fortune in the wine business ("Start with a large fortune," she and Roger agree, "and wait a few years."). Roger did not start with a large fortune but,

after searching in the Okanagan and on Vancouver Island for two years, he found a lovely, sloping, ten-acre parcel that faces southwest in the Cowichan Valley, and set to work.

He has stuck to his mandate: "to produce wine only from grapes grown in our vineyard." Beginning with 30 varieties, he has narrowed them down to 15 that perform well. Roger describes the business as "slow as you go," meaning that you don't know until you try if things will work or not.

What certainly has worked for Roger and his wife, Nancy, who runs the wine-tasting room, is that they have created a viable business and healthy (all that hard work and fresh air) lifestyle. They are contributing to the local economy by providing jobs for five workers in season, and they are giving wine connoisseurs and even amateurs like me the benefit of their considerable skill.

The vines are heavy with grapes at Alderlea Vineyards.

We stopped to taste the talk of the town, the vineyard's fruity, ruby-style port called Heritage Hearth. Roger set out a nice piece of Stilton and some fresh filberts from a farm down the road, and we quietly imbibed. Frances declared the nectar "rich and lush, with good acidity," and immediately ordered a case for the restaurant. I bought a bottle that I have practically hidden at home to enjoy with my cheese course.

Other offerings at Alderlea include Bacchus (a riesling/sylvaner cross), Angelique (a blend of optima and siegerrebe), pinot auxerrois, pinot noir, pinot gris (partial French oak barrel fermentation) and a claret that Frances describes as "a big, fat juicy fruity" wine.

We talk about defining Vancouver Island wine, and Roger suggests that "it will take at least another ten years to see what the island industry really is." He points out that, even within the Cowichan Valley, the locations of vineyards "vary greatly in their ability to grow grapes." One day, say Frances and Roger, it will be nice to see a flavour profile, to be able to say what's typical of the area.

For now, we can enjoy the journey from vineyard to vineyard and winemaker to winemaker, and make our views part of the exciting evolution of this area's style.

Blue Grouse Vineyards

It's one of those heart-stopping, big-blue-sky days in the Cowichan Valley, as Daniel Beiles and I pull into what is arguably Vancouver Island's prettiest vineyard. In the tasting room, we are warmly greeted by Sandrina Kiltz, who introduces herself as the "DOB — daughter of the boss."

The boss is Dr. Hans Kiltz, microbiologist, biochemist and former veterinarian for the United Nations, who brought his family to the Cowichan Valley in 1989. The timing was ideal; provincial legislation was just changing to allow for small farm wineries to operate commercially. The Kiltz family began to test different varietals for suitability, eventually settling on Ortega, Bacchus, pinot gris,

A welcoming sign at Blue Grouse Vineyards.

"Here with a loaf of bread beneath the bough, a flask of wine, a book of verse and thou ..."

— *Omar Khayyam*

Sandrina Kiltz offers wine tastings at her family's Blue Grouse Vineyards.

siegerrebe, pinot noir, gamay noir and others suited to the relatively cold climate. They planted in earnest in 1992 and 1993.

The vineyard is truly a family affair: Hans and his son, Richard, both European-trained winemakers, make the wines; Hans' wife, Evangeline, lovingly tends the vines by hand; and Sandrina, a graduate in international business, is responsible for the marketing and daily public wine-tastings. Now 27, Sandrina tells us it was wonderful growing up at Blue Grouse: "My brother and I did the weeding, thinned out the grape clusters and learned how to drive a tractor before a car. I think it's given us a really good work ethic, and the kids at school thought it was cool that we lived in a vineyard."

Before we turn our attention to the business at hand — wine tasting — we catch a parade of white swans on one of the lower slopes. Then, a couple from North Carolina drops by, and all eyes and ears are fixed on Sandrina, who pours the first selection: Ortega 2000. Daniel notes the "tropical fruit in the nose — lychee, as well as fresh, ripe peach; low acidity on the palate; and a clean fruit-driven finish."

Next up is the winery's Müller-Thurgau 1999, a relation of riesling, from which Daniel gets "soft, white peach and Bosc pear on the nose; petrol [typical of fine riesling] on the palate, and a faint herbal, lemon-balm finish." He tells me it would pair perfectly with a light fish (Sandrina recommends halibut) or shellfish.

The Pinot Gris 2001 is a big hit, and the entire tasting group appreciates what Daniel declares its "floral aspects and figginess." He identifies geranium, white peach, ripe cantaloupe and even a slight nuttiness, and suggests its low to medium acidity would pair well with lamb or fatty fish such as salmon. We learn that Blue Grouse was the first winery in the valley to produce pinot gris and they have been winning awards for it in the prestigious Oregon wine festival ever since. This is the wine we stock up on before reluctantly saying our goodbyes.

Cherry Point Vineyards

Helena Ulrich apologizes for not being available the day Frances and I are going to visit. She's off to Alberta for a week with the grandchildren, and her daughter has already persuaded her to jet-set back for a day in the middle of her holiday to accept the Lifetime Achievement Award from the British Columbia's Institute of Agrologists that she and her husband, Wayne, have won. So, Frances and I pull up chairs at the kitchen table with Wayne and ask how he came to be running a 34-acre vineyard that produces some 5,000 cases a year — the largest operation on Vancouver Island.

He'd always kept a decent cellar of mainly Italian wines. When he and Helena married, he pulled out several cases and his reds went first, before the whites and hard liquor that the caterer had recommended. He worked as an agricultural engineer and Helena was a lab technician and co-owner of the well-known 17-Mile House restaurant (on the road to Sooke) when the couple decided to follow their entrepreneurial spirits.

They moved to Victoria and ran the Victoria Lampshade Shop. However, having a small farm had always been a dream for Wayne. While he was still working for the federal agriculture department, he had been sent to the Okanagan to evaluate a request for funding from a fledgling winery. He visited several vineyards at that time and figured "those guys were enjoying life more" than he and Helena. Like many Vancouver Island vintners, he points to 1989, when the government allowed farm wineries to start up, as the pivotal year in his decision to follow his dream.

They bought the Cowichan Valley property in 1990 and intended to be selling wine by 1993. However, their business plan hadn't factored in the birds that descended in 1992 and put the whole operation back a year. By 1994, Cherry Point was fruitful and fully licensed.

There's a lot going on at this vineyard. In addition to the grape growing, wine production and wine tasting, there are a well-stocked gift shop, outdoor patio wine bar, tours with lunch and wine tastings, catered private parties including a recent dinner for the Confrérie de la Chaîne de Rôtisseurs (Helena and a neighbouring chef are the talent behind those events) and fabulous summer concerts in the 160-seat pa-vilion. People are encouraged to at-tend the concerts with their own picnics or buy a casual meal at the vineyard. The concerts are regularly sold out, so it's advisable to call well ahead for tickets.

Wayne has learned to make wine "just by doing it." He has re-cently been assisted in the winemaking by Hilary Abbott of neighbouring Hilary's Cheese, and has help in the vineyard. Wayne tells us that, as an engineer, "so much of the vineyard is in my head that I frustrate new employees because not much is written down."

We sample the well-received new blackberry port, which Christie Eng of the Shady Creek Ice Cream Com-pany included in her Blackberry Lav-ender Trifle recipe (I found it hard to save some for the trifle!). Made with wild blackberries from the Cowichan Indian Reserve, it's not the sweet, cloying drink one might expect; Frances praises its dryness and tanginess. The Cuvée de Pinot,

Diners revel in the moment at Steeples in Shawnigan Lake, where the menu notes which wines are produced entirely from grapes grown in the Cowichan Valley.

a blend of pinot blanc, pinot gris and Auxerrois has "a spicy nose, with acid from the pinot blanc and a nice long finish;" the Pinot Gris 2001 won a People's Choice award at the island's wine and oyster festival; the non-vintage Valley Sunset is notably fruity; the Pinot Noir 2000 has "less fruit, more structure and length," and Frances suggests it would match well with our West Coast salmon. With all of these tastings under our belt long before breakfast, we make our next stop Black Coffee at Whippletree Junction for a couple of Moriss' serious Americanos.

Glenterra Vineyards

John Kelly was a traffic-safety signmaker and his wife, Ruth Luxton, a Dubrulle-trained chef who cooked for the fabulous Meinhart food store in Vancouver when the couple decided to make a move. John had been commuting for two years to Okanagan University College to take a diploma in viticulture and oenology and had also volunteered at several Okanagan vineyards to learn the trade. When a 17-acre parcel became available on Vancouver Island, they moved the family across the pond.

Ruth does catering with her good friend Connie Papin of Cumberland's Chez Cuisine Kitchen, and also cooks at Livingstone's restuarant in Duncan. John tends the 4.5 acres of vines and makes the wine. They are both involved in the promotion of their vintages; I first met Ruth at the Harvest Bounty Festival where she turned me on to their pinot noir. Even though the property was originally a vineyard, John has done his share of experimentation. Early on, he determined that the Alsace varieties would do best: gewürztraminer, pinot blanc, pinot noir and pinot gris. He tells me about the Duncan Project, a practical research project in the

The entrance to Glenterra Vineyards' tasting room.

Owner John Kelly pours for two Seattle samplers at Glenterra Vineyards.

early 1980s in which vintners from the island's first wineries did a range of test plantings to determine the suitability of grape varieties.

It's a very cold day when Frances and I visit John in his tasting room, but we are soon warmed up with good conversation and samples of his Vivace 2002, a blend of Ortega, Auxerrois, Bacchus, Siegerrebe, Schonberger, et al., that Frances finds to be "almost sweet at the start with a kick of acidity." We both enjoy the Gewürztraminer 2002 straight from the barrel with its lychee, rose petal and grapefruit notes. Frances is impressed with the acid in the wine, as she is always looking for a good structure to stand up to Peter Zambri's dynamic cooking. Another tasting is of the Brio 2002, again from the barrel. John says its herbaceousness comes from the Dunkelfelder grapes. He will add some cabernet sauvignon to round off the flavour.

My ears perk up when John says he is applying for organic certification for his vineyard. He has stopped spraying, started controlling weeds with organic fertilizer mulch and will be switching to metal posts. It's a long road, and one that winemakers seem slower to travel than farmers. John says he's "trying to get there because the wine tastes better, cleaner." He also points out that he is working in the vines and doesn't want to be around pesticides and herbicides.

Glenterra has already won a silver medal for its Pinot Noir 2000 at the prestigious North West Wine Summit. John says they are producing 400 to

600 cases now, and will eventually increase production to ten acres and 1,200 to 1,500 cases. John and Ruth are also hoping to add some type of food service on their property — possibly barbeque, which I've told them would be well-supported by urban hunter-gatherers like myself.

In addition to the estate-grown vintages, a visit this spring will be rewarded with tastings of the Meritage 2001, a classic blend of cabernet sauvignon, merlot, cabernet franc, malbec and Petit Verdot.

Venturi Schulze Vineyards

We all know that there's balsamic and then there's balsamic. Venturi Schulze produces Aceto Balsamico, a nectar that attracts calls from all over the world. I first sampled it with a group of travel writers one overcast day, and I swear the sun came out.

Michelle Schulze tells us that the family's vineyards were originally planted for vinegar, and "then we found we were able to make wine. You see, for vinegar, we need use grapes that are as high, if not higher quality than for wine. If you have faults or a moldy taste, it is so huge after 12 years that you have to throw it away. You can't use pesticides, or the poisons end up in the vinegar. We like to do things the difficult way, and if there's a harder way, well, we'll find that too."

She passes around samples of the vinegar on silver spoons, and tells us: "You're looking for sweetness, and you have to have some acid in there. These

can be fairly high in acid, say 5 to 6 percent, but you won't be able to tell because they're so sweet. This one can be almost 50 percent sugar. A lot of people expect something quite acid, but they say: 'Wow, it's so good. It's sweet!'" I find it delicious — a dessert in itself. We all want to buy bottles to stash in our purses.

Michelle says they like their balsamic vinegar because it maintains some flavour of the grape. "We really enjoy a lot of the Italian ones, but they don't taste quite as alive. Our woods are younger than theirs. You're looking for some wood flavour, and often people don't recognize that. If you put your nose in there, you can smell cherries."

Michelle recommends serving it over strawberries or on really good ice cream. If you're going to use it in a sauce, she advises adding it at the end, as it's already so concentrated. One doesn't want to boil it down and destroy the

Barrels of the famed Aceto Balsamico in the vinegary at Venturi-Schulze Vineyards.

flavour. We also learn that the Venturi Schulze vinegar is not as black as some of the commercial vinegars because there is no added colouring.

We wander out to the vines to admire the healthy clumps of Madeleine Sylvaner, a white-grape variety used for the vinegar. Says Michelle: "We'll go through there seven times in a certain season. You can basically tell by July how your fruit is set and how it's going to ripen. Sometimes you can pick everything at once in one or two days; sometimes it's over three weeks. You get in there, and start picking those bunches that have ripened first. Giordano [Giordano Venturi, her stepfather], will say, 'I need more acid,' so sometimes, we even pick portions of bunches."

Sometimes they have to let the grapes over-ripen because they need higher sugar and lower acid to make it work. Once picked, the grapes are crushed as they are for wine, and the juice is simmered in 60-gallon pots for about three days. Michelle says: "It's really kind of a fun process. It's like making a broth,

Balm

"Balm is good for your health. Mix together with some ice and feel it cure all!" — *Michelle Schulze*

glass of club soda
drop of Venturi Schulze's Aceto Balsamico

and the proteins come to the top. They have to be skimmed off or they'll turn brown and have a bitter flavour. We're looking for a clear product."

When Michelle opens the door to the vinegary, the aroma pulls us inside. The neat rows of barrels represent more than 30 years of work. Giordano made his first barrel of vinegar in 1970. He comes from a very poor family and had never had the real stuff. His first batch went mouldy and had to be thrown out. Michelle tells us: "He ended up going back to Italy and bringing back a live culture. He put it in a barrel, and basically forgot about it. It was many years later that he tasted it and that was it! It was just sort of a fluke that it happened that way, and it took off from there. That's the little barrel right there — the mother barrel. We didn't make another vinegar until 1986." Although they've slowed down the evaporation from that original barrel, basically, the whole stock comes from it.

Michelle laughs as she points to the flowerpots on the property, barrels cut in half with geraniums in them. "Each represents $30,000 in lost revenue. When there's mould, you just have to throw the vinegar out and that's all they're good for. It's hit and miss, really."

Michelle's mother, Australian-born Marilyn Schulze, received a National Research Council grant to obtain certain Italian documents regarding vinegar production. She was able to make sense of them, and worked side by side with Giordano to create their special vinegar.

The current release is a blend of vinegars between six and 32 years old from the various barrels. Barrels are laid on their sides, side by side, and holes are cut in the top for evaporation. It gets fairly warm in the vinegary, so there is intense evaporation. They lose up to 30 percent volume a year, depending on how hot it is.

Each barrel gets topped up from the barrel beside it. That's why each barrel is slightly larger than the one next to it; it's also a year younger. The vinegar moves down the whole line, which is why they have to keep the grape production up. It takes a long time.

Vinegar barrels are traditionally made from mulberry wood, but it's a protected tree so it's now unavailable. Venturi Schulze uses oak, acacia, cherry, chestnut and ash barrels.

Michelle puts the whole production into perspective: "If you start with 1,000 gallons of juice, in 12 years, you will have between 25 and 30 gallons which is why it's so expensive. This is Giordano's dream, and it's working out. We're the only ones who are doing this commercially in North America."

Venturi Schulze is also highly regarded for its wines: a Brut Naturel that was chosen for the Queen's 1994 visit to the Commonwealth Games in Victoria; Millefiori, the ultimate tropical fruity siegerrebe; Brandenburg No. 3, a rich dessert wine that pairs perfectly with my favourite course, the cheese course. They are all estate-grown, and Marilyn is adamant that this is the only way to develop a regional identity for wine. She is concerned that some local winemakers are buying their grapes from other parts of the province and not declaring their origin. She sees huge potential for the Cowichan Valley wine area, and just wants it to be true to itself.

Vigneti Zanatta

A visit to Vigneti Zanatta should properly be combined with a meal at the vineyard's farmhouse restaurant, Vinoteca, so Daniel and I, together with friends, make time to do both.

Loretta Zanatta is the kind of thoughtful, intelligent vintner you want making your vino. The care and pride she takes in what she does and her obvious depth of knowledge are inspiring. We ask how she got into the business in the first place.

"We're an Italian family," she tells me, "so we have always grown grapes and made wine." Her parents emigrated from Treviso, which is north of Venice, in the 1950s. They found a 120-acre dairy farm just south of Duncan,

The enchanting farmhouse restaurant at Vigneti Zanatta vineyard.

and decided it would be "a great place to raise kids," so they raised dairy cattle and their own children. The family always grew their own vegetables and grapes.

By 1981, Loretta's father was experimenting with grapes in earnest. The family turned an acre of land over to the Duncan Project, a government-sponsored effort to determine which grapes would really grow well in these parts. Loretta says she spent a lot of time "testing the acids and sugars" of what was planted. She and her husband, Jim, had acquired degrees in plant science from the University of British Columbia. Loretta had also obtained a Master's degree in winemaking from the university in Piacenza, Italy. They were more than prepared when the provincial government introduced legislation that enabled farm wineries.

In 1992, Vigneti Zanatta became the first licensed commercial vineyard on Vancouver Island. Loretta is known for her sparklers that she makes "in the champagne style." She calls sparklers "the cleanest wines," because they contain no sulphur and are based on unadulterated wine fermented only with naturally occurring yeast and sugar. At Vinoteca, you can enjoy a champagne-tasting of Loretta's three sparklers paired with an appetizer plate, and I can think of no merrier way to begin a leisurely afternoon on its veranda.

Daniel tastes but, as I'm driving, I opt to take the three sparkling beauties home and make a dinner around tasting them — one of my more delicious excuses for a party. So, at a later occasion, my friends and I happily imbibe Glenora Fantasia Brut (made from 100% Cayuga grapes; aged up to six years), Alegria Brut Rosé (Loretta's personal favourite, a light rosé made from pinot noir and auxerrois grapes) and Taglio Russo (made from cabernet savignon grapes, a deep red sparkler that's based on the still wine Loretta used to make for her grandmother). All of us are most taken with the Fantasia Brut, the sparkler Daniel describes perfectly as having "a fine, light pale yellow complexion with thin, persistent streams of bubbles; a nose of fresh bread and Granny Smith apple; followed by a medium mouth feel with a crisp and tangy citrus finish." The Zanatta winery also produces pinot grigio and Damasco, an appetizer or sipping wine that's made using auxerrois wine refermented on Ortega skins.

Loretta is proud of what her family vineyard produces. They only make wine from their own grapes and will not bring in product from other grape-growing areas like the Okanagan. She recognizes that wine is a new industry in the Cowichan Valley, but would prefer to see more estate-based operations. "Ideally," she says, "all vintners in the valley will grow all their own grapes or buy them from other Cowichan Valley growers, and then we'll have a true sense of what Vancouver Island wine is."

Vinoteca at Vigneti Zanatta

Chef Fatima da Silva sleeps with her menu. "No, really," she tells me, over a cup of tea in the restaurant. "I often think of something in the night, switch on the light and scribble it down."

On the day I visit, the restuarant is two weeks away from opening for the season, and that menu is still a work in progress. Fatima is expecting the delivery of a sample of smoked duck, which she is keen to offer to customers. She will use Cowichan Bay Farm's duck. "I'm planning to serve a smoked duck open-face sandwich with fig and caramelized onion chutney for lunch, and smoked duck and arugula risotto finished with goat cheese and toasted pine nuts for dinner."

In the meantime, there's lots of preparation afoot to ready the restaurant for its opening. Everything is being cleaned and polished around us as we chat about what brought Fatima to this magical place. She arrived in Quebec City from Portugal in 1997, worked as an au pair and studied French at Laval University. She often cooked for her host-family, and

Chef Fatima da Silva gets a helping hand in the kitchen of Vinoteca.

they offered to send her to cooking school, but Fatima thought that sounded like "too much of a girlish thing."

Instead, she followed her sister to Victoria, where she studied English at Camosun College and worked at the old French Connection restaurant in James Bay. "I began as a dishwasher, but was soon cooking the lunches." Then, she made a career change from the food industry to the home-care field. All the while, she and her friends would have wonderful dinner parties at which they'd try new wines. At one party, someone brought a bottle of Glenora Fantasia Brut from Vigneti Zanatta, and everyone loved it. Fatima loved it so much that she decided to visit the winery. She and her friends tasted the wines and ate at Vinoteca, the charming restaurant in the Zanatta family's 1903 farmhouse. They returned many times to eat at Vinoteca, and one night overheard someone say the chef was leaving. Fatima's friends encouraged her to apply, and she is now running the place.

She loves being able to work with some of the finest local ingredients the Cowichan Valley has to offer: produce from the restaurant's own gardens and from Engeler Farm, chicken and duck from Cowichan Bay Farm, venison from Broken Briar

Fallow Deer Farm and lots of other wonderful things that simply arrive at the kitchen door from local growers. Fatima offers a select menu based on what's in season.

Says Fatima: "We've noticed in the past year that people are eating more and staying longer." The reasons are obvious. I can think of no better fare — fresh, and cooked with an ample dose of the chef's good humour — and certainly no better setting. On a beautiful day, nothing beats a table on the restaurant's large veranda with its expansive view of the vineyards, and a bottle of house-made wine and trademark Vinoteca antipasto platter between me and my husband.

The ultimate al fresco dining room at Vinoteca restaurant in the Vigneti Zanatta Vineyards.

Château Wolff

Harry von Wolff pulls up a chair in the late fall sunshine and welcomes me to his "little piece of paradise." He'd had the local women's Francophone association here the night before. They come every year, bringing cheeses and pâtés to enjoy with Harry's wines. The evening had ended, as always, "with a great deal of singing."

This afternoon, he's relaxed. The day's work is done. We range over many topics, from modern parenting to late marriages, but central to our conversation is the wine. The vineyard has been a long time coming for Harry.

Born in Latvia, he immigrated to Canada in 1953. He'd been fleeing west towards "a society of democratic freedom" since the outbreak of World War II, and working on his uncle's Peace River ranch was a good place to land. He soon sponsored his mother and grandmother, who began their new life in Vancouver.

Harry moved about a lot — 59 jobs in 11 years. From fixing fences, picking rocks and threshing in the Peace River district, he moved on to become an apprentice typographer. When lead poisoning sidelined him from that trade,

Harry von Wolff in his tasting room.

The expansive vineyards at Chateau Wolff — Harry von Wolff's successful hobby.

he worked as a compass man on the railway on Vancouver Island. He always had his eye on hillsides, and began looking for one with southwestern exposure, but several more careers came up before he would finally have his vineyard.

Stints as a wine steward and then barman at some fancy golf clubs in Vancouver got him thinking about proper training. He attended hotel school in Switzerland, then took positions running hotels in Haiti, the Queen Charlotte Islands and Jasper. His next venture was a shoe repair and western shop in Nanaimo where he met his future wife, Helga.

After he married, Harry began growing grapes and experimenting with wine making. Friends raved about his apple and blackberry wines, telling him he "could sell them to the public." When eight acres came up with what Harry considered to be the right combination of latitude, climate and soil, he began his current venture.

Describing his vineyard as "my 40-foot, mahogany yacht in Hong Kong harbour," really puts it into perspective. It's a hobby for Harry. People come to the winery for tours and tastings on the weekends. Some enjoy their picnics in the vineyard and everyone buys the wine, but Harry really just wanted to prove he could do it. "It's about living and having fun," he tells me.

I leave with a bottle of Harry's "new wine for the world," his Grand Rouge Demi-Sec, the Viva! pinot noir and a bottle of Grand Rouge dessert wine, which he advises me to enjoy with someone I love. It's late September, but Harry is not picking his grapes just yet. This year, he will wait until the last week of October so he can bottle late harvest wines.

Mermaid mosaic, designed by Karen White, in the gardens at Sooke Harbour House.

A plane delivers travellers to their ultimate destination — Sooke Harbour House.

131

Chef Edward Tuson of Sooke Harbour House happily displaying a rockfish — will this catch wind up on your plate tonight?

Reawaken your taste buds at Sooke Harbour House with skate wing with alaria and sea lettuce.

Gastronome Sinclair Philip of Sooke Harbour House exhibits a choice vintage.

A palatable plate at
Hastings House on
Saltspring Island.

Clipping herbs at the Hastings House
gardens. Tall fences surround the
garden to keep out bold deer.

The gardens at Engeler Farm, the "farm of angels," located in Cowichan Valley.

"Mead is the oldest art of fermentation. Consumed by all, from kings to peasants, mead has gained a reputation as a giver of life, wisdom, courage and strength down through the ages."
— *Tugwell Creek Honey Farm, Sooke*

Salt Spring Flour Mill flours and grains are innovatively packaged in boxes reminiscent of Chinese food takeout.

Darren Cole flambés while dinner guests warm to the atmosphere at Steeples in Shawnigan Lake, a stylish yet cozy restaurant offering food that is sublime.

These tidbits at The Aerie are as artfully presented as they are scrumptious.

Chef de Cuisine Christophe Letard surrounded by the bounty at The Aerie, located on the scenic Malahat.

Chickens roam free at Fairburn Farm near Duncan.

Rows of vegetables at Engeler Farm.

A view across the pond at Engeler Farm.

Master cheesemaker Paul Sutter and assistant Haiden Smith at Natural Pastures Cheese Company in Courtenay.

Employee Leslie Shann adds a round to the cheeses ready for shipping at Natural Pastures Cheese Company.

Paul Sutter proffers a tray of his award-winning Camembert at Natural Pastures Cheese Company.

Mid-Island

Denman Island Hornby Island

19

4

Qualicum Beach

Nanoose Bay

Parksville

Lantzville

Gabriola Island

Nanaimo

Cedar

Cowichan Lake

Ladysmith

Chemainus

Cowichan Valley

18

Duncan

Cobble Hill

N

14

The Malahat

he Mid-Island is truly the tummy of Vancouver Island — a noticeably warmer and contented stretch from Shawnigan Lake in the south to Hornby Island in the north that is blessed with unique farms, vineyards and eateries. Of late, this area has attracted a number of significant gastronomes from across the pond, including chef (and now farmer) James Barber; restaurateur John Bishop; host of CBC's "Pacific Palate" Don Genova; and chef, author and mushroom expert Bill Jones.

SHAWNIGAN LAKE

Steeples

I cannot believe it's taken me this long to discover Steeples, the stylish yet cozy restaurant in the heart of Shawnigan Lake Village. When I finally step through the door, I feel a sense of déjà vu — based on the many reports I'd read and the good things I'd heard, I must have been here before.

Steeples was born just two years ago, when locals Daphne and Michael Francis realized the village needed a proper restaurant. They're not restaurateurs, but they had the vision necessary to renovate the former Sylvan United Church. Despite a change in the nature of its business, the building has somehow retained a sense of spirituality. The dining room soars with light and colour. The altar is now a modern open kitchen and the pews have been replaced by tables and chairs at which patrons can dine on divine creations like roast duck breast with blackberries, grilled vegetable and goat cheese torta and prosciutto-wrapped filet mignon.

Partner and manager Darren Cole describes the renovation and decoration of the former church as "one big art project." Experienced in starting restaurants from scratch (including Mill Bay's

Chef and co-owner Darren Cole in the dining room at Steeples.

Fridays and Sidney's McGinty's), he clearly enjoyed the process. His cooking experience has come in handy, too — from stints at Victoria's Fogg 'n' Suds, Six Mile Pub and the short-lived but brilliant Classical Pig Café. Before Darren worked in the restaurant industry, he was a motivational speaker and I expect that training stands him in good stead in a business where not everyone knows what to order.

Like Brasserie L'École in Victoria, this is a very social room. I always enjoy dining by myself when a dining room is a-buzz with interesting conversation and table-hopping around me. I can feel part of the action without actually having to engage in conversation. All the more time, I gleefully think, for enjoying my food and drink.

Top: Chef and co-owner Darren Cole flambés at Steeples. Above: The dining room at Steeples was once a church.

What impresses me immediately is Darren's commitment to showcasing local producers. Chicken comes from Cowichan Bay Farm, greens and pears from Engeler Farm, free-range turkey from Kilrenny Farm, vegetables from Apple Bear Farm, mussels from Saltspring Island and oysters from Fanny Bay. The wine list reads like my wine route for this book: an entire section is devoted to the best of Alderlea, Blue Grouse, Cherry Point, Glenterra, Godfrey Brownell, Vigneti Zanatta and Venturi Schulze vineyards. And Darren has gone one important step further: he has noted on the menu which wines are produced entirely from grapes grown in the Cowichan Valley (versus those that have been made with grapes imported from the Okanagan). Darren tells me he loves selling the Vancouver Island wines, and I take great pleasure hearing him turn other diners on to a new merlot from Alderlea and the refreshing Millefiori from Venturi Schulze.

I start with a fabulously flavourful thin-crust pizza with duck confit, goat cheese and red onions and then try Darren's favourite, the grilled prawns and Digby scallops atop avocado with a summertime salsa of pineapple, mango and cilantro. The ultimate filet mignon served with a portobello mushroom topped with meltingly sinful Cambozola and mashed potatoes, whole carrots and asparagus spears is one of the restaurant's most popular entrées. I ended with a chocolate pâté with orange custard from local pâtissier Gerald Billings' significant repertoire.

There's a lot to like at Steeples, including the heated deck where it was warm enough for dinner on Valentine's Day; the enclosed garden with its pretty pond and kiwi vines where diners can play croquet before or after their meal; and the sense of occasion that seems to permeate every table in the place. I particularly like the fact that servers actually serve the excellent house-made focaccia one beautiful, warm slice at a time, and don't need to be asked to bring more, and that they take the time to prepare Caesar salad and a host of dessert flambés tableside.

Steeples may no longer be a church, but food is sublime here and the service is appropriately divine.

THE MALAHAT

The Aerie

The drive up to The Aerie feels like a turn off the autobahn, and suddenly one is in a romantic, almost fairy-tale setting. Yet this is more than a *haus* on the hill; an exclusive European destination resort awaits. A member of the prestigious Relais & Châteaux group and recently voted top resort in North America by the readers of *Condé Nast Traveler*, The Aerie is sitting pretty.

I check into my vast room, which, for one person, seems hugely extravagant until I begin to use and then appreciate every indulgence. In the sunken living room, I sink into the couch to take in my surroundings and find a bowl of strawberries and freshly baked organic oatmeal cookies within handy reach. The cookies are made with Millstream flour from the organic mill in Victoria's

James Bay. I decide to put on the kettle and savour tea and biscuits while enjoying the view across Finlayson Arm. After tea, I need no encouragement to run a deep bath in the round Jacuzzi by the window. Keeping my eye on that view, I slip in to soak and dream until dinnertime.

The dining room is set dramatically high above Finlayson Arm, and the views are spectacular from every table. From across the room, Brad Prevedoreos, the internationally renowned guitarist and recording artist, strums softly. I'm dining this evening with ten people including Alicia Richardson of Williams Sonoma's *Taste* magazine; Paige Herman of *Gotham and Hamptons*; Emily Benson of the American Food Network; Markus Griesser, the resort's general manager, and Mara Jernigan of Engeler Farm. It's a convivial group of people who are knowledgeable about and appreciative of good food.

> "What inspires us is the curiosity of our guests. People are now very curious about what they are eating, what goes into their food."
>
> — Markus Griesser,
> The Aerie

We begin with Spiced Red Wine Cured Chicken Breast and Foie Gras Spring Rolls with Sesame and Ginger Tossed New Zealand Spinach and a Thyme and Spring Morel Mushroom Infusion. Markus tells Mara that he wishes someone in the valley would produce foie gras, so great is the demand from their guests and, naturally, they would prefer to buy local. The meal continues through many inspired courses, finishing with Torrefazione coffee, a ten-year-old tawny port and one of the most inventive desserts I've encountered: "Trio" includes Tangy Grapefruit Jelly and Dark Chocolate Tart with Minted Fromage Blanc Sorbet; Long Pepper and Coconut Sorbet with Fresh Strawberry on a Spiced Wild Strawberry Syrup; and Chicory Root and Dried Candied Fruit Nougat

Glacé with Licorice Sauce. Had I not known the chef, I would have guessed its maker to be Titania, the Fairy Queen.

As a food writer, I've learned that the best stories are found right in the kitchens or on the farms — in other words, where the action is. When Executive Chef de Cuisine Christophe Letard invited me to don an apron during dinner preparation one evening, wings couldn't have carried me there faster. I quickly discovered that backstage at The Aerie is a well-choreographed, happy set. And all the players are unbelievably (to me, anyway) young, talented and dedicated.

Letard is a wiry, handsome, 30-something Frenchman who operates in perpetual motion for the three hours I'm at his side. I join him just as he begins to prepare the Pommes Anna for tonight's tasting menu. Never have I seen a chef so cleanly and exactly peel a potato, slice it into mere breaths and then create perfect rosettes from those slices. The rosettes are lightly brushed with olive oil, and sprinkled with salt, then popped into the oven to come out golden and crisp. I ask about his knife. "Ah, this. Everyone uses it. It's just a knife I'm comfortable with, that I started with in France." No lock and key here, no one assigned to carry the chef's knives. Later, Letard takes a moment to sharpen his knife before filleting some Arctic char. He uses his father's stone ("Actually, my father usually sharpens it, but I haven't been back for three years").

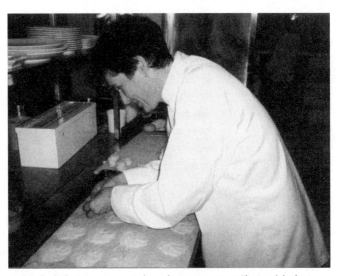

Author Elizabeth Levinson is recruited to make potato rosettes in The Aerie's kitchen.

Back to the rosettes. Three will be stacked with Summer Truffle Tartufo and Grain Mustard Beurre Blanc to form a base for the Grilled Ling Cod Pavé. Letard turns the rosette making over to me, and deftly prepares the truffle paste. In the middle of his work, he stops briefly to give me a taste, and a comment about three oils: huile de truffe ("fantastic"); huile d'olive Provence

Spiced Red Wine-Cured Chicken Breast and Foie Gras Spring Roll with Sesame Oil and Ginger Tossed New Zealand Spinach and Thyme and Spring Morel Mushroom Infusion

CHRISTOPHE LETARD, THE AERIE

Serves 4.

Don't let the long list of ingredients stop you from making an appetizer you'll become famous for!

Spring Rolls

6.5 oz	chicken breast	182 g
4 oz	Quebec foie gras	114 g
4	bright-lights chard leaves (or similar leaves)	4
1	celery root	1
4	spring roll wrappers	4
1	bunch New Zealand spinach	1
0.35 oz	minced ginger	10 g
1 c	sesame oil	240 ml

Infusion

1 tbsp	butter	15 ml
2 oz	morels	57 g
2	shallots	2
1	clove garlic	1
	thyme, bay leaves, black peppercorn	
6.5 oz	chicken marinade	195 ml
10 tsp	chicken stock	50 ml
10 tsp	cream	50 ml

Marinade for Chicken

4 c	red wine	1 L
1 c	brandy	240 ml
1 c	port	240 ml
	black peppercorns, bay leaves, thyme, garlic, shallot, juniper berries, cloves	

Chicken: Marinate the chicken breast for at least 24 hours. After marinating the chicken, clean and wash the chard and spinach. Peel celery root. Cut the foie gras and celery root into thick batons.

Blanch the celery root. Blend the ginger with the sesame oil and reserve. Take the chicken out of the marinade, dry on a cloth, and remove the skin. Sear the chicken with a little olive oil and season at the end. Cool. Cut the chicken into long batons similar to the foie gras.

Spring Rolls: Place one chard leaf on a flat surface. Place chicken, foie gras, and blanched celery root on the top of the chard. Roll together. Place the rolled chard onto a spring roll wrapper. Roll the spring roll wrapper and seal with a paste made of water and flour. Repeat until all four spring rolls are done. Reserve.

Infusion: Sweat chopped shallots, garlic, thyme and bay leaves with a teaspoon of butter for a few minutes. Add the morels and cook for three more minutes. Add marinade and reduce down. Add chicken stock and reduce by half. Add cream and reduce by two-thirds. Blend and pass through a sieve. Taste and season if desired.

Deep fry the spring rolls for about four minutes. Warm up the morel sauce. Blanch the spinach and toss it in the sesame emulsion. On the plate, put a spoonful of sauce in the middle. Place the spring roll (sliced diagonally) on top of the sauce and top with the spinach.

("for cooking"); and certified organic golden olive oil from Greece ("for taste!"). Finally, I taste the truffle tartufo, which is deep with truffle and garlic. Letard notes that the garlic will mellow with cooking, but says the paste "is me; that's my flavour."

While some chefs are shying away from the labour of tasting menus, Letard is planning to stay the many intricate courses. He loves "the little dishes — they're beautiful, like tapas," and he has a clientele that appreciates the small-plate experience.

Organics are very big in this kitchen. Letard reckons he is cooking with 80% organic produce (including meat, poultry and dairy) in the summer months. He is delighted to be cooking a menu that "happens with the seasons," and has come to depend on his local and on-site suppliers — from a monk who brings fiddleheads, sorrel and stinging nettles to his kitchen door, to David Groves who produces the meltingly tender fallow deer meat, to Jackie Morrell who runs the resort's vegetable and herb gardens. Asparagus are feverishly anticipated every year from The Asparagus Farm. As Markus Griesser says: "They arrive 15 minutes old. We don't even cook them. Then, there's the

gentleman who delivers quail, a Czechoslovakian with a triple doctorate. He's very modest. And the morel and chanterelle pickers. Figs and artichokes are growing here, things you wouldn't expect at first glance." The restaurant uses all local meat except beef, which comes from the Nicola Valley.

Griesser notes that the location of The Aerie means they "don't have the luxury of farmgate shopping. In the beginning, it was quite a challenge to seek out the quality ingredients." But many producers come to the door now, and Letard says his challenge is to space out the deliveries, so he is not overwhelmed with, say, mushrooms. He preserves as much as possible of the summer fruits, including some 20 types of heirloom tomatoes.

I ask Letard what the differences are between his work in Europe and in Canada. He says the training he received in France was more extensive and the equipment was more sophisticated, but he speaks highly of the cooking experiences he's had in this country (The Inn at Manitou and Langdon Hall, both in Ontario).

Letard was raised on his family's farm in Normandy. They had a bit of everything and were largely self-sufficient. There were cows, vegetables. His father made his own calvados. Letard took an early interest in "the science and the art of cooking," helping his mother prepare meals for his father and six older brothers. He went on to Hotel Savoie Leman, France's oldest cooking school, where he trained for four years. He says of that time: "I was small, and they didn't think I would last, but I came out with a degree of server."

He then focussed on pastry, working at establishments in Les Deux Alpes. When he landed the job of pastry chef at La Réserve in Albi, he was starting to think about becoming a chef. He made a deal that he would teach pastry to the chef, and the chef would teach him to cook. After that, he went back to Normandy to become chef de partie-saucier at La Ferme Saint Simeon, where he "worked so hard under an old-school chef" that he really respected. "I had 13 sauces to finish every night, but that was a great learning experience." While he was at Saint Simeon, the restaurant was awarded its first Michelin star.

Feeling he should travel and have some new experiences, Letard came to Canada, spending a couple of seasons at The Inn at Manitou in McKellar, Ontario, under the tutelage of Jean Pierre Chalet, the chef he holds up as his mentor. He credits Chalet for teaching him to cook using styles from many countries, but incorporating local flavours.

After that, he worked at the Normandie Hotel in Manchester, which was awarded England's first Michelin star (and where he served the Queen Mother for a week). Then, a stint cooking on a luxury cruising barge in Burgundy and the Upper Loire, where he met his wife. The two came to Canada, where Letard was the working chef at The Domain of Killien in the Haliburton area. Someone told him he should see British Columbia, so he headed west.

Letard and I are standing in the dining room, inhaling that big, blue view. He tells me when he came to The Aerie with his wife, he stood in this very place and thought to himself: "One day, I would love to work here." He didn't introduce himself at that time, but sent in a résumé after returning to Ontario.

Today, he is executive chef. His sous-chef is Christophe Alain, with whom Letard worked at The Inn at Manitou. They are a formidable pair, with the talent and drive to keep The Aerie's restaurant on the world's gourmet trail for a long time. At the same time, Letard is charmingly self-effacing: "I'm not a genius. Sometimes it goes well, sometimes not. It takes a lifetime to put everything together to make sense."

A Day in the Life of an Executive Chef

At noon, Letard is in the kitchen, checking that breakfast went well, and noting any concerns. From there, he checks the evening's reservations, the fridges and the day's supplies. He orders tomorrow's supplies, returns calls, sets the tasting menu and determines what needs to be prepped for the evening meal.

In the early afternoon, he has meetings with hotel management (and pesky food writers!), and helps to prep and instruct prep for the evening menu.

By 4:30 P.M., he leads a menu discussion for guests dining that evening, often passing around samples of fresh ingredients. He is joined by Markus Griesser who presents the evening's recommended wine pairings. Says Letard: "You learn a lot about the people you are cooking for, so you can change a dish to suit what you think they would like."

By 6:00 P.M., Letard is on the line and I am in gastronomic heaven, sitting in the luxuriously appointed dining room and enjoying his creations all the more now that I have seen up close his impressive devotion to the food he prepares.

The Aerie's Garden

The Aerie's gardener has a long history of vegetable and herb growing. Jackie Morrell and Carol Sowerby began Thetis Island Salad on Thetis Island. When Jackie and her husband, Ches, decided to grow for restaurants, they moved to Chemainus and founded Island Gourmet Salads four years ago. Sadly, Ches died, but Jackie has continued to grow the beautiful herbs and vegetables they had become known for.

Jackie now works exclusively for The Aerie, a position she relishes. "This is such a wonderful place to work," she tells me. "The staff call this the castle in

Jackie Morell and Christophe Letard in The Aerie's garden.

the mountains." She is actively developing the vegetable, herb and edible-flower beds. Guests enjoy touring the beds, either independently (everything is conveniently labelled) or with Jackie herself, and then discovering something on their dinner plate they've just seen growing.

Jackie says her biggest challenge is making the weather work for the garden. She has a small greenhouse to get plants started, double-covers everything and relies on her extensive experience to know what to plant and where. She consults regularly with Chef Letard to determine what the kitchen will need, and goes from there. Macro-greens, time consuming to grow but incredibly beautiful and nutritious, are a specialty of Jackie's. She loves growing fenugreek and arugula this way. "It's a form of sprouting, really — taking only the first two colten leaves of the plant, and then starting all over again."

An interesting new vegetable in her spring garden is the rat-tail radish, with a taste and texture between a snap pea and a radish, which the kitchen will use as garnishes and for snacking.

Jackie's organic-gardening methodology includes the use of red wriggler worms for composting, digging in the previous greens as green manure, mulching with straw, using baking soda to control mould and introducing herbs and edible flowers to encourage bugs as a natural insecticide.

COWICHAN VALLEY

The Asparagus Farm

Charles Ford and his dog, Asta, are just returning from picking up mail at the end of the road as I pull in to The Asparagus Farm. It's still a little early in the year, but my visit is partly designed to add to my own anticipation of the short, six-week asparagus season. Standing at the farmgate, I visualize myself right at the front of the long lineups that occur here every day from about mid-April through May. People travel from as far as Vancouver to buy the Fords' asparagus, and Charles says it's not unusual to have 50 cars parked at the gate before he opens it at 10 o'clock in the morning. One man, crossing the Atlantic on the *Queen Elizabeth II*, complained to his tablemate that he couldn't find white asparagus in North America. The tablemate sent him to Charles.

What is all the fuss about? To me, it's two things: you can't get any asparagus any fresher (these are picked daily in season and only hours before the gate opens), and you can buy white asparagus here. Freshness and the way the asparagus is handled mean everything to the connoisseur: the tenderest shoot can become woody from being stored too long, or stored in the wrong conditions. That "woodyness" can actually climb up the stalk after it has been picked and, if the asparagus is not chilled immediately after picking, its sugars turn to starch.

The white asparagus is a whole other story. Long prized by Europeans, white asparagus or spargel arrives with great fanfare every year. It is traditionally served with a white sauce and boiled

White Asparagus with Balsamic Vinegar Mayonnaise

Carole and Charles Ford, The Asparagus Farm

During asparagus season, I'm always looking for new ways to enjoy the king of the lily family. This presentation is always well received.

White asparagus requires different preparation and cooking methods than green asparagus. While it is not necessary to peel green asparagus and cooking is minimal (three to five minutes) so as to produce a bright green, tender-crisp product, this is not the case with white asparagus. Raw, (it has a sweet nutty taste, and crunchy texture) white asparagus may be eaten as is. If cooked, white asparagus MUST be peeled first, so that no skin remains, and steamed until completely tender (20 minutes or more).

To peel, begin lightly at the tip and peel deeper as you get toward the butt end. If peeling is done too timidly or cooking time is inadequate, the asparagus will be stringy. While there are special white asparagus peelers available in Europe, a potato peeler works fine. As with green asparagus, the more fibrous portion on the butt end should also be removed. Snap at its natural breaking point. Do not despair — the peeling goes quickly!

Make a mayonnaise substituting good quality, traditional balsamic vinegar for the regular vinegar and lemon juice. Peel and cook white asparagus as detailed above, then chill. Serve mayonnaise with the chilled white asparagus tips. The balsamic mayonnaise will lose its flavour within a day so do not make it too far in advance.

potatoes. Charles has answered the prayers of many here who grew up in Europe with a taste for white asparagus.

We take a walk across the ten-acre property. Asta bounds ahead and has a wonderful time chasing the California quail out of the asparagus patch (Charles encourages the quail as they eat many of his weeds). I ask how he got into this much-sought-after product in the first place.

Charles has always farmed, but mostly cranberries in Pitt Meadows on the mainland. He says he was lucky to be growing cranberries "during the boom time when Ocean Spray was buying tons of fruit." When his wife, Carole, accepted a teaching position at the University of Victoria in 1989, the couple decided to look for land on Vancouver Island. The Cobble Hill farm fit the bill, and Charles planned to grow asparagus and apples. He planted the apples first, but they got blight, and he focussed on the asparagus.

Charles is also experimenting with growing the coveted black truffle, as well as black elderberries, which are known for their health properties. As he collaborates with a botanist on the truffle project, Vancouver Island chefs are holding their collective breath.

Black Coffee and Other Delights

Okay, it's true. Coffee is what fuels the urban hunter-gatherer, which is probably why the people who know me best know to find me in the island's cafés. One favourite re-fuelling stop is Black Coffee and Other Delights at Whippletree Junction, south of Duncan. Even when I'm pressed for time, I still stop for a takeout giant cinnamon bun and an Americano — such is my addiction.

Located in Cobble Hill's former general store/post office building, which was moved to the Whippletree Junction site along with buildings from Duncan's old Chinatown, Black Coffee has been in business since March 2001. It's run by baker Andrew Simonson, coffee maven Morris Cleveland and Morris' wife, Corrine Wilson, a local pharmacist who is involved "behind the scenes."

The men both grew up in Calgary, where as teenagers they worked for Heartland, a busy general store/bakery/café in Kensington, a well-established coffee district there. Corrine tells me it was at Heartland that Andrew began to hone his baking skills "under the watchful eye

Black Coffee beckons just before Duncan at Whippletree Junction. Don't forget to order a cinnamon bun!

of Alice Kichik," the cook who, it seems, really kept him in line ("No soup served before 11:30 A.M. even if it is ready! No cutting out the centre cinnamon bun before the side ones!"). Andrew bakes all those amazing "other delights" — hearty food made from scratch like the soup, chili, muffins, date squares, big cookies and even bigger (and quite sinful) cinnamon buns. Morris is the coffee guy, using the great Caffé Fantastico beans from Ryan and Kristy Taylor in Victoria.

In summer, the place hums with tourists who love shopping at Whippletree Junction's antique and curio shops. Part of the attraction of Black Coffee for me is that you can also stop there in the middle of winter, early in the morning when most Whippletree shops are closed, and have a coffee with the locals and the truckers. It has great warmth and charm.

Corrine says they support local producers for dairy, berries and produce in season, particularly Engeler Farm, which is just down the road. They have copies of the cookbook Andrew contributed to during his time at Heartland: *Heartland Country Store Cookbook* (Centax Books, 1995) by Alice Kichik and the restaurant's owner, Nonie Sundstrom. And let me know if you've ever tasted a better cinnamon bun!

Broken Briar Fallow Deer Farm

The very first fawn David Groves raised was called Briar, and she became a family pet. Unfortunately, she lost her life to a careless hunter, but her name lives on.

The farm, originally called Barkley Farm, was a whistle stop on the Canadian Pacific Railway line. David's father, Tom, bought the farm from Kitty Barkley. Tom's father, whom David describes as "a genuine remittance man," also had a farm in the area. "He did anything for sport, including logging and fox hunting." He used to say to Tom: "No Englishman ever got up at 4:00 A.M. to milk cows." Tom wasn't afraid of milking cows, but he ended up taking a degree in forestry engineering at the University of British Columbia, then built bridges all over the country.

Later, David took a Ph.D. at Purdue and became an animal nutritionist. He began to study protein synthesis and mammary tissue culture, and taught animal physiology and biochemistry at both the University of Alberta and University of Victoria. He'd always been interested in farming and enjoyed applied research.

David believes in raising animals in conditions that are as natural as possible. The number of fallow deer he raises "are in direct proportion to the capability of

David Groves offers an afternoon snack to one of his fallow deer at Broken Briar Fallow Deer Farm.

the land to produce feed." While their ancestors came from the Middle East, these hundred or so fallow deer are offspring of David's original herd, which were brought from Sidney, James and Saltspring islands. His neighbour had trapped some of the deer on those islands and sold them to both David and the Douglas Ranch near Merritt.

I tasted David's venison at The Aerie, and liked venison for the very first time. The meat is very tender and mild tasting, without that strong gamey flavour. Other restaurants have standing orders, including Saltspring Island's Hastings House, the Inglenook in North Cowichan and the Mahle House in Cedar. The First Nations people buy hides from him, and "there are always roasts in the freezer for people who just drop by."

With the restaurants demanding the saddles for ribs, Dave says he and his wife eat a lot of bone-out shoulder. He barbeques it, always serves it medium rare, and only sometimes adds a glaze such as maple syrup and garlic. It's delicious meat on its own, so he doesn't advise marinating or drowning it in sauce.

David and I take a walk out to see the deer. He picks a bunch of burdock, and only has to wave it once before they come leaping over for their "candy."

Cowichan Bay Farm

Mara Jernigan loves the fact that she can grocery-shop by "just going from farmgate to farmgate" in the Cowichan Valley. This doesn't mean only fruit and veggies, but also local wines and cider, and top-quality pastured chicken, chicken sausage and duck at Lyle and Fiona Young's Cowichan Bay Farm.

When we arrive at the farm, we are treated to the sight of a movie being shot. The juxtaposition of actors in World War II attire and crew running around against the original farm buildings on a pastoral 43-acre backdrop is quite fun. We stop to chat and discover that this is a locally based production company of young people who are shooting their first pilot, which they hope to sell to Hollywood.

The farm buildings are fascinating. There is the 1920s butcher shop, erected by Lyle's grandfather, Nigel Kingscote, to process his own pork. It has a wooden walk-in fridge, sloped tables for ease of cleaning after he rolled the pork into sausages and earthenware urns for immersing special cuts of meat in brine. Behind is the wooden smokehouse where the hams and bacon, as well as Cowichan Bay salmon, were cured. The butcher shop is still in operation, and this is where local customers come to pick up the farm's pastured poultry, lamb and beef.

There's the newlywed cottage, where Lyle's grandparents lived after their marriage in 1935. Across the way is Nigel's workshop, where Lyle spent many hours straightening and sorting bent nails for his grandfather. He says he "remembers fondly the subtle lessons of an old man passed on to a young boy, simply by being fortunate enough to be there." Other original buildings include the Chinese labourers' shack, the granary, the horse barn, the dairy and the cow barn. The creamery boasts Lyle's grandmother's interesting collection of milk bottles.

Every Father's Day, the Youngs host a

One of the rustic farm buildings at Cowichan Bay Farm.

Grilled Chicken Sausages with Red Onion Marmalade

BILL JONES FOR COWICHAN BAY FARM

Serves 4. Cowichan Bay Farm's chicken sausages have become a regular feature on my appetizer tray. I simply grill and slice them into bite-sized pieces, stick in toothpicks and serve them with a coarse-grain mustard. I first enjoyed this presentation at Mara Jernigan's Engeler Farm. Bill Jones's onion marmalade is another perfect match.

8	grilled chicken sausages	8
	(preferably from Cowichan Bay Farm)	
Marmalade		
2 tbsp	olive oil	30 ml
4	medium red onions	4
1/2 c	sugar	120 ml
1/4 c	red wine vinegar	60 ml
1/4 c	raspberry or balsamic vinegar	60 ml
	salt and pepper to taste	

To make the marmalade, heat oil in a pot set over medium heat. Add the onions and cook until very tender, about five to six minutes. Sprinkle in the sugar and stir to dissolve. Season with salt and pepper. Add vinegar and reduce until it begins to glaze around the onions. Remove from the heat. Serve with the grilled sausages.

NOTE: The marmalade can be served warm, or made several hours in advance, refrigerated and served chilled. Leftovers can be served with roast meats, ham or poultry. It will keep for two to three weeks, stored in a tightly sealed jar in the refrigerator.

wonderful art show, with over 30 local artists represented. It's always thrilling to walk through the old farm buildings, their walls laden with the impressive talent of painters like Grant Leier, Adam Noonan and Wendy Bradshaw, and to sample delicacies such as gelato from Victoria's Italian Bakery and sausage dogs containing Cowichan Bay Farm's own chicken sausage.

We trek out to the fields to see the pastured-poultry operation, and run into Jerry, one of the farm hands. He used to work for Lyle's grandfather and still enjoys his work on the farm. He shows us the method the Youngs use to raise their birds. First developed by Joel Salatin, a Virginia farmer, it's a model

Farm memorabilia at Cowichan Bay Farm.

that Lyle chose to use for its humane practices. The chickens are housed in large moveable pens that are set out in the pasture. Jerry demonstrates how the pens are moved every day, thereby giving the birds an always-fresh source of food. They stay together and behave in a natural way, in contrast to chickens caged indoors. Whereas many chicken farmers follow the modern agricultural model of getting the animals to market as fast as possible, the Youngs are focussed on taking the animals to their own food in a natural environment. Birds that are allowed to develop naturally turn out happier, healthier and tastier.

The Youngs' chickens and ducks are featured on some of the area's top restaurant tables including Victoria's Herald Street Caffé, Café Brio and Brasserie L'École and Tofino's Long Beach Lodge. They can be bought from the island's better butchers including Victoria's Fourways Meat Market and Slater's First Class Meats. Mara Jernigan calls Cowichan Bay Farm "simply the best for roast chicken, clean healthy liver, delicious handmade chicken sausages with no mystery meat or additives and pasture-raised duck, which many chefs consider the best they have ever had."

When the Youngs first took over the farm, they raised veal calves in addition to the poultry, but they felt they were looking for something else. On a trip to England some years back, they began to take an interest in rare breeds of livestock, and when they returned to the farm, decided to invest in a few San Clemente goats, Navaho Churro sheep and Dexter cattle. The goats were brought by explorers from Spain to the coast of California, and left there as a food supply for whenever they returned to that part of the world. In Spain, the goats became extinct, but they lived for another 200 years on San Clemente Island until the American army used the island for bombing practice. Most of the stock was moved, and the Youngs ended up getting theirs from Boston. Today, there are probably only a hundred San Clemente goats in the world.

Engeler Farm

When a group of fellow foodies and I arrive at the top of the long driveway that leads to Engeler Farm ("farm of angels"), Mara Jernigan can be seen lifting a pizza to her shoulders and walking through the vineyard to the outdoor oven. The image is both evocative and startling, as I find myself checking my location: Cowichan or Loire valley? We're all hoping that pizza is on the menu for lunch.

Mara's husband, Alfons Obererlacher, first gives us a tour of the farm, starting with the two acres they've planted with pinot noir and pinot gris grapes. In mid-August, it's a pretty sight with the vines laden with grapes, but Alfons doesn't hesitate to point out the "incredible amount of work" that goes into growing an organic vineyard: "We weed by hand here, you know!"

Across from the vineyard is the wood-fired oven, which Mara and Alfons bought from Cliff Lier when he installed a larger one at his Wild Fire Bakery in Victoria. When the oven was hauled off the back of the truck, Alfons says, "The truck nearly fell over." We confirm that the pizza cooking inside it is in fact ours, then head over to see the various raised beds containing vegetables and over 20 varieties of salad greens.

The herb garden, which is punctuated with great stands of artichokes and cardoon, was designed with help from Noël Richardson and Andrew Yeoman of Ravenhill Herb Farm on the Saanich Peninsula. Finally, Alfons takes us over to sample golden raspberries straight from the bush. He remembers Toronto restaurants paying $70 a flat for these golden beauties ten years ago. They are both pretty and delicious. On our way to the farmhouse, we are checked out by the animals: Tamworth pigs, Muscovy ducks

Engeler Farm, the "farm of angels".

Sparkling Wine Sabayon with Summer Berries

MARA JERNIGAN, ENGELER FARM

Serves 4 to 6. Whenever I make this lovely seasonal dessert, I remember watching Mara Jernigan preparing it in her farmhouse kitchen. The dessert doesn't really need enhancement, but Mara's suggestions of a fresh mint sprig, shaved white chocolate or a thin wafer make it very special.

6	egg yolks	6
1/4 c	medium-priced sparkling wine such as Prosecco, Asti Spumante, a Spanish Cava or a British Columbia sparkling wine	60 ml
6 tbsp	white sugar	90 ml
3 c	fresh ripe berries of your choice	720 ml

Pour approximately four cups of water into a medium saucepan and bring it to a boil. You will need a stainless steel bowl that fits on top of the saucepan but does not come into direct contact with the water.

Separate the eggs. You will only need the yolks. Combine the yolks, the sugar and the sparkling wine in the bowl, whisking thoroughly to mix the ingredients.

Once the water has boiled, turn the element off and place the bowl over the steaming water bath. Whisk the mixture in a back-and-forth motion until it becomes light yellow in colour, thick and frothy. This will take approximately four minutes. If, at any time, the mixture looks as though it is beginning to cook and congeal, remove it temporarily from the heat. When the mixture falls slowly from your whisk and has doubled in volume, it is finished.

Pour the sabayon immediately over six portions of fresh berries. You may serve the sabayon and berries in martini glasses with sugared rims, wide-mouthed wine glasses or in bowls. Garnish and serve immediately.

♙

and chickens. Only the family cat, stretching on the back patio, pays us no regard.

It's only the second time I've been in Mara's kitchen, but both times it felt like home. She's renovated to accommodate the extensive roster of well-known guest chefs who give cooking classes here. There's a big, central island with prep area and Ultraline stove. Class participants pull stools up to the island for close-up demonstrations by chefs like James Barber, Karen Barnaby, Peter Zambri, Sean Brennan, Edward Tuson, Christophe Letard and, of course, Mara herself.

Today, we all have front-row seats to watch Mara prepare that sabayon she promised us earlier, out in the saskatoon berry fields. Jonna, an innkeeper from the Hudson Valley, pitches in to clean the berries while Mara commandeers the whisk and begins beating the sugar, egg yolk and sparkling wine mixture over a double boiler.

As she works, she tells us about the two Zimmermann (carpenters) who helped to build their new porch. One of them had worked for Mara's friend, the noted Canadian chef Michael Stadtlander. None of us had heard of the Zimmermann phenomenon before. It is a long-held tradition in Austria that the apprenticing Zimmermann must stay away from home for three years and one day (the one day is the time it takes them to leave home). Tradition holds that if you see a Zimmerman walking along the road, you should stop and take him home. In exchange for room and board, he will work for you. Mara said she had a fascinating experience taking her two workers to the local hardware store, where she provided the English translation as they gathered materials for her porch.

The sabayon is set aside, and we are invited into the vibrant red dining room for lunch. On big earthenware platters, Mara sets out two types of wood-baked pizza: one has

"Here on Vancouver Island, we have it all: fresh wild seafood, pasture-raised meats, artisan cheese, outstanding organic produce and wild foods from the forest."

— Mara Jernigan, Engeler Farm

tomatoes and fresh pesto made from her basil; the other, caramelized red onions and Courtenay's Natural Pastures' Amsterdammer cheese. There is a salad of several varieties of greens, just picked. We are delighted to find some saskatoon berries that we picked earlier in Mara's vinaigrette. The pièces de résistance are

Mara Jernigan tempts author and fellow foodies with a mouth-watering pizza creation.

succulent slices of Cowichan Bay Farm's chicken breast and chicken sausage served with whole-grain mustard. We feast as though we've been working all morning. (Well, we actually *had* picked the saskatoon berries.) The meal's finale is the sabayon, which swirls around the beautiful red and purple berries, and feels like little bubbles in the mouth.

We are happily satiated with food and drink, and stimulated by the conversation Mara dishes up: the "dumbing down" of people's taste buds by processed food; the fact that our economic system is built to accommodate the big guys like Kellogg, for example, when the consumer wants choice in the cereal aisle; and the increasing problem of obesity in children due to fatty diets.

As Vancouver Island's representative for the Slow Food movement, Mara is a strong advocate for social issues around food, including food security and sustainable agriculture. She says she is proud to "do everything the Slow Food way — I can say where everything on my table comes from." And that really sums up Mara Jernigan, a chef who is parlaying her considerable talents into educating people about eating well, and practising what she preaches.

Fairburn Farm

Who said you can't roller skate through a water buffalo herd? It was Darryl Archer, whose dry humour came in handy through a very difficult time at Fairburn Farm. Two years ago, Darryl and his wife, Anthea, imported 18 Bulgarian Murrah River water buffalo from Denmark. Their dream was, and still is, to launch a buffalo dairy that would sustain their farm and "create local jobs and new opportunities from the many spinoffs" of that dairy.

An unfortunate, and largely political, intervention by the Canadian government has put them back two or three years. Because their animals were imported just prior to the first outbreak of Bovine Spongiform Encephalopathy (BSE) in Denmark, the Canadian Food Inspection Agency ordered them destroyed. The pertinent facts were largely ignored: worldwide, there have been no cases of mad cow disease in water buffalo, and the Archers' animals had been quarantined and monitored on a Danish farm prior to export and had never eaten feed with any animal by-products.

Anthea and Darryl, with the local farming and restaurant communities, fought a long, hard battle to keep their water buffalo. Support poured in from all over the world and there were major fundraising events to help defray the legal costs. On July 28, 2002, they lost their fight and the original 18 animals were destroyed. Subsequent tests of the buffalo showed they were not contaminated with BSE.

The light is beginning to glimmer from the end of

The farmhouse and garden at Fairburn Farm.

An inviting dining room at Fairburn Farm.

that long tunnel. The Archers' Canadian-born buffalo have been released from quarantine, and they are now continuing with their plans. When I visited the herd with Darryl, I could see how hard it must have been for them to have parted with the other buffalo. The animals are incredibly loving and each is named. Of the herd, I met Ferdinand, Kimberly, Teresa, Ashley, Karina and Murray. The Archers can now begin to construct their dairy, and look forward to producing milk, ice cream and the much-anticipated bocconcini. Their dairy will be unique in Canada.

My first visit to Fairburn Farm was on a wild, windy December night. My husband and I, with many other members of Vancouver Island's Slow Food convivium, had gathered in the 1894 farmhouse to celebrate the season. The storm was so severe that we drove from Victoria with most of the highway traffic lights out, and arrived to find the 130-acre farm in complete darkness.

We inched our way into the house, where we were greeted with much merriment. The kitchen had been lit with candles. Mara Jernigan of Engeler Farm and Peter Zambri of Zambri's were joyfully preparing a feast, seemingly oblivious to the lack of electricity and water. Within an hour, Darryl had managed to start the generator and the crowd began greeting each other in earnest. We spent that night in one of Anthea's cosy bed-and-breakfast rooms, and woke to see what Sooke Harbour House's Sinclair Philip describes as "one of the most beautiful farms in the world" through our window.

Fairburn Farm was originally settled in the 1880s by John and Mary Jackson. Mary, who hailed from Scotland, named the farm Fairburn which means "beautiful stream." Most of the 1200-acre farm was sold to MacMillan Bloedel in the late 1940s by Mary's son, Edwin. In 1955, Jack and Mollie Archer, Darryl's parents, bought the remaining 130 acres.

Mollie founded the Vancouver Island Organic Vegetable Cooperative in 1955, and the family learned to farm the hard way. The farm went through many incarnations (in the 1960s, Mollie ran a children's summer camp there), but has stayed in the family. Today, Darryl, Anthea and their six children run the farm and bed and breakfast.

A hearty country breakfast followed my sound sleep: yogurt and muesli; homemade banana muffins with cherry jam; soft-scrambled farm eggs with Anthea's whole-wheat bread (she grinds the flour just before baking). I downed several mugs of hot coffee, then went out to meet the buffalo.

Feast of Fields

Vancouver's Island's foodie event of the year highlights the strong links between our local growers and chefs, and dishes up some of the best food you may ever eat. Set at a different island farm each time, the event is the ultimate gastronomic walkabout. Ticket-holders are greeted with a plate, a wine glass and a large linen napkin and invited to stroll from stall to stall to eat (all items are designed to be eaten by hand) and imbibe over the course of a long, leisurely afternoon.

The area's best chefs and vintners purvey their wares: one moment, you are savouring ostrich kebabs straight off the grill from Sidney's Dock 503 restaurant; later, you are enjoying the bouquet of a lively pinot gris from Cobble Hill's Glenterra vineyard or cooing over an almond Johnny cake drizzled with poaching sauce, enhanced with a dollop of cinnamon crème fraîche with lemon verbena and a rosette of slivered caramelized poached pear, and sprinkled with candied ginger and a confetti of pansy blossoms, created by David Feys of Feys & Hobbs Catered Arts.

Feast of Fields is a fundraiser for Farm Folk, City Folk, a nonprofit organization that recognizes and promotes "the connection between those who grow our food and those who eat it, and the interdependency of all living things." Among its many projects, FFCF is active in the development of food policy around food security; supports sustainable agriculture; and conducts a broad public-advocacy campaign to project awareness of food issues in British Columbia.

The indefatigable Mara Jernigan of Engeler Farm is Vancouver Island's representative for FFCF. She has organized successful Feast of Fields at many of the island's stellar farming operations including Oldfield Farm and Ravenhill Herb Farm in Saanich and Cowichan Bay Farm. It's a sell-out event every year, so if you are planning to be on the island in mid-September, call for tickets well in advance.

The Mushroom Guy

I'm heading into the hills behind Shawnigan Lake with Bill Jones, geologist, former chef at Sooke Harbour House and other superb restaurants from Alsace to Vancouver, author of eight cookbooks and busy food consultant. We're going way off-road to stalk the much-lauded chanterelle, a trumpet-shaped wild mushroom that emerges after the rains from mid-August through mid-November or until the killing frosts start. Not being too specific about our location is all part of the adventure: once a picker has found good foraging ground, he is not about to tell the world. I agree to keep the code.

It's a beautiful day in the woods. We've waited the requisite three days since the last rain to ensure there will be lots of new mushrooms, so we grab our bags and Swiss Army knives and make our way through the underbrush. It's fun, and a highly aerobic process. Bill steers me toward mossy beds where the chanterelles are most likely to be found, telling me that when I find one, I'll certainly find more. The yellow-orange ones (*Cantharellus cibarius*) are fairly easy to spot, and today there are white ones (*Cantharellus subalbidus*) as well — a real treat. I'm quickly hooked.

This is perfect territory for chanterelles, which, it turns out, are one of the hardiest mushrooms. Bill tells me that pharmaceutical companies are looking at the chanterelle's composition in their antibiotic research as they are almost never attacked by insects or worms, and don't tend to rot.

Picking mushrooms, I discover, is a tactile, organic experience. Once the specimen has been identified as edible, you knock off any debris that may have settled on it. Then, firmly holding the stalk, you pull the whole plant out of the ground, cut a small slice off the bottom of the stalk to perfect it, and pop the plump, spongy mushroom into your bag. It feels like a grown-up Easter egg hunt. With the retail price of chanterelles in my head, and the prospect of a mushroom feast that evening, I have no problem staying out in the woods for the rest of the afternoon — eyes roaming the forest floor, knife at the ready.

By the time our bags are full, we've spotted at least two dozen of the 2,000 or so varieties in the world including the Zellers bolete (*Boletus zelleri*) and honey mushroom (*Armillaria mellea*). On an old nurse log, we spy a bouquet of angel wing mushrooms (*Pleurcybella porrigens*), so named because of their shape. We eat them right away, their disarmingly fresh, nutty taste bringing the beauty of the forest to our palates.

At the end of our hunt, we climb back to the logging road and snack on organic apples from Bill's farm before heading to Engeler Farm. Later that day, Bill will cook up Phyllo Packets of Roast Chanterelles, Farm-cured Bacon and Leeks; Mushroom Risotto with Saltspring Island Cheese Company's Montana Cheese; Cured Salmon on Three Kinds of Kale and Porcini Mushrooms in Tomato Sauce; and a grand finale of Heritage Apple Tart with Vanilla Rosemary Ice Cream.

With a menu like that and a chef like Bill, I'm devastated to be double-booked and having to miss the meal. Still, I have a bag of fresh chanterelles and within hours they're merrily sautéing in a little olive oil with garlic and a splash of wine. Since I'd picked them myself, they were of course the best I'd ever eaten.

Bill has done extensive renovations to his heritage farmhouse where he caters for private parties. His real love, though, is everything mushroom, and

Mushroom expert, chef and author Bill Jones.

Grilled Oyster Mushrooms on Mixed Greens with Balsamic Vinaigrette*

BILL JONES, MAGNETIC NORTH CUISINE

 Serves 4 to 6. "The slight charring of the mushrooms works well with the sweetness of the balsamic vinegar. You can buy a pre-made salad mix like mesclun and have good results. Make sure the greens are crisp or refresh them in a bath of cold water. A salad spinner works well to rid the leaves of excess moisture. Place in the fridge for 5 to10 minutes after washing and even tired greens will be revitalized." — *Bill Jones*

Mushrooms

1 tbsp	minced fresh ginger	15 ml
1 tsp	sesame oil	5 ml
1 tsp	hot sauce	5 ml
2 tbsp	extra-virgin olive oil	30 ml
1 lb	oyster mushroom pieces	454 g
	salt and pepper to taste	

Salad

6 c	mixed salad greens, washed (lettuce, mustards, radicchio, arugula, etc.)	1.4 L
2 tbsp	balsamic vinegar	30 ml
2 tbsp	light soy sauce	30 ml
2 tbsp	extra-virgin olive oil	30 ml
	toasted sesame seeds for garnish	
	shredded nori for garnish	

In a bowl, combine ginger, sesame oil, hot sauce and oil. Stir to mix well and add the mushroom pieces. Season with salt and pepper and toss well to mix. Place on a hot grill and cook until soft and slightly charred at the edges. Transfer to a salad bowl and set aside. Add the salad greens and drizzle with vinegar, soy sauce and oil. Season lightly with salt and pepper and toss to coat. Serve family-style or transfer to four plates and garnish with a sprinkling of sesame seeds and nori.

*Reprinted with permission from *The Savoury Mushroom* by Bill Jones, Raincoast Books, 2001.

his company runs foraging tours and cooking demonstrations in season. In addition to the chanterelle run, there are morels from March through April (Bill says the first crocus in spring is a sign the morels are out) and pine mushrooms in the cold season.

Saskatoon Berry Farm

On a summer Sunday, I join one of the popular farm tours offered by The Aerie. I feel like a real tourist as the van pulls out and host Mara Jernigan begins to tell us about the day's program. "We'll stop by a cidery, a vineyard, a pastured chicken farm and how about a mystery stop this morning?" Naturally, we all agree. The mystery stop is one Mara hasn't been to yet, either, and it turns out to be a highlight.

It's the Saskatoon Berry Farm, a relative newcomer in the area. Alwin and Connie Dyrland moved to the Cowichan Valley from Edmonton, thinking it would be a great hobby to grow the berries of their native prairies, but the farm's popularity has exceeded their expectations. With so many prairie folk having moved to British Columbia, and the annual influx of "snowbirds" every

Connie Dyrland picks saskatoon berries at her Saskatoon Berry Farm.

winter, the berries are in high demand. "On any weekend, you can meet most of Alberta and Saskatchewan at our farmstand," Alwin says.

The Dyrlands bought the farm six years ago, and started the six-acre orchard with 14,000 to 16,000 seedlings from southern Alberta. The plants take eight years to fully mature. Alwin shows us the extensive drip-irrigation system he's devised for the fields ("That was about the fourth mortgage," he jokes). Connie keeps busy producing jams and the best saskatoon berry pies this side of Edmonton. Every weekend, they sell from their farmstand, and the cars never stop pulling in. Even though the season is short, it's a year-round operation and, as Alwin says: "We don't get off the farm much."

Across Canada, saskatoon berries go by a variety of other names including chuckleberries or Indian plums. As Alwin says: "They don't like wet feet, so that's why you don't usually see them out here [on Vancouver Island]." He is lucky to have land with a 20-foot slope from one end to the other. Also, the land has been covered with weeping tile to ensure good drainage.

Alwin takes us straight to the fields where the berry bushes are ripe with fruit, and invites us to "eat and enjoy." We are like kids in a candy store, and soon our mouths and hands are stained from the succulent, dark purple fruit.

The ultimate saskatoon berry pie and jam at Connie and Alwin Dyrland's Saskatoon Berry Farm.

Saskatoon Berry Pie

CONNIE DYRLAND, SASKATOON BERRY FARM

Serves 8. I took my first saskatoon berry pie to a dinner party in Youbou on Cowichan Lake and was immediately invited back. Make the pie yourself, and you be the judge: was it my scintillating company or the irresistible pie?

	pastry for a two-crust pie	
3 c	saskatoon berries	720 ml
3/4 c	sugar	180 ml
1/4 c	uncooked minute tapioca	60 ml
1 tsp	lemon juice	5 ml
4	drops of almond flavouring	4

Line a 9" pie plate with pastry. Combine all ingredients in a bowl and mix until slight juice forms. Pour into pastry shell and cover with other pastry, cutting openings in crust for steam to escape. Bake 450°F for 15 minutes, then 350°F for 45 minutes, until pastry is golden.

♕

Mara suggests picking a quantity, promising us sabayon to go with the berries, which she later prepares in her farmhouse kitchen. We pick with gusto, everyone thoroughly enjoying this real hands-on farm experience.

The fresh saskatoon berries are available from early July for three to four weeks. While they last, frozen berries are available direct from the farm.

CEDAR

Cedar Farmers' Market

The Cedar Farmers' Market features mainly organic growers from the surrounding area including Yellow Point Orchards, Bensons' Olde Tyme Farm, Limberlost Orchard, Golden Maples Farm, Big D Emu Farm and Munro Creek Farm. There are some crafts and great bread and baked goods from the Cedar Women's Institute.

To make a wonderful day of it, combine your visit to the market, which is located on the field next to the Crow and Gate Pub, with a nice pub lunch and afternoon visit to the nearby Barton Leier Gallery, featuring the paintings of Grant Leier and Nixie Barton, and their magical, whimsical garden and giftshop.

Mahle House Restaurant

I arrive early for dinner, and Maureen Loucks bounds out of the kitchen to greet me. "You must see our gardens first," and she walks me around the colourful vegetable and herb beds, stopping to show off various plants ("Look, have you ever seen white borage? Juliet tomatoes. Aren't they just perfect? Every kind of carrot, Maxibell French filet beans, Florence fennel"). She shows me zephyr, Costa romanesco and pale green pattypan squash, saying: "A chef can't create something wonderful out of inferior products."

Maureen established the kitchen garden to ensure she would always have high quality organic veggies. The garden has been tended by Kate White, who also gardens for the folks at Hazelwood Herb Farm. She's off to Arizona to take an herbalist course, and in her absence, Scott, a local orchardist will take over.

We wander over to the house itself, a Queen Anne beauty built in 1904 and surrounded by immaculate flower beds. These gardens are cared for by Maureen's sister-in-law, Ginny Horrocks. In July, Mahle House holds its Summer Wine and Garden Party. Maureen's brother and partner in the restaurant, Delbert Horrocks, organizes a dozen or so wine reps to proffer their wares, and a huge alfresco brunch is set out for guests. I immediately mark my calendar for the second Sunday in July.

Once inside, I am impressed by the hominess of the restaurant

Chef Maureen Loucks of The Mahle House proffers freshly picked tomatoes at the Harvest Bounty Festival.

and the clubbiness of its patrons. Fine dining takes on an appealing friendliness in the country, and the air is vibrant with greetings. It really is a close-knit place. Not only is it run by a brother and sister, but the next generation is involved. Delbert's daughter waits tables; Maureen's daughter worked in the restaurant before moving to Victoria where she now runs the venerable Bengal Lounge in The Fairmont Empress.

I take a seat by the window with a lovely view of Ginny's flower beds, and then count six of Grant Leier's richly textured food paintings on the walls around me. One can only hope that food emulates art here.

It seems I've timed my visit well because tonight is the famous "Adventurous Wednesday," when ordering from a menu is thrown out the window, and the chef gets to surprise diners with things they might never have considered ordering before. The concept took off from day

The Mahle House Restaurant and organic garden.

one. People come from all over the island with friends and family, and everyone at the table is served something different for each of four courses.

Even though I'm dining alone, I can vicariously enjoy the reactions from tables around me. The two couples opposite are obviously thrilled as the appetizer is set down: prawns with cannellini beans for one man, Kataifi-wrapped prawns with wasabi sauce for another; steamed mussels and calamari Dijonnaise for the women, one of whom says: "I can see a food fight coming."

I've given Chef Loucks a bit of a challenge with my request for "no pork or shellfish," but she certainly rises to the occasion. I begin with a salad of tomatoes from her garden, topped with melted fontina and shredded basil and follow with a delicately flavoured carrot-ginger soup. The accompanying molasses bread is locally made for the restaurant.

My main course, lamb tenderloin with a basil and Dijon mustard sauce, is served with some of those beautiful baby zucchini and red cauliflower from the garden. Delbert, winner of a whole wall full of wine awards, gets to have fun on Wednesdays, pairing new wines with the food. I enjoy Lang Pinot Auxerrois 2001, Hogg Fumé Blanc from Washington State and Wolf Blass Yarra Valley Pinot Noir 2000 and Yellow Tail Shiraz (all in very small amounts, as I'm driving myself back to Victoria).

The pièce de résistance is a chocolate triple sec pâté with raspberry purée, and a good cup of coffee. Earlier, Maureen told me: "I am really happy when I'm cooking," and her food is a winning reflection of that.

LADYSMITH

Hazelwood Herb Farm

Sitting under the arbour with the heady fragrances of clematis, ahebia, cidergum eucalyptus and passion flower lulling me, watching the fantastical mating dance of hummingbirds, and looking over a gentle lily pond to the herb gardens beyond, I am transfixed. This peaceful place is a dream come true for Richard White and Jacynthe Dugas. He is originally from Leeds, England, and was a maintenance mechanic for the local sawmill; she hails from Val d'Or, Quebec, and worked for the federal government. Richard says he had fixed every piece of equipment at the mill many times, and it was time to find a new challenge.

It was his idea to start growing herbs for the local restaurants, but that didn't work out. In those days, the restaurants were only looking for a little bunch here and there, so the venture didn't pay. Not one to be deterred, Richard quit his job and the couple began growing herbs in earnest, improving the gardens and buildings as their budget allowed. Jacynthe soon left her job, and

 the two have thrown themselves into creating a multi-faceted business whose success, they say, is sometimes overwhelming.

By the end of May, there are over 400 different culinary, landscape and medicinal herbs proliferating, from what Richard calls the

Owners Richard White and Jacynthe Dugas and their delightful gift shop at Hazelwood Herb Farm.

Simon and Garfunkels (parsley, sage, rosemary and thyme) to some very unusual varieties. Many people come looking for alternative health cures, and what the couple don't already grow, they are always game to try. Richard says if a medicinal herb hits the news, they are flooded with requests: evening primrose, St. John's Wort and milk thistle are in constant demand.

Word of mouth brings people from all over Vancouver Island, and there are many out-of-country visitors in the summer. It is not unusual for people to bring in plans for herb gardens, to seek Richard's advice and stock up on plants. Everything is conveniently labelled to help people orient themselves to the many types of herbs. There are historical herbs like germander to treat gout; camphor for the stomach; every imaginable variety of thyme; Tucson blue rosemary; calamint; lemongrass; angelica; sweet cicely, a sugar substitute appreciated by diabetics; red bugle, a styptic; bloodroot, a native plant for medicinal purposes; red-flowered comfrey to rejuvenate skin cells; and lavender, which finds its way into Jacynthe's soaps and soothing eye masks.

The formal garden is just the beginning. Beyond are raised beds of herbs and a lath house — an open-slatted nursery with plastic roof that allows watering to be manually controlled. The building is full of herbs, lined up row on row. We are joined at this stage of the tour by Saffron, the resident golden lab who politely leads us to the first greenhouse. Here, many plants begin their growing cycle heated by the wood-burning stove. The greenhouse's thermostat is set at 60°F, and when the stove cuts out, the oil furnace kicks in. Richard says this hothouse is also a wonderful place to hang out in winter with a glass of brandy.

In addition to their generous free advice, Richard and Jacynthe have hundreds of potted herbs for sale, and there is a fabulous gift shop brimming with all things herbal.

Herb Wise

Last summer, my niece Lizzie and I were amazed by what we found at the end of a driveway on Pender Island: a gift shop brimming with herbal candles, potpourri and cosmetics for her, and the discovery that this was the home of Bruce Burnett for me.

Bruce is a chartered herbalist from London, England, and author of *Herb Wise* (Joyful Symmetry Country Cottage, 2002), a book of advice about growing

Roast Lamb with Blackberries and Lavender
BRUCE BURNETT, HERB WISE

When I originally visited Bruce at his home on Pender Island, he told me about a delicious lamb preparation he'd invented the night before. As we walked around his herb garden, he gave me the recipe out of his head.

	leg of lamb	
1/2 c	lavender flowers (not lavendine)	120 ml
2 c	blackberries	480 ml
1/2 c	sweet red vermouth	120 ml
6	cloves garlic	6
	juice of 1/2 lemon	
1 tsp	salt	5 ml
	splash of Worcestershire Sauce	

Preheat oven to 325°F. Place the leg of lamb in roasting pan. Combine all marinade ingredients in a blender and pour over the lamb. Cover with foil. Bake to desired doneness.

herbs, some great recipes that include herbs and an exploration into the mythology and etymology of herbs.

We were thrilled when Bruce and Delaine offered to walk us through their herb gardens. The tour started in Delaine's basil greenhouse, then up to the orchard and lavender field, where we stopped to eat golden plums straight from the tree. The couple's main herb beds are contained in a lovely wheel-shaped garden next to their house. From the herbs, they make a range of herbal products called Love 'n' Herbs, and Bruce experiments with different herbal combinations for food and healing.

Thirteen years ago, they bought their Pender Island home on four acres as a weekend getaway. It didn't take long to leave the Vancouver rat race altogether, and create their new business and tranquil lifestyle on the island. Recently, the Burnetts made another lifestyle move, this time to Ladysmith.

Kiwi Cove Lodge

When I arrive, Peggy Kolosoff is saying goodbye to some of her bed-and-breakfast guests. They are six women who have been kayaking down the coast for two weeks and are singing the praises of her bathtubs and showers. There are 12 rooms at the inn, all facing the orchard, and beyond it, Ladysmith Harbour.

It's a lovely fall morning, so we take a walk through the vines. Peggy and Doug Kolosoff bought this ten-acre property six years ago with the intention of making it into a campground. The zoning didn't happen, so they built a lodge and planted a thousand Christmas trees.

They gave a lot of thought to producing a crop that "would be fairly low-maintenance and would work with having the public on our property." Kiwis came to mind, and the result is a three-quarter acre orchard of

Owners Peggy and Doug Kolosoff of Kiwi Cove Lodge.

Kiwi Chutney

PEGGY KOLOSOFF, KIWI COVE LODGE

 Makes about 1 cup. This yummy chutney makes a good marinade for grilled chicken or fish. Peggy suggests adding 1 3/4 cups (320 ml) cooked rice to the chutney to make a spicy filling for wraps. Spread cream cheese on a tortilla, then top with some of the chutney-rice mixture and add sliced sweet potatoes, mushrooms, chicken — whatever you wish.

Mix together:

2 tbsp	lime juice	30 ml
1 tbsp	olive oil	15 ml
1	jalapeno pepper, seeded and minced	1
1 tsp	honey	5 ml
1	garlic clove, minced	1
1 tsp	curry powder	5 ml
1 tsp	cumin	5 ml
1/4 tsp	hot pepper flakes	1.2 ml
Add:		
6	kiwi fruit, frappéed	6
1/4 c	finely chopped purple onion	60 ml

immaculate design. Doug, a forestry worker who has kept his day job, chose the site wisely and has developed an irrigation system that waters the plants while ensuring that the leaves don't get wet. He created slight valleys between the rows of vines and the whole orchard slopes toward the water, all of which is essential for run-off during heavy rains.

In addition to the standard fuzzy varieties of kiwis, the Kolosoffs are growing Hardy Anna argutas, which are "smaller, sweeter and grape-like," says Peggy. "The chefs love them, and there is no fussing with the fuzz!"

There is no spraying and very little threat of predators. Peggy says the deer don't like kiwis (finally, something they don't like!), and the birds could care less about the fruit. Only the rabbits are interested, but Doug wrapped the bottom of the vines in chicken wire to prevent any major damage.

The planting was done five years ago, so the vines are really filling out and bearing fruit — 200 pounds this year. In another three or four years, Peggy expects each vine to bear 100 pounds. Peggy tells me that kiwis are picked unripe in the first week of December, then placed in cold storage.

When she needs some for use at the inn or for a local restaurant, she simply brings them to room temperature for a few days. Guests at her bed and breakfast enjoy a variety of kiwi dishes, from kiwi glaze on fruit salad and pancakes to kiwi tarts and cheesecake. The night before my visit, Peggy's kiwi milkshakes received rave reviews from the kayakers.

Page Point Inn

The best food experiences are often revealed, not anticipated, and such was the case at Page Point Inn. I'd heard about the 1940s charm of the place, the magic of chef Steven Mugridge and the friendliness of the staff. I enjoyed it all, but was blown away by a sailboat — or more specifically, by the prospect of dinner on a sailboat under a starry sky.

The inn has a long and colourful history, dating back to 1873, when David Page homesteaded 160 acres at Page Point. Page raised oysters in Oyster Bay (now Ladysmith Harbour). It's amazing the chap lasted as long as he did, given the cougar dens on his property and the Indians who regularly threatened his life, but he lived at Page Point until 1911 when he moved to Ladysmith. The property was bought by an American doctor who leased it to the Krjivitsky family. The family's daughters, known as the "Russian Marys," rowed across the bay every day to attend school in Ladysmith. Their father planted asparagus, flowers and fruits: cherries, peaches, currants and apples. When he died in 1938, the family moved to

The Dame Pattie, *a private dining room with no fixed address.*

Local wines on display in the dining room at the Page Point Inn.

Vancouver and Page Point fell into disrepair.

Harry and Zella Olmstead bought it in 1947 and built Manana Lodge the next year with help from a local artist, Ron Grouhel. Grouhel was responsible for the totem pole art still on display in the older guest rooms and an interesting rolled copper mural that was uncovered in 1999 during a renovation of the dining room. Zella Olmstead had a pet deer called Bambi that had the run of the lodge's dining room, and it was Zella who claimed there were singing fish in the bay.

Fortunately, much of the colourful past lives on in Page Point Inn's new incarnation. Owners Lawrence and Lexie Lambert were former next-door neighbours who had their eye on the property and were able to purchase it in 1998. They've made some improvements, like new docks for the many boaters who come to stay or eat at the inn, and they've introduced first-rate dining, but happily, they're keeping the rustic, original guest rooms and the leisurely pace of yesteryear.

I arrived in the middle of the night, having dined in Nanaimo, and was shown to one of the original guest rooms facing the marina. I took a welcome hot bath, and a tipple of the sherry that is thoughtfully put out in the bedrooms, and went to sleep to the gentle clink of boats' masts in the bay. Rose, a neighbour and Page Point's morning waitress, served me a continental breakfast in the oceanside Harbour Room, and then I was off to explore the grounds. Just as I headed around to the hot tub, Rose called out: "Lexie has something to show you down on the dock."

That something was something else — the 65-foot Australian *Dame Pattie* that had competed in the 1967 America's Cup. It seems that Lawrence, an avid sailor, had found the boat in bad shape in Victoria and brought it home to Ladysmith to restore. I climbed aboard and swooned at the quality finishings inside, and the prospect of returning in summer for a dinner cruise. This big, beautiful sailboat can be chartered for an afternoon or several days and comes equipped with staff and chef.

Back on shore, I dined again in the Harbour Room. This time, Chef Mugridge was on the line, and I thoroughly enjoyed his lunch offerings of spicy French lentil soup with tomatoes, spinach and sour cream; a generous sampler plate of spinakopita, chicken satay and fish cakes with orange and jalapeno chutney; and a sublime blackberry cheesecake. Mugridge brought an impressive résumé to Page Point. He apprenticed at Claxtons in Surrey, England, and worked for the Hyatt Regency chain throughout Australia as well as in one of my favourite hotels, Lillianfels, in the Blue Mountains, the Four Seasons Yorkville in Toronto, and The Aerie. He believes in "good honest flavours with a twist of French," and is a big supporter of local producers including the Cowichan Valley wineries.

NANAIMO

Glow World Cuisine

With so few see-and-be-seen dining rooms around, I was thrilled to find one had opened in Nanaimo — in a 110-year-old, well-preserved brick building that used to be the city's fire hall. The main dining room exudes stage-set décor: bright, high-ceilinged and lavished with gauze curtains and banquettes in appetite-stimulating colours like tomato, violet and lime green. A sweep of stairs made of plexiglass and dotted with tiny lights takes customers to a smaller, mezzanine dining room. I was equally thrilled to find the congenial Mark Wachtin, formerly of The Marina restaurant in Victoria, ensconced as manager.

One sunny day, my parents and I opted for a window table in the main room, with views across the city. We came with good appetites, having heard that the tapas brunch was more than worth

Eggs Benedict Glow Style

GERD VOIGT, GLOW WORLD CUISINE

Serves 4.
Thank you, Gerd, for giving me the ultimate eggs Benedict recipe.

Eggs

4	medium eggs	4

Poach for three minutes in 4 litres (16 cups) of boiling water with 4 tbsp (60 mL) of sherry vinegar. Remove the eggs, trim and set aside.

Ham

6 oz	cooked honey ham, sliced	168 g

Hollandaise Sauce

1/4 tsp	shallots	1.2 ml
1/4 tsp	crushed pepper from pepper mill	1.2 ml
3 tbsp	white wine	45 ml
2	egg yolks	2
8 oz	clarified butter	227 g

Place first three ingredients in saucepan and reduce over medium heat to 1 1/2 tbsp (360 ml) of liquid. Remove from heat and add 2 tbsp (30 ml) cold water. Strain and add the egg yolks, whisking constantly. Add the butter until the sauce is thick and creamy. Season with salt and 2 to 3 drops of lemon juice.

Scones

4 1/2 c	all-purpose flour	1.1 L
1/2 c	pastry flour	120 ml
	pinch of salt	
1 1/4 tsp	baking powder	6.2 ml
3 oz	soft butter	85 g
5 oz	buttermilk	150 ml

Mix all dry ingredients and butter. Add buttermilk and mix as little as possible. Roll out to approximately 1" high, and cut into 2" diameter rounds. Bake at 425°F for about 15 minutes. To serve, cut the scones in half, butter and toast them, top with the poached eggs and ham and cover with the hollandaise sauce. Streak each serving with aged balsamic vinegar.

the drive from Victoria. At $20 for eight selections per person, we were impressed with the value, and we had fun choosing and sampling from each other's plates. Our all-round favourite was the classic eggs Benedict in a novel form. The eggs and hollandaise topped light, home-baked scones, and a drizzle of balsamic vinegar and sprinkling of chives were nice, modern additions. The chef's hor d'oeuvres was a pretty composition of local quail eggs stuffed with pâté and rolled in ground pistachios, foie gras piped into choux pastry, salmon tartar, a king prawn and caviar on a slice of cucumber. Among 12 other choices were a grilled lamb chop over yam mash, local organic greens from Nanoose Edibles dressed in a pesto and truffle vinaigrette, a gyoza of Cowichan Bay Farm chicken

Glow World Cuisine's glowing interior.

The old Nanaimo fire hall now houses Glow World Cuisine.

and vegetables with ginger dipping sauce and a substantial slice of leek, apple and fennel tart topped with pear confit. We finished with pumpkin cheesecake and black cherry kirsch trifle, and asked to meet the chef.

Chef Gerd Voigt is a partner with long-time Nanaimo restaurant owners Eric and Larry Lim (they own Saki House and Blue Ginger). He hails from St. Galo, Switzerland, where he lived on his grandparents' farm, and learned to cook. At 19, he set off on a cooking apprenticeship that took him to Austria, Africa and, by way of a job with Pan American Airlines, to Montreal. He cooked at Vancouver's Truffles at the Hyatt, Le Crêperie and Chez Joel before moving to Lantzville on Vancouver Island where he started his own catering company. Known for catering huge events, he is now delighted to be working with fresh, local ingredients in smaller quantities at Glow.

Voigt is a strong proponent of local, organic growers and food producers. "I always want to see where the ingredients come from," he tells us, "and I am enjoying having no boundaries in my kitchen here." The result is an eclectic mix of European and Asian dishes that easily pleased our palates, and left us asking if he might consider moving the whole operation to Victoria.

Island Natural Markets

I suppose I've always been under the impression that it takes a large population to support large, full-service organic grocery stores. I am now happy to admit that's wrong. Courtenay has Edible Island Market, there's a Lifestyles Select Market in Sidney, and in the middle of sprawling mall country just north of Nanaimo, Island Natural Markets has been doing a booming business for three years.

The store has a very open, almost tropical feel to it (although there are four walls and a ceiling). Shelves are lined with all things organic and there's a

A tasty cornucopia of fruits and veggies complements the deli counter at Island Natural Markets in Nanaimo.

bustling deli serving veggie and fruit juices (wheatgrass is optional), fruit smoothies (with or without protein powder), yummy energy balls made by Trish Vet of Hornby Island and homemade gourmet pizzas by the slice.

I enjoy my first Creekmore's BuzzRight coffee of the day and watch the locals shop.

McLean's Specialty Foods

I can never decide what brings me back to McLean's more — the food or the humour, but of course, it's both. Nowhere outside of England have I found the range of foods near and dear to my homeland than here, where Baxter's soups, Bird's custard and Rose's lime marmalade share shelves with pickled fish, rémoulade, fried onions and lingonberry jam from Scandinavia and passion-fruit pulp, rooibos and beef biltong from South Africa.

There are over 100 cheeses and smoked meats. In the fall, Eric holds convivial wine- and cheese-tasting evenings. As early as July, people like me start ordering whisky and cherry brandy Christmas cakes and deluxe puddings that are brought in specially from the Old Country. The selection of German stollen and English chocolates, jams and chutneys is remarkable. As I ooh and ahh my way around the store with Eric one December afternoon, he keeps darting to the back room to replenish things that he can't keep on the shelves.

My road trips are never quite complete without a stop at McLean's for a cup of tea and an excellent, housemade "bap," a white English roll that's slighly crunchy on the outside and soft inside, filled with cheese, salad cream, lettuce and tomato. The teapots have hand-knit cosies and the china has roses on it. For fleeting moments, I'm back in Britain as I chat with Eric and Sandy, the seriously fun owners.

The couple had lived in Maple Ridge on the mainland where Eric was an account representative for Cadbury-Schweppes, and Sandy was an office manager for the provincial government. Fifteen years ago, their Nanaimo friends invited them across for a look around. "They took us to the pub, and we liked the feel of the town — less anonymity." They were fed up with big-city living and wanted to be near the ocean, so they made the crossing permanently.

Owners Sandy and Eric McLean always have a smile and often a good joke for their customers at McLean's Specialty Foods.

Eric worked for a food distributor for a while, but became frustrated: "That was when you couldn't get

The huge selection of cheese at Eric and Sandy McLean's Specialty Foods.

grocers to stock extra-virgin olive oil, good-quality Italian pasta, Parmigiano-Reggiano or balsamic vinegar." From years of doing business with grocers, he realized: "Few people actually knew what they were selling." His frustration led to the opening of McLean's Specialty Foods, a cornucopia of food and sociability.

Eric was raised in a little Scottish town. The family didn't have much money, but he remembers things like the fishmonger apologizing to his mother if there were still bones in the fish. He appreciated the interest that people took in what they were eating. He believes people need to be educated about their food, and he and Sandy love helping their customers find more interesting alternatives. He doesn't sell mozzarella which "you can buy everywhere," but rather, recommends something new for a

"If we don't have it, you don't need it."

— Eric McLean, McLean's Specialty Foods

Cullen Skink

Serves 4 to 6. This is Eric's mother's recipe for a traditional Scottish seafood soup. He cooks it from memory, but kindly worked out the quantities for this book.

6.5 oz	smoked haddock or smoked cod	182 g
4 c	light cream	1 L
2 oz	butter	60 g
1	large onion	1
3	medium to large potatoes	3
4 c	vegetable stock	1 L
2 tsp	flour	10 ml
2 c	water (approximate)	1/2 L
1 tsp	chopped parsley	5 ml
	salt and pepper to taste	

Peel the potatoes, boil and drain. Peel and dice the onions. Sauté in a little olive or vegetable oil till soft and golden, but not brown. Flake the fish. Drain the potatoes and very lightly mash them. Mix them in large pot with the cooked onions and the butter, flour and fish. Add the vegetable stock and water. Bring to the boil, then reduce heat to medium and simmer gently for 10 minutes, stirring often and adding the light cream to adjust the consistency (consistency should be reasonably thick, not runny, with small pieces, not chunky). Adjust seasoning. Sprinkle with the parsley and serve.

pizza: fontina, asiago, pecorino. And they keep coming back.

McLean's picnic hampers are still a bit of a secret, but those in the know (such as chef James Barber) rely on Eric and Sandy's creativity and quality foods whenever they want to venture forth into nature or need provisions for the ferry ride back to the mainland or a long-haul flight. How do the McLeans know what to put in a hamper? "We ask a lot of probing questions," says Eric: "Are they wanting food of a particular ethnicity? Is this a special occasion? Are they serious foodies?"

Ah, serious foodies. You're home.

Shady Mile Farm Market

Before the Shady Mile Farm Market sprang up, small farms in the area never had an outlet, beyond the farmgate, to sell what they grew. Bill and Sharon Earthy have changed that with their open-door policy of buying surplus fresh produce from the locals.

Bill is a former welding instructor and landscaping contractor; Sharon managed a wholesale food company. They both wanted to open a country nursery, but recognized that it wasn't a year-round proposition. They could see a growing interest from urban dwellers in the "country experience," so when the opportunity came up to lease seven acres of the historic 118-acre McClure Farm, they decided to combine a nursery with a food market and café.

Their big, sunny establishment includes a couple of production greenhouses and a 5,000-square-foot greenhouse selling annuals, perennials and hanging baskets. Indoors, there is a butcher shop, and dry-goods and fresh-flower sections. The cosy café serves small-batch, custom-ground coffee and treats from popular Lila's Specialty Bakeshop of Ladysmith. Lila is known for her fruit pies, cinnamon buns and bread, and her Kahlua-raisin butter tarts have a loyal following. There's a fireplace and lots of good gardening-related reading material, which makes the café a perfect spot to relax.

The café will eventually double as a demonstration-kitchen and seminar room, where Bill says they'll offer cooking classes, including some for men only. As someone who always travels hopefully, I have already signed my husband up.

Out in front is the large produce area, protected from the

You can pet the deer at Shady Mile Farm Market near Nanaimo.

Pick a peck of peppers at Shady Mile Farm Market near Nanaimo.

elements with a courtyard wall and heaters in winter. It's an inspiring place to shop on a cold day and still enjoy the ambiance of an outdoor market.

The McClure Farm was first homesteaded in 1892. Bill is in the process of bracing the original farmhouse and adding a few heritage elements, like a replica hand pump, so children can learn about how the place used to operate.

The Wesley Street

Gaetan Brousseau studied political science at university, but decided he didn't want to be a starving student, so he learned how to cook. He took his chef's training in Lausanne, Switzerland, and his sommelier training in Bordeaux. He and his wife, Linda, worked in the wine-distribution business, then in a restaurant in Arizona. Keen sailors, they ended up in Vancouver where they ran the successful Granite Café, which was awarded best restaurant status in Vancouver two years running. From their sailing jaunts, they learned of an opportunity at Silva Bay on Gabriola Island and ran their restaurant, Latitude, there for five years.

"And then," says Gaetan, "we decided we were ready to take the boat to Mexico." What changed that plan was another opportunity to take over a restaurant, this time in Nanaimo. The Wesley Street is relatively new to the scene, but has established itself quickly as the place to dine well on the mid-island, for both lunch and dinner. I arrive early for dinner, in order to spend time with Gaetan and his charming chef, Daniel Caron. Daniel is formerly of the Château Laurier in Ottawa, and Vancouver's Waterfront Hotel and the Vancouver Club. He tells me he is thrilled to be cooking on a more intimate scale now. Daniel's wife, pastry chef Tammy Deline, is working at Nanaimo's Scotch Bakery.

My first question, as always, is about their ingredients. What are they sourcing locally? The answer puts The Wesley Street on the same page as restaurants run by the chefs of the Island Chefs Collaborative (ICC) that "emphasize locally-grown, organic, seasonal and minimally processed ingredients." Says Daniel: "We all have our own conscience to answer to. It is our preference to serve locally grown and raised foods in the restaurant." He's known about the quality of Vancouver Island ingredients because "when I worked in Vancouver, we ordered many things from the island."

The charming Wesley Street restaurant and co-owner Gaetan Brousseau.

The menu features pork from nearby Errington, chicken from Cowichan Bay Farm and venison from Qualicum Farms. Greens are supplied by Nanoose Edibles and the cheese course showcases Courtenay's Natural Pastures cheeses. Gaetan has put his sommelier training to good use on the wine list, which is garnering a lot of favourable attention. I'm pleased to see featured selections from Alderlea, Glenterra, Blue Grouse and Saturna Island vineyards.

Gaetan pours me the Victoria Estate Vineyards' Madeleine Sylvaner 2000, and presents the house-made warmed egg bread as I consult the evening's menu. There is a good choice, pleasingly French-leaning, with some personal favourites of mine like bouillabaisse and grilled rack of lamb. I start with delicate slices of venison carpaccio served with mustard aïoli, Nanoose Edibles' mesclun and toast points and then two large ravioli filled with peas and mascarpone and served with small, sweet scallops and seared prawns, finished with basil and chili oils. Both appetizers are first-class.

Gaetan and I have a lively discussion about eating wild versus farmed fish (he favours wild, and serves wild salmon). Hearing he has a good supply of sockeye from Barkley Sound, I decide to go for the salmon baked on a cedar plank, and served this evening with a warm citrus chutney, a nice slice of eggplant, zucchini and onion tart, carrots and perfect rice. I realize I have eaten everything on my plate and can't even contemplate dessert or cheese. That momentary catastrophe was soon remedied; I will just have to come back, and soon.

As Gaetan attends to other diners, I reflect on my excellent meal and think how fortunate Nanaimo is that he and Linda postponed their journey to Mexico.

GABRIOLA ISLAND

Gabriola Gourmet Garlic

Anyone who plays continuous classical music to his chickens is all right with me. As Ken Stefanson gives me a tour of his tranquil Gabriola property, I am particularly taken with his animals: those sophisticated Araucana chickens,

Mr. Gabriola Gourmet Garlic, Ken Stefanson.

a dear miniature horse named Peter and two Angora goats who vie with each other to have their photo taken. Then there are the prize-winning schnauzers. I lose count of how many there are as they frolic around me. Ken's wife, Llie Brotherton, is a professional dog-groomer, and the couple has always raised show dogs.

It was Llie who found their Gabriola property. The couple had been living in Vancouver when she paid a visit to the island with a girlfriend. Says Ken: "She came home and reminded me that I'd once said I could live on an island." They are now happily settled in their island home. Llie has a prolific vegetable garden and makes beautiful baskets. Ken, who had previously sold computers, furniture and real estate, and bought and sold 18 restaurants, has found a new profession in garlic and chocolate.

The garlic was his doctor's suggestion. After Ken had suffered four strokes, she told him to get his blood pressure down by eating more garlic. That led Ken to grow garlic, which led to his growing a lot of garlic — more than 6,000 pounds a year. He grows it mainly on the south, warmer part of the island and has a barn over on Vancouver Island for drying it. Ken tells me he'd always enjoyed garlic, but "I didn't know how much I liked it until I started growing it." Also on Vancouver Island is the chocolate factory where he and his business partner, Ille Jocelyn, produce their amazing array of chocolate bars and truffles.

The chocolate was Ken's own idea. He'd been experimenting with garlic dipped in chocolate. He met Ille, a chocolatier, and they launched The Original Gabriola Bar made of dark chocolate and garlic. The range of Gabriola

Gourmet chocolate bars now includes The Exquist Gabriola Bar (ginger and garlic), Red Hot Chili Bar, Gabriola Island Orange, Gabriola Island Mint and Gabriola Island Espresso. I arrive just as the mint and coffee bars are being launched, and add my praise to the mix between orgasmic bites of each flavour. Speaking of orgasmic, Ken's new maca bars are infused with the recommended daily dose of Peruvian maca, which he tells me is known for its energy-producing and aphrodisiac qualities. There are also divine truffles.

Other products are the hugely popular garlic chutney, pickled- and hot-pickled garlic, three- and four-year aged garlic and garlic salad dressing and marinade. Ken also sells fresh and dried garlic, seed, greens and braids. You'll find this charming gentleman and his garlic products all over the island including at the Nanaimo and Duncan farmers' markets. In season, you can always find him at the Gabriola "Agi Hall" Farmers' Market on Saturdays and the Silva Bay market on Sundays, and at the Saltspring Island Garlic Festival in August. If you have the chance, go directly to the source; Llie's gardens and the irresistible chocolate studio are open year-round. And don't forget to pay your respects to the animals.

Gabriola Agricultural Association Farmers' Market

Tannie Meyer, one of the founders of the Gabriola Agricultural Association Farmers' Market, is showing me around her farm. We're meeting here because it's January and the market is closed for the season, not least to give the busy vendors a break.

The Gabriola market is one of the area's largest with 85 regular and up to 20 "casual" stalls. Tannie says the casual vendors are those who take their chances on market day, bringing whatever they have an abundance of in their gardens that week. "After winter," Tannie says, "the market is a big social event. It's like coming home again."

Vendors include Ken Stefanson and Llie Brotherton of Gabriola Gourmet Garlic with their wonderful garlic products and Llie's beautiful baskets; Ike MacKay of Berry Point Fruit and Honey, who brings apples, pears, cherries and honey; Jocelyne Boulanger and Michael Bean of Auld Alliance Farm, who are well known for their herbs and attractively bottled vinegars; Helen Cox and Dale Ferguson of Early Dawn Farm with cucumbers, flowers, peppers, strawberries and more; and Jacinthe and Peter Eastick of Freedom Farm who come with eggs, greens, chickens and pheasants. There is also a full-service kitchen for snacks and lunch.

Tannie's "6 Meyer Farm" is well represented at the market. Tannie, her husband, Jeff, and her three young children have a regular stall where they sell potatoes and their popular "Meyer corn." The whole family is up before the sun

> # "We want the kids to be able to pick food directly from the garden and eat it without any concerns."
> — Tannie Meyer, G.A.A. Farmers' Market

on market day to harvest, and then have a big breakfast before heading down to the Agi Hall. Tannie tells me they have always grown organically because "we want the kids to be able to pick food directly from the garden and eat it without any concerns."

Heavenly Flowers & Good Earth Vegetables

There was a good rain the night before I went to visit Rosheen Holland. "Bring your gumboots," she advised me. I parked on the road and tramped down a muddy path into the woods. Her home appeared in a clearing, smoke wafting from the chimney. Rosheen was at the door, inviting me in for freshly brewed green tea.

I'd heard great things about the vegetables and flowers grown by Rosheen and her husband, Bob Shields. They had worked in the landscape-maintenance business in Vancouver for 12 years, then thought it would be better to have their own land and grow for themselves. The original idea was to grow ornamentals and trees, but they found their land was best suited to annuals. Actually, they have two pieces of land on Gabriola. The small parcel on the island's warm, south end is ideal for "starting a lot of our babies." The plants are then moved to the couple's mid-island property, which sits on a flood plain. There, they flourish in the rich soil.

Rosheen and Bob began selling their wares from the Gabriola Farmers' Market when it started eight years ago. Their produce and flowers were instant successes, but, as the market grew from a handful of stalls to over 100, they found it more difficult to serve their loyal local customers. Rosheen says that the huge crowds at the market meant "people were struggling to find us, and then actually get to us." So they decided to operate exclusively from their farmgate and by special order.

The special orders are often for Rosheen's extraordinary floral arrangements.

She's popular with brides who visit her flower gardens ("a riot of colour in summer") a week before their weddings, usually with their mothers, to choose the blooms for their big day. Rosheen displays her arrangements at the farmgate, each thoughtfully wrapped in water-filled bubblepacks. Rosheen tells me her flowers are so hardy that they can last up to two weeks.

Rosheen and Bob grow an impressive range of vegetables, many larger than life, like the giant onions Rosheen pulls out of her cold storage to show me. She attributes their quality to the fact that they are organically grown. The couple is always feeding the soil with good things like seaweed, which they get from the east side of the island. "Our soil is 80 percent humus, which acts

Rosheen Holland of Gabriola's Heavenly Flowers & Good Earth Vegetables shows off a bouquet of her famous flowers at the Gabriola Agricultural Association Farmers' Market.

like a giant bag of peat moss on the plants and makes things grow big and healthy." Rosheen feels they have a responsibility to produce high quality produce. "After all," she tells me, "our customers are our neighbours."

Before I leave, we have a wonderful conversation about cooking for oneself versus eating in restaurants. Rosheen loves cooking from the bounty in her garden. She believes "a meal doesn't go anywhere without the best ingredients, and organic ingredients make a meal ex-

Veggies from Heavenly Flowers & Good Earth Vegetables on Gabriola Island.

ceptional." Taught by her mother to understand "what good food is and what it tastes like," she, like me, finds it a challenge to eat out unless the food quality is exceptional.

I leave Rosheen's cosy cottage in the woods, and run into Bob cutting firewood. Even though Rosheen has impressed on me that farming "is not as romantic as people think," for the moment, I am enchanted by the appearance of their rural idyll.

LANTZVILLE/ NANOOSE BAY

The Book Worm Café

There are certain cafés one simply must know about, that serve the kind of food Oscar Wilde might say "causes happiness." For a peripatetic foodie like me, there is nothing more gratifying than knowing where to find wholesome, delicious and creative food just off the beaten track. The Book Worm Café is such a spot, and I am indebted to Barbara Ebell of Nanoose Edibles for pointing me in its direction.

Poached Salmon Salad with Blueberry Salsa

CHRIS THOMAS, THE BOOK WORM CAFÉ

Serves 4.

A great luncheon salad, whose flavour is matched by its beautiful combination of colours.

2 lb	fillet salmon, poached in wine, water and fresh herbs	910 g
6 c	mixed salad greens	1.4 L
1	red pepper, julienned	1
4 tbsp	creamy lemon and chive dressing	60 ml
1 c	blueberry salsa	240 ml

Dressing

Combine in food processor or blender:

1	egg	1
2 1/2 tbsp	lemon juice	37.5 ml
1 tbsp	Dijon mustard	15 ml
	salt and pepper, to taste	

With motor running, slowly add:

1 1/2 c	olive oil	360 ml

Stir in:

1/4 c	finely chopped chives	60 ml
	zest from 1 lemon	

Blueberry Salsa

Mix together and let sit one hour:

1 c	fresh blueberries, coarsely chopped	240 ml
1/2 c	finely diced onion	120 ml
4 tbsp	chopped cilantro	60 ml
1 tbsp	fresh lime juice	15 ml
1/2	jalapeno chile, finely diced (or more, to taste)	1/2
1 tsp	sugar	5 ml
1/2 tsp	salt	2.5 ml

To compose the salads, make a bed of greens on each of four plates, drizzle each with 1 tbsp (15 ml) of the dressing, top each with 1/4 of the salmon left in big chunks, and spoon over 1/4 of the blueberry salsa.

Owner and chef Chris Thomas of The Book Worm Café sets up a stand at the Harvest Bounty Festival.

The café is owned by sisters Vicky Adamson and Chris Thomas who grew up in Nanaimo. Vicky is an art teacher who helps out in the café when she can; Chris is the chef. Chris spent 15 years in Prince Rupert where she also cooked in a café. Moving to Nanoose five years ago, she began looking for a place of her own.

The Book Worm Café had sold used books and served food, but only from a hot plate. Chris and Vicky put in a new kitchen, and introduced the neighbourhood to some very good cooking, what Chris calls "casual, West Coast contemporary." She makes everything from scratch except the bagels.

She relies on local suppliers and enjoys changing her menu with the seasons, running with what's available. Nanoose Edibles is the vegetable and fruit source. They provided such lovely strawberries last summer that the café served strawberry shortcake every day. A farmer supplies the eggs, another the chicken and turkey, and local fishers bring in sockeye salmon and shrimp. Chris serves organic, fair-trade Karma Coffee from nearby Errington.

Morning coffee is incredibly popular at The Book Worm Café, and Chris' customers have her trained to make them a different type of muffin every day. One group of retired gentlemen meets there every morning at 10 o'clock, and Chris says the conversation is fascinating. I'm reminded of my father's Kaffee

Klatsch that also meets at 10 o'clock precisely, behind Oak Bay's tweed curtain, to discuss their portfolios and other weighty matters.

On one side of the café, Chris exhibits local artists' work. As with the food suppliers, she is committed to providing a venue to local artists. She also holds music evenings on Fridays to showcase local talent.

I dropped in on a June afternoon and enjoyed the café's Thai Noodle Salad with Nanoose Edible's greens and asparagus, then left with the only portable piece of pie I've encountered. The café's pie-shaped O'Henry Bar is a sinfully solid creation of chocolate, peanut butter and Rice Crispies that's perfect for road trippers like myself. Next time, I'm looking forward to trying Chris' famous lemon meringue pie.

Harvest Bounty Festival

Like Feast of Fields on the island's south end in September, the Harvest Bounty Festival is well worth the price of admission. It's co-ordinated by Debbie Schug from Parksville, who proves to be a wealth of information about all things agricultural and foodie in the area. Also like Feast of Fields, it's a good idea to call well ahead for tickets. In 2003 Nanoose Edibles hosted the event.

The Island Farmers' Alliance organizes this fabulous celebration of local agriculture, food, drink and the culinary arts in late August. Last year, I drove up early, and was actually first in the gate of Dave and Marnie Evans' 350-acre farm in Qualicum Beach.

Getting there early proves to be beneficial that Sunday, because many of the churches are still in session, and I have beaten the crowds. It gives me the opportunity I most enjoy: meeting one-on-one with the growers and chefs, and enjoying their exquisite food offerings in a relaxed way.

I find myself grazing first for food and wine, then gravitating to a bench or picnic table where I can enjoy not only the food, but also the other people. I manage to eat and drink my way around the whole exhibition! The Harvest Bounty Festival has a homey, small-community feel even though the exhibitors come from all over the island.

I meet up with Mary Ann Hyndman Smith and Edgar Smith of Natural Pastures Cheese; Christie Eng of Shady Creek Ice Cream, who calls me over to "try this tuile with roasted banana ice cream" as it is "just right" to eat — and it is delicious; and Carol Mann of The Earthshake Café, who, with her assistant, Jessica, a Malaspina culinary arts student, is serving up a colourful summer salad. Sandy and Eric McLean of McLean's Specialty Foods join me for a sample of the 2001 Pinot Gris from Ruth Luxton at the Glenterra Vineyard table.

The Landing at Pacific Shores

Chef Christine Lilyholm comes by her way with seafood honestly. After graduating from the chef's training program at Winnipeg's Red River Community College, she headed to the West Coast to serve her apprenticeship through Camosun College in Victoria. A stint in the kitchen of the city's popular seafood restaurant, The Marina, was followed by five seasons at Campbell River's April Point Lodge, also known for its fruits de mer. She is particularly excited about the wonderful seafood available to her in the Parksville area, and, as she points to the ocean, tells me: "I want people to enjoy what's out there, specifically what is caught in these waters."

Top: *Chef Christine Lilyholm slides a pizza into the wood-fired oven at The Landing; left: the lunch brigade prepares for service; right: owners Susan and Andy Pearson in front of their state-of-the-art kitchen.*

So, you won't see lobster on this menu because it cannot be sourced locally, but you will be wowed by the local Qualicum Bay scallops that Christine loves to present with other shellfish in a beautiful copper cataplana that has been placed in the wood-fired oven, or serves steamed in a champagne broth finished with saffron cream. Jason Walmark, The Landing's personable food and beverage director, tells me how delighted guests are to learn that he personally picks up the scallops daily from the fisher in Qualicum Bay.

The Landing offers West Coast cuisine, which Christine defines as cooking that is based on what's available locally, with a nod to the Mediterranean; from the wood-fired oven come pizza and grilled vegetables, and the rotisserie can roast as many as 42 chickens at once. To understand why a 120-seat restaurant would need to roast that many chickens, is to see beyond The Landing itself.

It's situated within Pacific Shores Nature Resort, a 15-acre, time-share resort that also offers a teahouse, private dining room and state-of-the-art demo kitchen located in a gazebo in the garden. The Landing's kitchen does the majority of the cooking for these other facilities, so it's normal to have a full restaurant, a large wedding party outdoors and an intimate winemaker's dinner all happening at once. And even with that volume, Christine tells me proudly: "I'm part of every meal that leaves the kitchen."

I'm invited to join the resort's owners, Andy and Susan Pearson, for lunch in The Landing. I enjoy a bowl of carrot-ginger soup topped with a chiffonade of Nanoose Edibles' spinach, and a steaming hot bowl of bouillabaisse, chock full of all that's good from the sea in front of me: clams, mussels, scallops, prawns, salmon, tuna and halibut that have been steamed in a light saffron broth.

Susan is putting the final touches on a world-class spa that's due to open the next day, but the enormity of that doesn't prevent her from focusing her attention on me and her husband, and enjoying her cheeseburger. She is a certified real estate appraiser who worked with her husband in their real estate brokerage business and in property development before embarking on the development of time-share offerings. The couple own or have interests in four time-share properties, and are about to build an urban time-share in Victoria. The Landing is their first restaurant venture.

Andy Pearson studied botany and zoology at university, and I'm impressed when, walking with him after lunch, he can name every plant in every section of the property's extensive gardens (there are Japanese, Chinese, South African, North American and Mediterranean gardens; Australasian and South American sections are planned). He shows me the herb gardens that are located throughout the property and the vegetable and fruit garden, from which resort guests are invited to pick whatever they like. What a thoughtful touch from a man who is obviously passionate about plants and the environment (there is no use of pesticides or herbicides, and the resort makes its own organic compost). There are figs, hazelnuts, rhubarb, gooseberries, blueberries and greens ripe for the taking. Says Andy: "Guests often stop me to say thank you, or to ask questions about the gardens."

The Landing is the kind of place one wants to find on any edible journey: good food, great service, spectacular setting, and believe it or not, the best sweet potato fries this side of New Orleans.

Nanoose Edibles

It's 9:00 a.m. on a clear Monday morning in Nanoose Bay. I've ferried across earlier this morning from Vesuvius on Saltspring Island, excited to see Barbara and Lorne Ebell's popular Nanoose Edibles farm. Such is the quality of their produce that chefs like Michael Bebault of The Wickaninnish Inn actually have orders couriered to them.

I've been asked to join a culinary arts class from Malaspina College that is touring the farm with instructor Gordon Cower (formerly of Sooke Harbour House). They're a lively bunch of 20-somethings whose enthusiasm for the whole growing process is infectious.

Our hostess, the indomitable Barbara Ebell, is a former manager of women's programs for B.C.'s Ministry of Agriculture. Lorne holds a Ph.D. in agriculture and has worked for the provincial and federal governments. The couple retired a few years ago,

"We're still hunters and gatherers, still working with the basic tools."

— Barbara Ebell, Nanoose Edibles

realized longevity ran on both sides of their family, and worked out what they were going to do for the next 40 years. They turned to their 23-acre property in Nanoose, thought they would plant a few apple trees and some raspberries, and are now going full-tilt with a variety of herbs, 20 kinds of nutritional greens and other veggies, flowers and fruit, a box program and a large farmstand.

Located as they are, in a non-farming community, Barbara says it hasn't always been easy, but they are determined to make a go of organic farming. It's the lowest-lying property in the area, located on an old estuary, with some clay and some gravel base. When they took over the land, the soil was seriously degraded. They've spent a lot of time raising its nutritional level through cover-crop plantings that just get tilled in, and reverse rototilling. They have their own water supply, with a drip-irrigation system operating from six zones on the property. The drip system is used when the wind blows to ensure that water goes where it should and is not wasted.

Nanoose Edibles was certified organic in 1997. When Barbara is asked to explain the road to organic certification to the Malaspina students, she cites a lowly onion. The certification body (in her case, BCARA) requires detailed

Top: Nanoose Edibles' owner Barbara Ebell rings up a sale for Malaspina College's culinary arts instructor Gordon Cower; left: rows and rows of nutritional greens surround the greenhouse; right: resident chickens.

Farmer's Lunch

BARBARA EBELL, NANOOSE EDIBLES

Barbara says she loves this quick and easy shake when she's working in the fields: "With all the bending over, I don't want a heavy meal in my stomach."

In a blender, combine to taste:

> V-8 juice
> nutritional greens
> cayenne pepper

records on when it was seeded, transplanted and harvested. The way the food is grown and handled must be recorded every step of the way. It's a process that is both laborious and costly, but ultimately gives the consumers complete confidence in what they're buying.

Barbara learned her growing techniques through her association with the Pacific Northwest branch of the North American Direct Farm Marketing Association. At one of their meetings in Portland, Oregon, she happened to be sitting next to the owner of Nicky's Greens, a California business focussed on growing nutritional greens. Nicky befriended Barbara and took the time to explain how her business worked. It was a fortuitous meeting.

Barbara says her first taste of "bitter" herbs was at the Herald Street Caffé in Victoria where she ate a delicious salad of greens with quail eggs. To her, "bitter is one of the great tastes of the culinary arts," but she says most people want their greens devoid of bitterness. It's certainly a taste worth acquiring as the nutritional values are impressive.

Fresh is important to Barbara, who notes that green vegetables lose their nutritional value at a rate of 10% per day. She says: "Eating only a lettuce salad probably puts you in a negative nutrition mode." And, of course, eating fresh and local is also good for the economy. Local organic chard is ultimately less expensive because there's no waste. So the moral is, the closer you can get to the grower and the sooner you can eat that just-picked produce, the better.

PARKSVILLE

The Earthshake Café

Looks are certainly deceiving, and location ain't everything. The Earthshake Café is located on the main drag (actually, the old Island Highway) in Parksville, on the outskirts of the city centre, but it's a real find by any standard.

I begin with an Earthrise, a freshly made drink of orange, strawberry, ginseng and royal jelly that whets my appetite for the food to come. An "omelette to live for" with avocado, cheddar and salsa is accompanied by pumpkin toast and a spinach Caesar salad that's made without egg, anchovy or dairy, yet still packs a taste punch. The café uses organic ingredients where possible and serves free-range eggs and chicken, and wild salmon.

Chef Carol Mann started the café from scratch a year and a half ago, having spent 15 years cheffing in Vancouver at spots like Mulvaney's and Bridges restaurants on Granville Island. Originally from Parksville, she welcomed the opportunity to produce fresh, flavourful food for her hometown crowd. Above all, she says: "Food has got to have flavour. We all eat three times a day. You want to have the best possible experience every time."

Owner and chef Carol Mann and her assistant Jessica of The Earthshake Café in Parksville serve a colourful salad at the Harvest Bounty Festival.

There are only 15 seats in this tiny café, so it feels very homey. Carol says she likes it "small and personal" to ensure consistency of the food served. It seems to attract a real mix of people, young and old, who obviously condone Carol's philosophy: "To eat is human, to digest divine." On one visit, a woman next to me asked the waitress whether a particular dish is high in carbohydrates. The answer came back directly from the chef who takes a keen interest in her customers' dietary needs. I'm sure no one leaves The Earthshake Café feeling anything but satisfied and healthy.

QUALICUM BEACH

Creekmore Coffee

I once had the pleasure of sharing a stall at Victoria's Banana Belt Fine Foods' customer appreciation day with two wonderful fellas, Richard Lewin of Golda's Fine Foods and David Creekmore of Creekmore Coffee. Suffice it to say, I learned a few things about promotion from both of them. And I sure developed a taste for BuzzRight coffee, a dark-roasted, full-bodied blend that is one of Creekmore's most popular.

David and Elaine Creekmore have always been "coffee hounds," but their careers took them in other directions. David was a furniture maker and then a salesman for the largest beverage company in Alaska; Elaine was a children's librarian. Elaine says: "David and I are very different. If you had told me ten years ago that we'd be working together, I wouldn't have believed you, but we love it."

It turns out their differences have made them a great team. David is very gregarious, so he's responsible for the marketing, promotion and delivery of their coffee. Elaine enjoys the roasting process and has become so expert that she almost never refers to her daily logbook when roasting a batch of green beans.

Together, they are very proud of their Little Red Primo drum roaster, and treat me to an exclusive demonstration. They are rigorous about roasting in small batches to ensure the quality and consistency of the coffee they sell. Elaine turns on the machine and waits for the burners to reach a certain temperature. She is a petite woman, but has no difficulty shouldering 40 pounds of green coffee beans and pouring them into the roaster.

Each type of coffee requires a different starting temperature. Today, Elaine is roasting Peruvian beans, and she is able to tell by sight (the colour of the beans as they roast is visible through a glass window) and sound (at around 400°F, the beans start to pop like popcorn). There is also a "tryer," a small spout

Michael, Elaine and David Creekmore operate Creekmore Coffee in Qualicum.

that extracts a few beans from the batch as it's roasting. Depending on what she sees in the sample, Elaine may adjust the temperature up or down.

After the beans are roasted, Elaine releases them into the cooling tray where a continuous agitator with steel brushes kicks off the chaff. The chaff goes directly into a collecting vessel and is then put on the Creekmores' compost pile. It takes at least seven minutes to cool the beans, and then they are weighed. What started out at 40 pounds has been reduced to 33.5, as beans lose between 12 and 25 percent moisture in the roasting process.

Elaine records every batch in her logbook, taking note of how the different coffee beans from different countries react. David points to their many

sources of organic coffee: bags of beans from Peru, Indonesia, Sumatra and Colombia are stacked around the room. Their decaffeinated coffee is made from beans from the well-known Mexican Isman cooperative.

David says that, with coffee, "freshness is everything," and that's why he does his own distribution. This is a real family affair with their son, Michael, a science student at the University of Victoria, active in the business during school vacations.

Fore & Aft Foods

Years ago, I used to enjoy breakfasts at a little café on the dock at Brentwood Bay, just north of Victoria. In addition to serving meals, the café sold wonderful jams and condiments.

Wandering around the What's Cooking? cookshop in Qualicum Beach, I came across jars of the divine Fore & Aft antipasto, a taste from my past. The labels showed that the company was now in Qualicum Beach.

Medallions of Pork Tenderloin with a Ginger Grapefruit Sauce

BEVERLEY CHILD, FORE & AFT FOODS

Serves 4. Chris Tyrrell tested this dish on dinner-party guests, and declared the result "beautiful, tender, juicy, moist — perfect." He cooked the pork for 20 minutes, then let it rest for ten minutes before slicing. Says Chris: "This sauce is to die for!" Fore & Aft makes a good grapefruit marmalade.

2	whole pork tenderloins	2
Marinade		
1 3/4 c	grapefruit marmalade	420 ml
4 tbsp	soy sauce	60 ml
4 tbsp	medium sherry	60 ml
1 tbsp	sesame oil	15 ml
2 tbsp	finely chopped garlic	30 ml
2 tbsp	finely chopped fresh ginger	30 ml
1/2 c	water or white wine	120 ml
1	can good quality consommé	1
1 1/2 - 2 c	crème fraîche	360 - 480 ml

Mix ingredients together and pour over pork. Marinate for a minimum of three hours, but preferably overnight. Remove pork from marinade and set aside. Add consommé to marinade and bring to boil. Simmer to reduce by half. At this point, add the crème fraîche and continue to simmer. While sauce is thickening, sear to brown the two tenderloins in 1 1/2 tbsp (22.5 ml) olive oil. Transfer pork to roasting pan and bake 20 to 30 minutes at 350°F. Slice pork into medallions and drizzle sauce over meat. Serve with fresh greens and rice, and garnish with fresh grapefruit.

With no address or phone number to follow up, I had to do a bit of serious foodie sleuthing before I knocked on a door that was opened by Beverley Child, co-owner of the company. "When we left Brentwood Bay, we ran the teahouse at Filberg Lodge in Comox for five years, then started our own catering company." Actually, she and her husband and business partner, Patrick Brownrigg, had never stopped making their condiments.

Wine jellies, jams, vinegars, chutneys and that great antipasto are all available from their commercial kitchen, at Slater's First Class Meats in Victoria and at What's Cooking? in Qualicum Beach. The couple sources a lot of their ingredients locally, and most of the fruit is organic. Trained at Dubrulle in Vancouver, Beverley says she is delighted to be doing what she does and seemed pleased to be rediscovered by one of her old customers.

La Boulange Organic Breads

If you expect to find an elderly French gentleman behind La Boulange breads, you would at least be half right. Roger Floch had been a baker in Bordeaux before bringing the spirit of levain breads to Cumberland, British Columbia.

John Taraynor was a carpenter who happened to be working on a building project in Qualicum Beach with a fellow who knew Roger. At that time, Roger had his house on the market and was looking to sell his bakery and return to France. John was reminiscing about his epiphany over a sourdough bun in Zurich (when he ate that bun, he realized he'd never eaten good bread before). There was no doubt that John, looking for a change of careers, was in the right place at the right time. He and his wife, Jean Wilson, bought the business from Roger, who stayed nearly two years to train them. When he returned to France, the couple hired two locals, Ron Postl and Jamie Barter, neither of whom were bakers, and their success has pleasantly delighted them all. Ron formerly owned a local gift shop specializing in environmentally friendly products and Jamie is a musician.

Jamie says they're passionate about what they do, that "the weird thing is, it's about the bread. I'd be bored if I was making donuts, but this is a fascinating journey through 48 hours." They all seem to have inherited a certain fanaticism from Roger, who was obsessed with the microbiotic requirements of making the bread, and they turn out very impressive loaves: seven-grain flax, seven-grain raisin and nut, kamut/spelt multi-grain (my husband's favourite), 100% rye, rye with wholewheat flours, kamut, spelt, French and a new rice bread. There also are organic raisin squares that practically make a full meal.

The bakery is now located on John and Jean's six-acre property in Qualicum Beach, in what was once the horse barn. The property was formerly owned by Jean's parents; when they wanted a smaller place in town, the two couples agreed to exchange houses!

I arrive just as their baking shift is over, and Jean and the boys are having a cup of tea. We sit around in the bakery, surrounded by loaves of bread on the cooling racks, chatting about the importance of levain, the wild culture that's made from the flour itself. Roger used to tell them that, from a nutritional point of view, "Yeast is the enemy," so they are very rigorous about using their secret-recipe levain.

As we chat, local folk drop by to pick up their bread. Ron, a Vermont transplant, goes off with a loaf of multi-grain,

The mixing machine takes pride of place at La Boulange Organic Breads.

telling me: "This is real, artisan bread. I moved here to be closer to La Boulange." A woman who had picked up La Boulange kamut bread in Vancouver sent Jean an email when she got home: "Where's your outlet in Manhattan?"

La Boulange makes about 2,000 loaves of bread a week for outlets in Vancouver and the Lower Mainland, Victoria, Campbell River and on Saltspring, Hornby and Gabriola islands. Their Cinelli gas-fired, rotating-tray oven bakes up to 160 loaves at a time. It really is a 48-hour process to make each loaf, and John says they're taking expansion very slowly. Eventually, he would like to install a wood-fired oven to make some rustic loaves.

RainBarrel Farm

Mother and daughter Marilyn Mant and Tami Treit pick dahlias for four or five hours every Friday, in order to have enough bouquets for the Qualicum Farmers' Market on Saturday mornings. Whether they have 70 or 100 bouquets on their stall, they are quickly bought up.

Also on Fridays, they prepare beautiful baskets of fruits and vegetables from the farm for their brown-box customers. The baskets are so artistic that I was stopped in my tracks when I saw them at the Harvest Bounty Festival. They also supply the local Thrifty Foods and Quality Foods with their lettuce mix and other veggies.

When I visit Marilyn and her husband, Henry, on their 35-acre farm on the outskirts of Qualicum Beach, I can see that their exquisite produce comes from a long history of hard work. Henry's parents arrived in the Qualicum area from England in 1913 with very little money. Over the years, they slowly bought land, five acres at a time, until they had 150 acres.

Today, the Mants raise miniature horses, Muscovy ducks and hundreds of plants: 300 broccoli, 200 cabbage, 200 cauliflower and endless corn, beets, tomatoes, English cucumbers, zucchini, peppers, raspberries, strawberries and grapes. There are 700 dahlia plants, which Marilyn is getting ready to dig out for storage until next season.

The Mants have always farmed organically, but when Thrifty Foods said they'd buy a significant amount of produce if the Mants were officially certified, they went through the process. The soil and their farming practices were so exemplary that the certification process took less than a year. Like many farmers I've met, Marilyn would rather not have the cost and amount of paperwork that certification involves, but she is adamant that her family eat organics. "I've got a grandchild," she tells me, "so I'm not going to grow food with tons of junk on it."

Marilyn and Henry live in a most interesting home — their former hayloft. As we enter the house, Marilyn points to where the cows used to be milked. Local potter Larry Aguilar has recently moved into another house on the property and set up a studio for public visits.

FANNY BAY

Ships Point Inn

"These pears have been poached in white wine and finished with a little orange-flavoured cream cheese. Enjoy." Rod Milligan, former chef at Ships Point Inn in Fanny Bay, is presenting the first course of a four-course breakfast to 11 hungry guests.

Staying at the sumptuous inn during my trawl around the North Island, I met a gentleman farmer from Doncaster, U.K., who told me about various organic gardens and seed collectors in that part of the world.

The Ships Point Inn on Fanny Bay.

I also found an amazing number of dedicated organic-food producers in the area: vegetables, beef, poultry, pork, emu, fallow-deer venison, ostrich and dairy products are widely available. A trip to this area should properly include an excursion to Denman and Hornby islands where an invasion of hippiedom in the 1960s brought with it prolific organic growers and food producers. Happily, their traditions continue.

DENMAN ISLAND

Bien Tostado Custom Coffee Roasting

Over and over again, delicious food and drink surface where one might least expect them. I'd enjoyed Bien Tostado coffee beans in Denman Island Chocolate company's rich espresso chocolate bar in Victoria, and then in a cappuccino at the Cowppuccino Café on Denman Island while waiting for a ferry to Hornby Island. When I finally had some time to spend on Denman, I was determined to find the roaster of this wonderful organic java.

Elaine Head's story began in Colorado where she met her future husband, Colombian-born Steven Carballeira. Steve's grandfather was a coffee broker in New York, who introduced the lad to good coffee at an early age. When his grandfather passed away, Steve inherited his old German coffee roaster.

Coffee Pie

ELAINE HEAD, BIEN TOSTADO CUSTOM COFFEE ROASTING

Serves 8.
The filling is like pudding — rich and creamy. This pie
will satisfy any coffee maven's craving.

1/4 c	flour	60 ml
1/8 tsp	salt	0.6 ml
2/3 c	sugar	160 ml
1 c	very strong coffee	240 ml
1 c	milk	240 ml
2	egg yolks	2
2 tbsp	butter	30 ml
1	plain or nut pie shell, baked	1
2 c	whipped cream	480 ml
1	square semi-sweet chocolate	1

In a heavy saucepan whisk together the flour, salt and sugar; add coffee and milk and mix well.
Cook over low heat until thickened, stirring constantly. Quickly stir one cup of hot mixture into
beaten egg yolks and return mixture to saucepan to continue cooking. Stir while cooking one minute
longer. Add butter and cool. Pour into pie shell and cool completely. When the pie is cool, cover with
whipped cream and grate chocolate over top.

By this time, the couple had married. Steve missed living by the ocean and
Elaine wanted to live in Canada, so they headed out to find "home." They
chose Denman Island and began playing around with that coffee roaster. Says
Elaine: "We had no intention of going into business, but one thing led to
another."

Now, two years later, they are roasting over 6,000 pounds of organic Colombian coffee annually. Steve calls their business "a nano-roastery," in defer-
ence to the larger, but hardly huge, micro-roasteries. Elaine says they had three
goals when they started out: they wanted to roast wonderful-tasting coffee; they
wanted to roast only organic beans; and they wanted to have personal contact
with their customers, whether restaurants or individuals.

Elaine had been turned on to organics when her daughter developed sensi-
tivities to food additives. She claims her child's health improved 100 percent

through eating organic food, and she is now delighted that her grandchildren are being raised in the same way. She is concerned about the health of people who are growing crops with pesticides, and is determined not to handle any coffee beans that haven't been grown pesticide-free.

She tells me that they "don't want to be Nabob"; they want to stay small and high quality. Elaine keeps a record of every coffee that her customers buy, along with their comments and suggestions.

Bien Tostado roasts only seven certified organic Arabica Latin American coffees; Mesa comes from beans grown on a plantation on a Colombian mesa (an old, flat-topped mountain), all are mountain- and shade-grown. Two of the coffees are exported directly by small grower co-ops, which enable the growers to negotiate their own prices.

Elaine ships coffee throughout North America. They have a customer whose Caribbean-based yachts they supply and many individuals order regularly from New York, Colorado and California. British Columbia restaurants as far as the Queen Charlotte Islands brew their beans, and a Fanny Bay kayak-adventure company takes Bien Tostado along on its ten-day paddling and gourmet-food excursions around the islands.

Steve continues to work as a hydro-geologist, doing mainly environmental work. Elaine, who is now a lifetime away from her career as a construction manager for university and college laboratories, has never been happier, roasting small-batch fresh coffee.

Cowppuccino Café

The Cowppuccino Café came into view at exactly the right time for an organic Bien Tostado java before I boarded the ferry to Hornby Island. It's a little caravan with a deck, situated in Gravelly Bay where it attracts the ferry crowd, cyclists and many locals who make a regular stop for coffee, freshly baked muffins and brownies and lunch items like tacos made with veggies from the nearby farms.

Owner Evelyn Martins grew up on a ranch in California's Salinas Valley, and tells me she became a property owner on Denman Island 17 years ago "because of a ghost!" She had been visiting Expo '86, and came over to Vancouver Island to get away from the crowds. While staying at the Qualicum College Inn, she lost her car keys and was forced to spend an extra day there. She blames the inn's famous ghost for the loss of the keys, but thanks it for allowing her to tarry longer and discover the Gulf Islands. When she came to Denman, she bought a 67-acre waterfront farm close to the ferry terminal.

Evelyn and her daughter-in-law opened the Cowppuccino Café four years ago because "you couldn't even get a glass of water while waiting for the ferry," and it has been a popular seasonal meeting spot ever since. She has plans to open an eco-retreat at Driftwood Farms in the next year or so. A cancer survivor, she wants to "share what I've learned about nutrition, spiritual healing and alternative medicine" with people who could benefit.

Denman Island Chocolate

Ruth and Daniel Terry WWOOFed their way around Europe and the interior of British Columbia, got turned on to organics, and finally settled on Denman Island. Like many Gulf Islanders, Daniel worked a variety of jobs, including recycling-depot manager, firefighter and carpenter.

Ruth holds a Master's degree in English from Cambridge University. Four years ago, she made vegan truffles (no cream or butter) for the island's annual Christmas craft fair, and people went crazy for them. Having sourced high-quality organic chocolate from Belgium, hazelnuts and raspberries from the Fraser Valley's In Season Farms, fair-traded Nicaraguan coffee and pure orange and mint essences from England, Daniel began to develop the ultimate organic chocolate bar. He is a self-taught chocolatier and marketer, who clearly thrives on the business side of things. As Ruth, who continues to make truffles for special orders, says: "He likes selling chocolate and I like giving it away."

Their goal is to become a complete "bean to bar" chocolate factory, but for now, they're working feverishly to produce 1,350 bars a day, many for seriously addicted customers like myself.

The Denman Island Chocolate factory is not open to the public, but its chocolate bars are available at over 200 retailers on Vancouver Island.

East Cider Orchard

The sun is just beginning to dip in the sky as Anne de Cosson and I sit on her back patio, watching a promenade of peacocks through the orchard (seriously!) and sipping apple cider from the second pressing of her Gravenstein apples. Anne was happy to take a break from painting an upstairs bedroom to chat with a curious urbanite.

She and her husband, Larry Berg, had worked at Capilano College in Vancouver, travelled through India and then had the chance to house-sit for friends on Denman Island. Anne had been raised on her father's

Crabapple Jelly

ANNE DE COSSON, EAST CIDER ORCHARD

I bought a big bag of crabapples from the Cobble Hill Farmers' Market and enjoyed making Anne's jelly. It's the perfect accompaniment to pork and poultry.

Place about 6 lbs (2.75 kg) of whole, washed crabapples (Anne likes the Dolgo crabs) in a large kettle and cover with water. Boil until the apples explode and the water turns pink. Remove to a jelly bag, and let the juice drip out. Measure 5 cups (1.2 L) of the juice and combine it with 4 cups (1 L) of sugar in a large saucepan.

Boil the mixture for about ten minutes or until it reaches the jam stage (220°F). Pour it into sterilized rubber-ringed jars and let them sit until the jelly is set.

homegrown vegetables, and she was always aware of the marked contrast between garden-fresh and store-bought.

The couple lost no time finding a property on this very peaceful island. They bought their orchard in 1979 when it was nothing but a fallen-down house and 25 apple trees. They got together with two other families and formed a co-operative called Apple Lane Orchards. The co-op seemed like a good idea then, but over time, the families found differences in their growing philosophies, and the de Cosson/Berg contingent struck out on their own at East Cider Orchard.

It was always important to Anne to grow organically, so theirs is a fully certified operation, and all the juice, or soft cider as they call it, is pasteurized. Anne says they never know how much money the orchard will generate, as organic farming is much more dependent on weather and other forces of nature than conventional farming. They have 1,000 trees from which they make between 300 and 900 gallons of cider per year.

They take the apples by the truckload to Bill LePage, of The Cider Press in Courtenay. Bill presses it into four- and two-litre jugs, and then it's sold at Vancouver's Granville Island and East Vancouver markets and at the Courtenay Farmers' Market.

At harvest time, the whole family pitches in, together with eight to ten WWOOFers. As Anne says: "The world comes to work in our orchard, so it's been a really interesting experience for our family. We've had lots of workers from the Czech Republic when it opened up."

Jacquie's Ices

In 1970, Jacquie Barnett and her then-husband, having built a boat in their Chicago backyard, set out for three and a half years at sea. "We were anti-war protestors," she tells me. They had a friend on Denman Island and sailed on up. Thirty-three years later, Jacquie has a thriving ice-cream business on the island.

She started with cattle, but "it gets very hot on my side [the west side] of the island. It's hot until 10 o'clock at night," so she was looking for a cooler occupation. She spotted a 1957 white Dodge truck in Courtenay one day and thought it would make an excellent ice-cream truck. Fifty dollars later, the truck was hers. "It overheated all the time, so I would put ice cubes on the carburetor." Jacquie started making ice cream for local fairs, driving it around in the Dodge. Sometimes she had left-over stock on her hands, so Jacquie's Ices at the ferry to Hornby Island was established 20 years ago. It's a cute trailer with big photos of Einstein enjoying an ice cream cone just like you and me.

Jacquie picks the wild plums and rhubarb from her property and adds them, along with chocolate, vanilla and other gourmet ingredients to ice cream. She makes her own giant waffle cones, and "people just love them." She says she loves to watch tourists recharge on the island. People buy her ice creams, then sit on a rock and look out to sea. "It's a great form of meditation," she tells me, and I agree as I devour a rhubarb-chocolate double scoop (no worries: I'll work it off writing!).

Windy Marsh Farm

The contrast between the strip malls of any modern city and the back roads of any Gulf Island is startling. The malls offer a parade of predictable fast-food magnets — different city, but same fatty smorgasbord. Rural roads produce erratic offerings — a farmstand around the bend that only sells beans and flowers, and then nothing for ten kilometres. Ah, but the unpredictability of snacking from the back-road farmstands is the whole point. It's an adventure, and every trip is a clean canvas for the intrepid hunter-gatherer.

On a late summer afternoon, my husband and I were touring the back roads of Denman Island, enjoying the scenery, but feeling peckish. Up ahead, we glimpsed a farmstand. Beans and flowers? Well, yes and no. The Windy Marsh farmstand, a labour of love by Bob and Velda Parsons, has a range of produce to convert any hot-blooded, fast-food junkie. We dive right into a basket of sun-warmed raspberries.

The Parsons grow 100% organically, and Velda says they strive for variety: big, cream-coloured vegetable marrows, dill weed for a nickel a stem, shiny fresh snow peas, just-picked red raspberries, parsley, kale, beet thinnings, zucchini, artichokes, peppers, cucumbers, tomatoes, fat shelling peas, potatoes and lettuce. Their chickens produce enough eggs for, as the sign says: "one dozen per family, please."

A decorated can at Windy Marsh Farm.

She and Bob, a boat builder, bought the farm 12 years ago. They had been living on a float home in Genoa Bay, but says Velda: "It was in danger of sinking from the number of plants we had growing on it — especially tropical plants." A New Zealander, Bob has always grown tropicals and today coaxes papayas and bananas in his greenhouse.

Velda told me they looked around the Gulf Islands, and settled on the ten-acre Denman Island property because it was located next to a marsh, and "water is essential for growing veg." It's proven time and again to have been a wise choice. They bought the property with "every cent we had," cleared three acres, and have learned to grow what suits the soil.

Velda says they grow organically because it is "morally correct," but, like many local producers who sell to people who know them, they feel no need to certify. They grow primarily for their farmgate, and sell any surplus at the in-season Saturday morning farmers' market held next to the elementary school.

Hornby Island

The Flower Lady

Anna MacKay's beautiful smile radiates out from behind bunches of red, yellow and fuchsia gerberas in French florists' vases. I could be on South Granville, but wait — these flowers actually have fragrance. Anna and I chat as she nibbles on her lunch of pakoras from another vendor's stand.

She tells me there were 300 residents on the island when she moved here 30 years ago from Ontario, looking for an alternative lifestyle. She has raised three children on the island, and the population has grown along with them — to about 1,200 permanent residents.

Anna MacKay's radiant smile and gorgeous posies light up her stall at the Hornby Island Farmers' Market.

Like many growers, she is concerned that "people don't remember what good food tastes like." She and several others started the market 12 years ago so they wouldn't have to sell at the farmgate. She enjoys being in direct contact with the buyers, and thinks "the most positive thing that could happen [in our food-distribution system] would be to cut out the middle man, cut out the transportation." Like many others, she is concerned about the food miles, and advocates eating only what we grow locally.

Hornby Island Co-op

No visit to Hornby is complete without a stop at the co-op, the island's heartbeat, where shopping for groceries and supplies plays second fiddle to picking up your mail, checking out the bulletin board and meeting up with friends. It's the most social grocery store I know.

Produce manager Sue Horner, a former sign-language interpreter from Vancouver, is unpacking organic veggies, and stops to tell me where they all come from. The store buys a lot through Vancouver's Wildwest and Thrifty Foods' wholesale distributor, but when a resident arrives at the back door with a bag of plums, they're also set out for sale. The result is an impressive range of organic fruit and vegetables and a good selection of dry goods. Bread is baked fresh daily by the island's Cardboard House Bakery.

This is the best place to pick up picnic supplies before heading out for the day to Tribune Bay or Ford Cove.

Hornby Island Farmers' Market

Every market has its own special flavour. To me, the Hornby Island Farmers' Market is a vibrant statement of how things could be if the world didn't encroach. Certainly, it has that latter-day hippie look and feel, but once you've met the vendors and sampled their wares, you will appreciate the quality of food grown with great understanding, and lovingly prepared. The local musicians and an exotic belly dancer add an air of festivity.

Savoie Farm

Chatting with Andrea and David at the Savoie farmstand in the market led me to one of the most magical flower and vegetable gardens on the west coast. "You'll find Elaine at the farm today because she's setting up for tonight's art exhibit," said David. I will always remember my journey to the farm at the end of Carmichael Road, how the sea seemed to rise up and meet me when I stopped the car.

I found Elaine Savoie in her house on the property, cleaning up for 150 guests, including the renowned Vancouver restaurateur and Hornby Islander John Bishop, who were coming that evening for her annual art exhibition. The house originally had no electricity or running water, and she has only recently installed a phone. Her paintings are a unique style of chicken iconography, which has been well received by the artistic community and, not surprisingly, questioned by the religious sector. She welcomes me like an old friend, and doesn't hesitate to take me out to see the gardens and meet her sister and gardening partner, Mary.

We cross a nondescript field before I stop in my tracks at the first sight of their garden. I cannot believe that, just six years ago, this was also a field. Today, there are vast plantings of veggies and herbs: squashes, basil, thyme, blueberries, hot peppers, onions, asparagus, strawberries and more, mostly grown in raised beds to keep the roots out of the water. There are rows upon rows of cutting flowers like dahlias, gladioli, bachelor's button (Mary's favourite) and statice. On one section, local basket maker Alistair Hesseltine grows willow for his craft. To complete the picture, there are a dozen Hereford cows just nonchalantly wandering

Elaine and Mary Savoie tend their prolific vegetable and flower gardens at Savoie Farm on Hornby Island.

about. Mary and I walk over to the property's big pond, from which they run a drip-irrigation system. When the pond gets low, they cut the watering to every second day.

The farm was started in the 1920s by the girls' grandfather, Leo Savoie, who came from France with his Métis wife, looking for paradise. He certainly found it: 80 waterfront acres on the north side of the island. Their father continued the tradition of growing his family's food. When he passed away, the land was divided into two, 40-acre parcels. The girls, with their brother, Remi, hold title to both sections, and their closest neighbour is a cousin who operates a cattle ranch.

Elaine paints and tends the vegetable beds. Mary lives close by. She is the custodian at the local school, but her passion is the flowers. In summer, bunches of her fresh and dried flowers are sold at the market and also from a stand across from the Cardboard House Bakery. In the cooler months, Mary and her mother make dried flower sachets.

Mary tells me she started growing organic because she wanted to buy organic strawberries at a reasonable price. The farm offers fair prices, particularly on bulk orders over five pounds.

The Sushi Lady

Tania Hale has always gravitated to the island lifestyle. She spent years on Cortes before moving in the early 1990s to Hornby, where she says there is "freedom, but still an economy." She wanted to be part of the market, which she views as a wonderful creative outlet. She loves meeting the shoppers, and catching up with fellow vendors every Wednesday and Saturday.

On market days, she rises early to pick herbs and veggies from her own organic garden. Then, it's into the kitchen where she loves "making a big mess." The results of that mess are little jewel boxes of exquisite sushi, so beautiful that I looked at mine for several hours before eating it.

Tania makes different kinds of sushi every week, but she always has a vegetarian option. She decided on sushi because "it's fun to make," and she always has a good response. With a glass of her cool lemonade, this west coast foodie experience rates very high on my list.

Tania also produces a useful map of the island that can be purchased at the co-op.

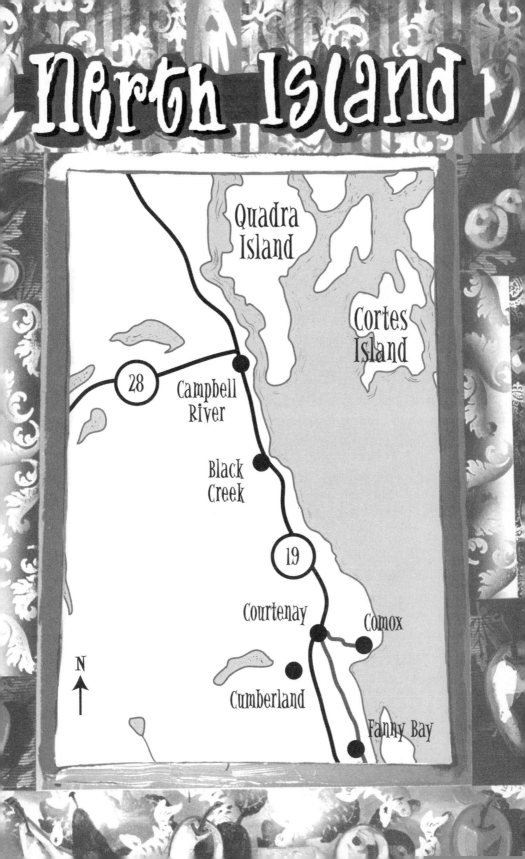

o an urbanite like myself, the North Island means the Comox Valley. Of course Vancouver Island extends farther north, but let's just say that will be another book. Immersing oneself in the valley itself and northern islands of Quadra and Cortes provides a wealth of foodie experiences, from the best doughnuts to a cheese factory that could be in the Swiss Alps to a world-renowned New-Age dining room.

CUMBERLAND

Auchterlonie's Bakery

Far be it from me to rate any non-organic food item this highly, but what can I say? I found the ultimate doughnut, right there on Cumberland's main street, and I can't keep it to myself. Auchterlonie's makes the biggest, freshest, tastiest glazed doughnuts for a mere 50¢ each. Roberta and John Auchterlonie are carrying on the baking tradition of his grandfather who started the shop in 1923. Connie Papin says that when the Auchterlonies take their five-day annual holiday, everyone in town has serious sugar withdrawal.

Chez Cuisine Kitchen

Connie Papin had cooked all over the world for 30 years, but when a heritage house with a commercial kitchen became available in the old mining town of Cumberland, she knew she'd come home. From there, she could offer her catering and cooking classes. Her husband Rodney, a talented pedal steel guitar player, began working with local musicians to produce a CD in support of preserving our rainforest, and Connie soon joined forces with Cumberland's The Cutting Edge butcher to purvey Cutting Edge Veg.

Ex-Vancouverites, she and Rodney missed their shopping excursions along Broadway, a street known for its dazzling displays of fresh fruits and vegetables. They decided to create their own little Broadway, and Rodney set to work building barrows. Made from recycled materials, they are placed in front of the butcher shop, holding the vegetables that Connie gathers six mornings a week from local farms.

She loves her hunting and gathering trips to local growers, which include On Line Farms and Kirby Road Farm in Courtenay and Siefferts Farm in Comox. On Saturday mornings in season, she shops at the Courtenay Farmers' Market.

Involtini di Salvia
(Sage Leaf and Anchovy Bites)

CONNIE PAPIN, CHEZ CUISINE KITCHEN

Often the simplest preparations are the most satisfying. I had fun making and munching these bites in one of Connie's inspiring cooking classes.

	anchovies, oil drained off and patted dry	
	fresh sage leaves	
1	egg, beaten	1
	flour	
	olive oil	

Sandwich one anchovy between two sage leaves and secure with a toothpick by threading the toothpick through. Dip the whole "bite" into the beaten egg, then in the flour. Flash-fry the bite in hot olive oil until crisp and puffed up, and eat immediately.

Being able to buy fresh farm produce in Cumberland has been well received by locals and visitors alike. Cumberland is an easy pull-off from the highway, and a delightful stop for quality meat and veggies.

If you time it right, you can stay at one of the town's charmingly restored heritage B & Bs and take a cooking class in the Chez Cuisine Kitchen. Connie offers Thai, East Indian, Mexican and California wine-country cooking classes, and will happily tailor a class to fit individuals or groups.

I attended one of the popular La Cucina Povera classes with a lively group of local residents. Connie's appreciation for eating in season and her determination to keep things simple were evident as we learned to make the delectable Involtini di Salvia morsels (a recipe given to her by a Florentine friend, Chris Guiffrida, who also made her elegantly rustic serving dishes); Fennel and Mushroom Salad with Pecorino; Fish Tacos that combined freshly made tacos, cabbage slaw, mango and avocado salsa, cilantro aïoli, grilled snapper and crème fraîche to rave reviews; and a decadent cranberry caramel sauce that topped dulce les leche ice cream. When we sat down to eat, Connie poured a chilled 2001 pinot gris from Cobble Hill's Glenterra Vineyards, a clean-tasting, partially French oak-barrel-fermented wine with distinctive apple and melon flavours.

Connie says she loves Vancouver Island: "the absolute bounty of it all." She describes the recent marriage of a fisher friend, at which the mountain of prawns had been caught locally that morning. "To have the great produce and then the mini-Napa Valley in Cobble Hill is all really swell."

Hazelmere Farms

When Lijen and Sherlene Hua emigrated from Taiwan three and a half years ago, they took their time finding the perfect farm and the perfect crop. They had never farmed — he was a civil engineer and she had worked for a consumer co-op back home — but they knew they "wanted to be close to nature and do something we really believe in."

They finally came upon 63 acres near Cumberland, where they are creating a certified organic, self-sustaining farm. They raise chickens, ducks and sheep and are growing Oriental vegetables including burdock and cucumbers, as well as garlic. Their number-one crop is wasabi, which I first sampled at the Harvest Bounty Festival in September. Sherlene encourages me to visit in the spring when her acre of wasabi "looks its most lovely." It is a mass of little white flowers, which, along with the entire plant, are edible. The leaves and flowers are slightly spicy and make lively additions to salad.

Wasabi takes at least two years to harvest, so Sherlene and Lijen are only just coming into their first big marketing year. They already sell their wasabi to several local restaurants and Edible Island grocery in Courtenay and will be expanding their distribution to other locations on the island.

COURTENAY/ BLACK CREEK

Edible Island Whole Foods Market

Another inviting organic grocery store is Edible Island, a shop that makes me want to become a resident of Courtenay. Begun 22 years ago by three entre-preneurial local women, Sue Tupper, Sue Clark and Jackie Somerville, it draws appreciative customers from all over the Comox Valley. It's also the perfect stop

for your picnic supplies when you're touring in that area. I picked up some La Boulange bread, Natural Pastures fresh curds and organic cherry tomatoes for a picnic.

The owners came from diverse working backgrounds: the recording industry, graphic arts and private- and public-sector accounting. Jackie says they share "a passion for healthy, clean food and a concern for the environmental impact of mass production." Their shelves are lined with between 50 and 75 percent organic foodstuffs, and they "choose organically grown and non-GMO certified products wherever possible."

Natural Pastures Cheese Company

Third-generation Comox Valley dairy farmer Edgar Smith was the former president of the local co-operative creamery, the oldest association of its kind in British Columbia. When the co-op was sold to a conglomerate, he was concerned. He wanted to ensure that the industry continued to be viable in his community and, most importantly, that it employed local people. He decided to make cheese.

With help from his wife, Mary Ann Hyndman Smith, and their partner, Rick Adams, Edgar founded the Natural Pastures Cheese Company just a year ago. They brought in a Swiss-trained cheese master, Paul Sutter, whose artisan cheeses have already gained national acclaim. Their Comox Camembert, Boerenkaas and Cumin Seed Verdelait were awarded gold medals at the prestigious Canadian Cheese Grand Prix.

I visited Edgar and Mary Ann, wanting to know the secret behind their seemingly overnight success. It was no surprise to discover that the secret was passion for their product, good planning and plain hard work. They are also devoted to their local market. Edgar says demand for their cheeses far outweighs supply at the moment, but they are committed to filling local orders first. Mary Ann, who takes their cheese to the Courtenay Farmers' Market, says she is touched by people with tears in their eyes who thank her for bringing them "a taste of their childhood."

No product is more likely to generate those tears than their fresh cheese curds, which fly off the grocers' shelves. Handmade curds

Pasta Primavera with Garlic and Chive Verdelait

MARY ANN HYNDMAN SMITH, NATURAL PASTURES CHEESE COMPANY

Serves 4.

This recipe makes the ultimate family dinner, served with a healthy salad and freshly baked baguette.

8 oz	rotini, twists, spirals or penne	225 g
1 tbsp	olive oil	15 ml
2	cloves garlic, minced	2
1/8 tsp	red pepper sauce (such as Tabasco)	0.6 ml
2	small zucchini, sliced	2
2	small yellow squash, sliced	2
1 c	thinly sliced carrot	240 ml
1	medium red onion, cut into eighths	1
1/4 c	chicken broth	60 ml
1/4 c	lightly packed fresh basil leaves, chopped	60 ml
1/2 c	oil-packed sun-dried tomatoes, chopped	120 ml
1 c	grated Natural Pastures Garlic and Chive Verdelait Cheese	240 ml
1/4 c	chopped fresh parsley	60 ml

Prepare pasta according to package directions; drain.

In a medium skillet, heat oil and garlic. Stir in pepper sauce, add zucchini, squash, carrots and onion and stir-fry until tender crisp, about five minutes. Add chicken broth and simmer one minute.

In a large serving bowl, toss together pasta, vegetables, basil and sun-dried tomatoes. Garnish with the grated cheese and parsley.

are noshed straight from the packet, but many people use them to make the popular Québecois dish, poutine. The curds are sprinkled over a plate of piping-hot french fries (organic potatoes, please!), then smothered with hot gravy.

Mary Ann was a caterer in Vancouver before marrying Edgar and moving to the valley. She brings a discriminating palate to the company, and tells me she is inspired by different ingredients and how they come together to create west coast fusion flavours. She works with Paul to develop the company's original cheese recipes. Case in point is the Wasabi Banzai. As I taste it with Mary Ann, she explains why I'm enjoying it so much: "First, you are hit by the wasabi, then the fresh garlic, and finally the rounded, curvaceous flavour of the ginger." Whatever the design, the outcome is addictive, and I'm not surprised that this is another cheese she can't keep on the shelves.

Once I'm appropriately attired in a white "spacesuit" and gumboots, Edgar takes me on a fascinating tour of the cheese factory. The simple story is that the milk comes directly to the back door from their own 1930s, heritage dairy farm in Comox. It is immediately pasteurized. One side of the factory is dedicated to producing semi-hard cheese; the other to soft.

We first enter the semi-hard production area, where the pasteurized milk is placed in a 4,000-litre vat. The curds are separated from the whey, pressed into moulds and placed in a brine solution for two days. They are then cured in the aging room at an average temperature of 11°C for a period appropriate to their type (from six to eight weeks, or up to ten months). After the aging process, some of the cheeses are also waxed.

A variety of cheese labels.

Across the way, the soft cheeses are made in smaller batches. They take less time to make and age, but need more attention. The cheeses are formed, left to drain, then turned over and drained again. When dry enough, they are placed in a brine bath for just 30 minutes before being set out to age for up to two weeks at 15° to 16°C. It is at this stage that the trademark white molds develop on the outside of the cheeses. In the final stage, the bries and Camemberts cure at 6°C. Natural Pastures buys a special paper from France to wrap the soft cheeses in. Edgar says the paper quality is critical: one layer has microscopic holes that allow the cheese to breathe and the other provides hygienic protection.

Edgar is committed to mastering his craft. He tells me how deeply satisfying it is to see the milk come directly from his cows, "a still-living biological system that produces the wonderful taste of the cheese." For him, the cheese-making "completes the whole cycle of the farmer in touch with the craftsman and the consumer."

Before I leave, he proffers a sample of Sky Blue Cheddar, another successful example of contrasting flavours created by Mary Ann and made by Edgar and Paul. I savour the combined creaminess of the blue Stilton and the solidness of the white cheddar, and realize how much the couple's commitment to make the highest quality hand-crafted cheese is reflected in their products. When, several weeks later, I serve only Natural Pastures cheeses on my cheese tray, friends think I've been around the world to please their palates.

On Line Farms

Price Lang was a house-husband in Royston before his life took an interesting turn. Having raised "two great kids," he remarried, moved to Abbotsford, and established On Line Farms. "This was long before the whole online Internet thing," he explains. "Our farm was located on Zero Avenue which basically is the line between Canada and the US border. We really were 'on line'!"

Price's wife, Marjan de Jong, draws on her Dutch dairy-farming background and had previously worked with Susan Davidson of Vancouver's renowned Glorious Garnishes. She is a natural grower. Price, on the other hand, had no previous farming experience, but they managed to hit the gourmet vegetable market at the right time, and, in 1988, their farm was the largest of its kind in the province.

So, how did On Line Farms end up moving to the Comox Valley? Price says they had concerns about the poor air and water quality in Abbotsford, so they drove around the valley looking for a property. They chose 24 acres in Black Creek, just north of Courtenay. They grow veggies on five acres and pasture other people's cows on the rest of their land.

When they moved the farming operation from Vancouver, they wisely started small. The local restaurants were big supporters, particularly the fishing resorts. Price says it was fun hearing from the chefs that Bob Hope, Eric Clapton, Bill Gates, George Bush and many other visiting sport fishermen were dining on their gourmet vegetables.

I find Price taking a well-deserved break on his front porch. There are bunches of horsetail drying overhead which he will later make into a tea to spray on the greenhouse crops to prevent fungus. Living and working on the farm, he says he has learned to schedule breaks like these. He and Marjan have always believed that "you are what you eat." He says they choose organics personally because: "It's the best and the healthiest food, the natural extension by our generation to get cleaner and more conscious, to find the ways and means to lead a healthier life."

He shows me the farm's Flowform, which they made themselves under licence through a biodynamic farm in Duncan. It's an intriguing sculptured

Owners Marjan de Jong and Price Lang at their On Line Farms market.

series of vessels based on the principle that water rejuvenates itself through its own natural movements. The Flowform is fed by their own well. De Jong adds a concoction of camomile, oak bark, dandelion and other organic composts and they spray the water on their plants to promote larger and healthier produce. Price encourages me to stop and listen to the water flow, its steady rhythm sounding like a heartbeat.

Biodynamics is the next logical stage for On Line Farms, which is already certified Demeter, the highest international level of organic certification. The Demeter standards determine the methods for plant production, including such things as compost and preparation usage and the outlawing of genetically modified material.

On Line Farms' vegetables are for sale at their own farmstand, at Courtenay's Saturday farmers' market and through Thrifty Foods' wholesale distributor.

What is Biodynamic Farming?

It grew out of anthroposophy, the spiritual science articulated by Rudolf Steiner, an Austrian-born philosopher, in 1924. He had been approached by a group of European farmers trying to solve the problem of soil decline. His holistic approach to agriculture "notes the interrelationship of all kingdoms — mineral, plant, animal and human — and their intricate correspondence to the rhythms and activities of the larger cosmos."* Biodynamic farming follows Steiner's ideals of self-contained farms, community-supported agriculture, quality over quantity, treating the soil as a live element and close observation of nature.

*from *What is Biodynamics?* by Sherry Wildfeuer at www.biodynamics.com

Seaview Game Farm

It's just starting to sprinkle as I pull in to the 175-acre Seaview Game Farm, but rain doesn't dampen spirits here. The horse-drawn wagons keep taking visitors around this stunning acreage, stopping to visit the 400 fallow deer and petting-zoo residents. Inside the food store, Seaview's general manager and well-known chef, Michel Rabu, is answering questions about the many products on offer: various cuts of venison, lamb and chicken; a seasonal variety of herbs and veggies grown on the property; and his own special-recipe herb and berry vinegars and vinaigrettes. There are some intriguing spice mixtures including one with juniper berries that he is recommending to a man for cooking venison.

I tour the extensive vegetable garden with Dan, who has been gardening for 16 years, mainly on Cortes Island. He tells me that they are determined to protect people from pesticides, so they use only fish compost and their own chicken manure. The produce is used by the food store and sold at the seasonal Courtenay Farmers' Market. In the tomato greenhouse, we come across the farm's owner, Paul Pflager, quietly picking fruit. He takes one look at my open-toed sandals and, with a twinkle in his eye, warns me that no pesticides means more snakes and spiders.

I sit down with Michel to commiserate about how people are eating these days. Michel grew up on the family farm in Brittany. He was a top hairdresser when he first came to Canada, but after a trip to Vancouver Island with his father, he opened Gourmet by the Sea restaurant in Campbell River. "My father and I couldn't believe this place: oysters on the beach, water-cress and chanterelles

Just-picked tomatoes at Seaview Game Farm in Black Creek.

Sautéed Venison

 My husband, Clive, gets the credit for obtaining this recipe. Understandably tired of having me overcook his venison, he asked Chef Rabu for a foolproof preparation. Rabu obliged, as we sat with him overlooking the vegetable gardens.

First, get your frying pan hot and add a tablespoon (15 ml) of olive oil.

Sauté some finely chopped shallots and a few sliced mushrooms. Michel says he would choose chanterelles when they're in season, but morels, oyster or portobello work well.

Sauté the vegetables until brown.

Add a couple of venison steaks or tenderloins to the pan. Sauté just two minutes each side — the worst thing is to overcook venison. Sprinkle with crushed black pepper and remove to warming oven.

Deglaze the pan with about 2 tbsp (30 ml) Madeira (Michel's preference), port, Cinzano or sherry, letting it reduce by about one-third (takes 4 to 5 minutes). Add 2 tbsp (30 ml) heavy cream and stir until the sauce is a rich, brown colour. Add 1 tsp (5 ml) butter to emulsify. Plate the venison and pour the sauce over.

growing wild." After running the restaurant for 25 years, he sold it to his son, Daniel, who continues to operate it.

Paul proposed to his future wife in Michel's restaurant. Every time he came in after that, he kept asking Michel to "come and run his farm." Michel said only when he retired from the restaurant would he consider that, and the rest is history. Michael feels he has come full-circle now that he is back working on a farm.

He loves being part of this whole agricultural-tourism concept because he can educate people about what food should taste like. He's "fed up with what looks good but tastes terrible," so he ensures that the food store only stocks what's in season — there are no forced crops sold here.

We agree that it's discouraging to stand in a grocery store lineup and watch people spend more than they need to because they're buying so much processed food. Michel is now teaching weekend cooking classes for small groups in which he shows that it is actually cheaper to cook from scratch with organic ingredients. The cooking classes include seaview accommodations.

Rows of kiwi plants form part of this spectacular view from Kiwi Cove Lodge, near Ladysmith. Luckily, deer and birds have no interest in this fruit, and rabbits are deterred by chicken wire on the vine bottoms.

The gardens at Fairburn Farm in the Cowichan Valley — described by Sinclair Philip of Sooke Harbour House as "one of the most beautiful farms in the world."

235

Co-owner and chef Mara Jernigan slices freshly baked pizza for her many guests at Engeler Farm in the Cowichan Valley.

Secret-recipe lavein loaves baking at La Boulange Organic Breads, Qualicum Beach.

Rows upon rows of nutritional greens at Nanoose Edibles — certified organic in 1997.

Chef Steven Mugridge, of Ladysmith's Page Point Inn, displays examples of his creativity.

The Landing's food and beverage director, Jason Walmark, in front of the restaurant's spectacular fish tanks. The Landing is located in Pacific Shores Nature Resort, Nanoose Bay.

The gardens at Clayoquot Organics near Tofino are run by Melanie MacLeod.

The gardens at Hollyhock on Cortes Island have been looked after for over 20 years by head gardener Nori Fletcher, using the biodynamic/French intensive (BFI) method.

A guest enjoying the peace at Hollyhock.

Head chef Debra Fountaine among the garden delights at Hollyhock retreat centre.

Arte and Lisa Ahier at their Sobo Global Cuisine catering cart in Tofino.

Raised beds and greenhouses make up the gardens at Tofino's Clayoquot Organics, which supplies top local restaurants and Salals Co-op & Café.

Meet Puddle Jumper, the new buck at Westerly Wynds Farm near Ucluelet.

Celebrated local artisan Henry Nolan designed and carved many features in The Wickaninnish Inn, including these impressive front doors.

A beautiful banquet table at The Wickaninnish Inn, between Ucluelet and Tofino.

An innovative creation from the award-winning kitchen team at The Pointe Restaurant in The Wickaninnish Inn.

Situated on a rocky point surrounded by water on three sides, The Wickaninnish Inn features direct access to spectacular Chesterman Beach.

QUADRA ISLAND

Bold Point Farmstay

"We don't do 'ta-ta' here, Elizabeth," says my exuberant Irish hostess, Geraldine Kenny. Bold Point Farmstay is as far from chocolates-on-your-pillow, five-star luxury as you would want to get, and, believe me, you want to get there. I stagger in at the end of a long drive along a logging road (part of which is single-lane) one dark winter night, and feel the whole place embrace me.

The woodstove is crackling away, with a big pot of coq au vin simmering slowly on top of it. Geraldine is washing kale, chard and beet tops and draws me over to see how beautiful they are — four kinds, all unblemished and best of all, just picked from her winter garden, her "greatest joy" just outside the kitchen door.

Geraldine's husband, Rod Burns, pours me a glass of his deeply satisfying blackberry-rosehip "juice," and invites me into his cellar. Neatly organized, it contains hundreds of units of food: smoked oysters off their beach, marinated chanterelles from their forest, dried nettles and mint from the fields, four-fruit marmalade (lime, lemon, grapefruit and Valencia orange), Sitka spruce-tip jelly, flowering currant jelly, pressure-canned local salmon (pink, chum and sockeye), apple-quince jelly, 200 pounds of dehydrated apples and

Top: Guests get in on the jam-making at Bold Point Farmstay; above: just one small shelf of Rod Burns' well-stocked pantry.

243

Coastal Winter Salad

GERALDINE KENNY, BOLD POINT FARMSTAY

 Serves 4 to 6. "Try to get as many organic ingredients as possible, especially winter greens that have been touched by at least one frost. Some vegetables are perennials, such as the Jerusalem artichokes. In general, the winter salad vegetables provide our table from September through the winter, and often into March and April until the air becomes too warm." — *Geraldine Kenny*

Salad

Pick 4 or 5 leaves each of New Zealand spinach, collard greens, curly or Russian kale, beet greens, endive leaves, and a big handful of arugula leaves.

Dig up some Jerusalem artichokes. Wash off the earth and worms, and peel. Shred 1/2 cup (120 ml). Finely chop about 1/2 cup (120 ml) of any variety of sweet apple. The peel adds a wonderful colour. Grate 1/4 cup (60 ml) of carrots.

Dressing

1/4 - 1/2 c	extra virgin olive oil	60 - 120 ml
3 tbsp	balsamic vinegar	45 ml
1 tbsp	or more locally produced raspberry jelly or honey	15 ml
	variety of roasted seeds such as soy, pine nuts, sunflower seeds (shelled)	
	calendula petals from 2 or 3 blossoms	
Optional:	1 tsp (5 ml) Dijon mustard	

Whisk together the oil and vinegar (and mustard if you're using it). Rinse and spin-dry the various leaves. Pour on the dressing and toss. Sprinkle the seeds and calendula leaves on top of the salad.

mushrooms, 200 bottles of stewed tomatoes ("We won't eat another fresh tomato until next July," says Geraldine) and gallons of homemade wine, apple juice and tomato juice. I think of some of the urban cellars I've been in, and take my hat off to Geraldine and Rod who have grown and produced all of this food themselves.

Geraldine says she was born with a gumboot on one foot and a high heel on the other. She was an English teacher and translator for the German government in Berlin during the Cold War, then travelled. When Rod, a Parks Canada naturalist, picked up Geraldine and her friend hitchhiking near Lake Louise, British Columbia, he never guessed they would end up living together in Nova Scotia six months later.

They crossed to Vancouver a few years later, then ran a well-known tour company in Victoria before heading to the islands to find peace. They found it on ten acres at the end of that logging road and it was perfect. Geraldine walked down to the beach that first visit and couldn't believe the oyster beds which reminded her of Galway, her home in Ireland.

Together, Rod and Geraldine operate a bed-and-breakfast, farmstay (guests participate in daily farming activities) and ecotours. With Rod's experience as the chief naturalist at Salmonier Nature Park, Nova Scotia, and his devotion to the land (the couple have put a covenant on their Sitka spruce trees), these are fascinating tours of discovery to sea, lakes and forest. Here, as at Madrona Valley Farm on Saltspring Island, there is a self-contained cottage where city families can stay to fully experience living (and working if they want to) on a farm.

When I sit down to dinner with Rod and Geraldine, it is to sup on the glories of sustainable living: Bold Point Farm butternut squash and watercress soup served with a huge, dense Irish soda bread; that coq au vin, which by now has cooked for 36 hours and is embellished with prunes, carrots, chanterelles and stewed quince; Jerusalem artichokes; golden russet potatoes; a winter salad that I beg to include in this book; and finally, deep-dish apple pie and mint tea.

The next morning, I help Geraldine feed alfalfa to "the gorgeous girls," her Friesian and Romney sheep, and have a good tour of her winter garden. She and Rod and their guests will eat from this garden and their prolific pantry until spring. She says it's all about eating what they can grow themselves: "Basic foods don't have to cross any borders."

The Spanish garlic is from Saltspring Island's Bright Farm; there are binge, Cariboo purple and Yukon gold potatoes; watercress growing in the stream; Brussels sprouts companion-planted with lettuces; Russian and curly kales; and hazelnut, apple and cherry trees. Geraldine shows me her wooden honey bee "condos" that hang from the barn. We come around the house to where Rod is already in full production dehydrating apples. I reluctantly say goodbye, realizing that I have found in them the sustainable-living ideal. They are dedicated to and knowledgeable about the land and willing to share their knowledge with anyone who knocks at their door. With such a bounty, who needs "ta-ta?"

Driving back along that winding road was a breeze in the morning light. I remembered the Irish blessing on Geraldine's tea towel:

"May the road rise up to meet you, may the wind be always at your back, may the sun shine warm upon your face and the rain fall soft upon your fields until we meet again." I knew we would meet again.

Topcliff Farm

Linda Lessard is puréeing vast quantities of cooked apples when I visit her. Her partner and children are away for the weekend, and she is gleefully preparing hundreds of jars of strawberry and raspberry jam and applesauce for the upcoming Christmas market. She's in full production mode with three large cauldrons of confection bubbling away, jam jars sterilizing and row upon row of filled, ruby-coloured jars cooling on her table.

Her foodstuffs are fully organic. When the local market had no organic lemons for the applesauce, she substituted limes that were. She uses no sugar, just the lovely Prima apples from her orchard and the lime juice, and the taste is sensational — tangy and refreshing. The jams are made with natural Nicola Valley honey and pectin. Berries in the jams are left whole, just the way I like them and hard to find in the sea of "fruit spreads" at most grocers.

Linda has come to operating an organic farm on a Gulf Island honestly. A teacher, she left Quebec 24 years ago looking for the rural life. She taught for a while in Campbell River, a ten-minute ferry ride from Quadra Island. Eventually, she and John, a silviculturist, bought their ten-acre haven on Quadra and they began organic growing in earnest six years ago.

Linda's focus is fruit: Totem strawberries, raspberries, blueberries, gooseberries and red and white currants are laid out in elegant formation on three-quarters of an acre. I think the Sun King himself would have had no better fruit gardens at Versailles. He certainly would have had no better scarecrows than the ones, fashioned by Linda's two children, that guard her large, sweet strawberries. In the one-acre orchard, there are half a dozen types of apples, plums, cherries, pears and hazelnuts, and she can step out of her kitchen door to the small culinary and medicinal-herb garden.

A vegetarian for over 20 years, Linda feels organic is the only way to go. Her children have known nothing else, and she is proud that, when they shop with her, they hold up items and ask, "Mum, is this organic?" before putting it in the cart. She taught them early on that McDonalds is "unacceptable." She also teaches them their lessons. Both children are home-schooled, not uncommon on these islands.

Linda learned to cook at home in Quebec, then put her skills to the test at a logging camp on Vancouver Island. Today, she is

popular on Quadra for her dairy- and gluten-free baking that she sells at thea-
tre and concert concessions. Locals and visitors can shop at her farmgate in
season. She has many repeat visitors, including a couple from Texas who drops
by every year for her strawberries. When her children are a little older, Linda
would like to add a bed-and-breakfast operation to her bucolic farm. I can tell
you now: it will be heaven.

CORTES ISLAND

Cortes Café

If you're lucky enough to be visiting Cortes Island on market day, or indeed, on any postal delivery day, then you'll want to eat at the Cortes Café.
Established in a cosy back room of Manson's Hall, full of local art and artsy
people, the café dishes up delicious fare.

I stopped shopping in the market to enjoy the last piece of their homemade
carrot cake and a good cup of coffee, and soak up some of the local colour and
chat around me. It was a warm haven on that cold winter's day, and I loved
listening in on the market-related conversations: "I bought some lovely Ribston
Pippins from Bill Wheeler," "Does L.J. have her brie en croûte today?" and
"What do you say we grab an ice cream before we go?"

Cortes Island Farmers' Market

The Cortes market runs year-round. Its offerings change with the seasons,
with a little island eclecticism thrown in. In summer, there's lots of fresh produce, but don't be surprised to be in a lineup for the organic ice cream in
winter.

John Gordon is a photographer whose lovely images of island flora and
fauna sell from his gallery at Smelt Bay. He and his wife, Ruby, decided they
should offer something in addition to the photographs and settled on ice cream.
It's proven to be a big hit, especially the organic berry flavours (made from their
home-grown strawberries, raspberries, loganberries, blackberries, even tayberries).

Lisa Jo Osland caught my eye with her mane of red hair and celadon silk
jacket. Her stall was laden with goodies, and she was surrounded by children,
four of whom turned out to be her own. Her story put the whole island lifestyle
into perspective for me. A caterer in the film industry, she and her family were

living the urban life in North Vancouver before they moved to Cortes for one reason: Linnaea School, the famed environment-oriented private school for children that operates from a 350-acre farm. L.J. caters the school's hot organic lunch program, in addition to her private catering and weekly market offerings. I only wish her lunch program could be instituted at all schools, in place of the unhealthy "pizza or hotdog days."

I meet a customer of hers, Bud, who says L.J. has "really made a job for herself" on the island. In addition to her catering, she will begin teaching an Asian fusion workshop at Hollyhock in the fall.

L.J. presents her goodies as "more fooling around from L.J.'s Kitchen," and on the day I visit, the selection is awesome: Giant Raviolis (for poaching and napping with a favourite sauce); pastry-covered Salacious brie ("for when your sweetie's coming over"); Garlic Cream (a "pasta positive" sauce that's also delicious on garlic bread); homemade fettuccini and bocconcini. As I'm on the road, I buy the bocconcini to nibble on. This generous helping of tiny mozzarellas marinating in fresh herbs and olive oil is sealed in an airtight bag and lasts me four road-trip days without refrigeration.

Brigid Weiler proffers a range of botanical body products. She is a cook who has worked in the island's tree-planting camps and also at Hollyhock. I buy a copy of her wonderful book (*Recipes from Garden, Sea and Bush*, Winnipeg: Rasmussen Company, co-written with Jill Milton), which is full of instructions for great back-to-the-land fare. Brigid leads mushroom-foraging walks on Saturday mornings in season.

Also on offer the day I visit the market are a huge selection of apples from Bill Wheeler and Mary Clare Preston's Inner Coast Nursery, incredible baking such as baguettes and cookies, and Wild Harvest smoked salmon from Andrea and Gary Block. The craft stalls are equally impressive with reasonably priced home-knit sweaters, slippers made from handspun sheep's wool and jewellery fashioned from elk antlers and feathers.

Hollyhock

The first time I visited Hollyhock, standing on its beach and looking out to sea, I felt I was standing on the edge of Planet Earth. The property has a special, indescribable quality that one has to experience to understand. And, of course, that quality and the array of New Age, experiential learning programs have kept people coming from all over the world for 20 years.

The next time I visited was to interview head chef Debra Fontaine for this book. It was in late November, when Hollyhock is essentially closed. There was

Wilderness surrounds Hollyhock, enhancing one's sense of sight, smell, touch and taste.

a small group of writers using the lodge for a retreat; it was otherwise quiet, but still magical. Debra invited me to sit by the fire with her, and we talked about her responsibility to feed up to 140 people every day, many of whom are on special diets or suffer from food allergies.

The week before, she had cooked the last dinner of the season for workshop participants: local salmon, sautéed local prawns with pesto made from Hollyhock basil, mushroom risotto with asiago, baked squash and chocolate mousse. She spent five hours stirring the huge pot of risotto, and loved every minute of it. "I choose what I am the most passionate about, what gives me the most joy," she tells me.

Debra first came to Cortes Island at three weeks of age when her father began appraising logging camps on the island. Then the family started holidaying there. When Debra was 29, she felt the pull of Cortes and left her busy life in Vancouver where she worked as an architectural draftsperson.

After some catering stints and private cheffing on the island (which she still does in the off-season), she began cooking at Hollyhock. Working with a brigade of 22 to 25 people, she says each meal "is like doing a big party." She approaches cooking like an artist approaching a canvas, telling her cooks she wants "healthy, fresh food with great taste that also catches the eye. I'm looking for lots of textures — soft and chewy and crunchy — and colours; and a

Thai Baked Tofu With Red Curry Sauce

DEBRA FONTAINE, HOLLYHOCK

Serves 8. "This dish is good served with jasmine rice and black Thai rice. If you make both rices, you can arrange them on a serving platter in a yin yang symbol, which looks beautiful. Serve with a stirfry of pea pods and red peppers." — *Debra Fontaine*

Baked Tofu

2	packages firm tofu, cut into 16 equal pieces	2
Mix together with a whisk:		
1/4 c	tamari	60 ml
1/4 c	vegetable oil	60 ml
1/4 c	lemon juice	60 ml
1/4 c	garlic purée	60 ml
1/4 c	ginger purée	60 ml
1/2 c	peanut butter	120 ml
1/3 c	brown sugar	80 ml
	(omit the sugar if there is sugar in the peanut butter)	
1	jalapeno pepper seeded and finely chopped	1
1 c	sliced shiitake mushrooms	120 ml

Coat the tofu with the above ingredients and put in a well-oiled casserole pan, cover and bake at 350°F for 1 hour. Stir every 20 minutes. Uncover for the last 20 minutes. While the tofu is baking make a red curry sauce to pour over it.

Red Curry Sauce

1/4 c	red curry paste	60 ml
1	can coconut milk	1
1 tbsp	sugar	15 ml
3	lime leaves OR	3
1 tsp	lime zest	5 ml

Sauté the curry paste in a little vegetable oil to release the flavour. Add the coconut milk, sugar and lime zest and cook on a very low heat. Do not allow to boil. When the tofu dish is plated pour curry sauce over.

balance of heat." It's important, she says, to think about food both visually and texturally, and to be mindful of "how it is going to sit in the stomach."

Hollyhock subscribed to a vegetarian-only kitchen until 11 years ago, when fish was introduced. Debra says she is open to free-range poultry. She cooked a big turkey dinner at Thanksgiving which was hugely popular. She wondered if the vegetarian model hadn't gone a bit too far when a guest asked: "Did you debone the tofu?"

Debra loves the veggies and herbs she cooks which travel only a few feet from Hollyhock's gardens to its kitchen. The growers provide daily lists for the cooks of what will be available from the garden the next morning. All produce is picked before the sun heats the plants. Menu planning follows what the earth provides, not what has been driven for three days up the I-5 from California.

Head gardener Nori Fletcher has worked the Hollyhock gardens for over 20 years using the biodynamic/French intensive (BFI) method she learned at the Farallones Institute in California. Her assistant, Myann Reid, is a graduate of Linnaea Farm's ecological gardening program. Their training and passion are reflected in their incomparable kitchen garden.

Debra took the culinary program at Dubrulle in Vancouver four years ago, and cooked at The Waterfront Hotel there, but she soon retreated to the ultimate retreat, Hollyhock. This, she tells me, is her home and she loves it. In the spring, she teaches a hands-on, deliciously passionate cooking workshop. "In prawn season, we take participants out on the boat, we pick our veggies from the garden, we dig for clams." Next spring, I hope to be one of those clam-diggers.

Reef Point Farm

When Queen Elizabeth II and Prince Philip stayed with their relatives, the Markgräf Max and Markgräfin Valerie von Baden, on the Twin Islands, just off Cortes, Ginnie Ellingsen was called over to cook for six weeks. Such is Ginnie's modesty that I wouldn't have known that had Debra Fontaine of Hollyhock, on learning I was spending the night at Reef Point Farm, not sent me off with a wink and a suggestion: "Ask her about cooking for the queen."

Not only did Ginnie tell me about that singular experience, but she kindly shared her photographs of the very relaxed sovereign enjoying her holiday. Of course, what was cooked and what was eaten by Her Majesty could not be revealed, but the story certainly gave me a window into the interesting world of Ginnie and her husband, Bruce.

Bruce's great-grandfather was the first white settler on Cortes — Michael Manson, for whom Manson's Landing is named. The property he and Ginnie live on, a 96-acre west-facing waterfront paradise, has been in the family since 1938. I had a stimulating morning walk with the couple through their apple, cherry, filbert and walnut orchard and vegetable gardens, and down to the beach. Ginnie planned to harvest seaweed for the gardens later that day, and wanted to check on the tide.

While their rambunctious dog swam out to annoy the seals, we stood at Sacred Point on their property and looked across to Mitlenatch Island, which had been owned by the Manson family prior to its becoming a provincial park. Bruce tells me that Michael Manson and his brother, John, used to row their sheep out to graze on Mitlenatch for the summer. "John's wife, Margaret, used to love staying out there. The lack of trees and its openness reminded her of the Shetland Islands where they came from. During the tough times of the 'Dirty Thirties,' they stopped grazing the sheep there because of the poaching that went on."

We walked to the beach on one of the remaining horse-logging roads. Horses were used to drag logs to the water to be floated off to buyers in the late 1880s when Japanese settlers logged the island. Bruce has worked in the forest industry, and now runs his own sawmill on the island with one of his four sons.

The bed-and-breakfast at Reef Point Farm on Cortes Island.

Breakfast Scones

GINNIE ELLINGSEN, REEF POINT FARM

 Makes 8 large scones. As a Brit, I take pride in the scones I make for teatime. Ginnie's recipe has replaced my own as the most delicious. I fantasize that these were actually served to Queen Elizabeth when Ginnie cooked for her on the Twin Islands, but of course, I will never really know.

2 c	unbleached flour	480 ml
1/4 c	wheat germ	60 ml
2 1/2 tsp	baking powder	12.5 ml
2 tbsp	brown sugar	30 ml
1/2 tsp	salt	2.5 ml
1/3 c	butter	80 ml
1/2 c	currants or raisins	60 ml
2	eggs	2
1/3 c	buttermilk	80 ml

Combine flour, wheat germ, baking powder, sugar and salt. Cut in butter with pastry blender or two knives until flour mixture resembles fine bread crumbs. Add currants or raisins. Beat eggs and milk together and add all at once to flour mixture. Knead a few strokes until dough holds together. Divide in two pieces and pat each into rounds, then cut each into quarters. Place quarters on ungreased baking sheet and bake at 425°F for 15 minutes or until golden brown. Take care not to overbake!

As a board member of the Cortes Eco-forestry Society, Bruce is committed to selective logging and logging in situ, meaning that he takes his own Mobile Dimension sawmill into the woods "on a light-duty road system, to cut logs from roadside piles or bunks." He built his own house from timber taken from the property. Bruce is also helping with the divestiture of some 4,000 acres of Weyerhauser-owned lands on Cortes.

I loved my cosy room at Reef Point Farm, and was honoured to have dinner en famille with the Ellingsens. Ginnie's interest in serving only locally produced foods (much from her own garden) shone through in her cooking, and I enjoyed a lovely beef daube (made with beef from the island's Linnaea Farm), mashed potatoes, Ginnie's French beans and pickled beets. There was a local birthday girl at the table that night so Ginnie had made a first-rate and not overly sweet chocolate cake, which she served with her own canned peaches. As it stormed outside, the rain sheeting down on the kitchen's tin roof, we were a very contented and convivial party inside.

Reef Point Farm has connections to the famed ReBar restaurant in Victoria: son David was a prominent fixture there before pursuing his photography career full-time in Vancouver, and Lizzie, the restaurant's longest-serving and seriously fun server, is a good friend of the Ellingsen family.

The morning I reluctantly left, I opted for the lighter version of breakfast: a fresh fruit salad, Ginnie's currant scones and steaming coffee. Everything was presented on good English china and everything was scrumptious. Reef Point Farm is a place to immerse oneself in peace and tranquillity as well as to eat and sleep like a queen.

The Tak

Every Gulf Island seems to have a particular casual restaurant where a cross-section of the locals hang out. None of them are about décor; all focus on good, hearty food at reasonable prices. There's Jan's Café on Hornby, Pistou Grill on Pender, Barb's Buns on Saltspring, The General Store on Saturna, and The Lovin' Oven on Quadra. On Cortes, it's The Tak, so naturally I headed there first.

Their lentil-walnut burger turned out to be a real treat: a piping hot, fat patty served on a toasted kaiser with lettuce, tomato, mayo and Dijon mustard. It was just the fuel I needed on a rainy day before hitting the famous Friday market across at the community hall. The Tak's owner, Scott Mercs, was on the line that day, so I met him later to chat about his restaurant and the food culture on Cortes.

He's owned the place for four years, having previously managed the island's Floathouse Restaurant, and cooked in Squamish and Whistler. He says Cortes is "an incredible food community," but it's more about people growing their own than active retailing.

There is a seasonal brown-box program run by the island's largest organic farm at Blue Jay Lake. In the winter months, the Cortes Connection truck picks up a load of organic food from ProOrganics in Vancouver, and it is divided up among a committed group of local residents. Scott hopes that venture will eventually develop into a permanent co-op market to increase islanders' accessibility to organic food.

Cortes has its share of natural living pioneers including Dr. Andrew Weil, who is a homeowner here and has often led workshops at Hollyhock, and Russell

Lentil Walnut Burgers

Makes 12 to 18 burgers, depending on desired size. I'm fussy about vegetarian burgers because they are often boring. The almond burgers at Victoria's ReBar restaurant and these lentil-walnut beauties are first-rate.

3	medium onions, diced	3
2	large carrots, grated	2
2 tbsp	cumin seeds	30 ml
1 tbsp	turmeric	15 ml
2 1/2 tbsp	coriander	37.5 ml
4 tbsp	basil	60 ml
4 tbsp	dill	60 ml
1 tbsp	pepper	15 ml
1 tbsp	curry powder	15 ml
1 tsp	cumin powder	5 ml
4 c	lentils	960 ml
5 c	walnuts	1.2 L
2	potatoes, cooked and mashed	2
2 c	breadcrumbs	480 ml
2 tbsp	salt	30 ml

Cook the lentils until soft, then drain well for one hour. Roast walnuts in oven until lightly browned. Sauté onions, carrots and cumin seeds until soft. Add all the other herbs and spices and sauté gently for five more minutes. Mix all ingredients in a food processor. The mixture should hold together when formed into a patty. If too dry, add some water. If too moist, add more breadcrumbs. Sauté the patties and serve immediately on a whole-grain bun, with lettuce, sliced tomatoes, mayo and mustard.

Precious, who founded Caper's organic grocery in Vancouver, and originally ran a food store on Cortes.

Scott feels his restaurant "fills an important function" in such a small community as Cortes, where, in the winter months, some people feel a sense of isolation. There is always a friendly welcome and hot cup of coffee when they open the door.

West Coast

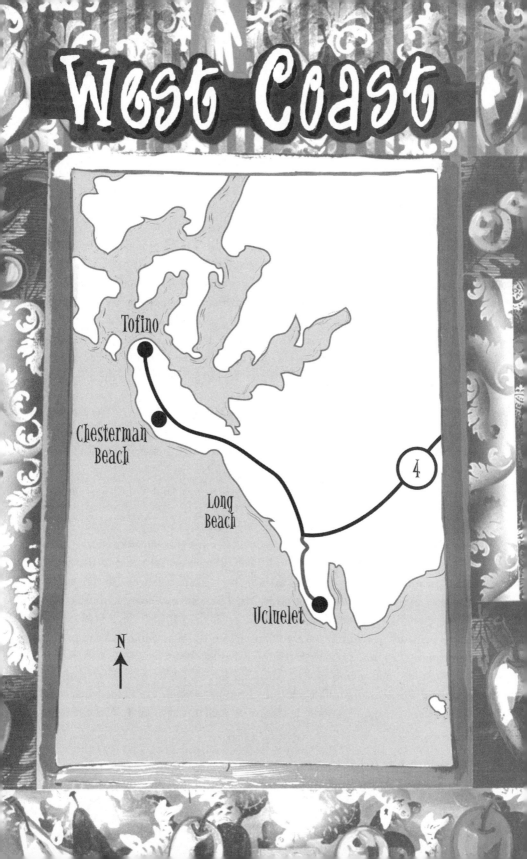

n this trip, I'm in the company of two New York food writers and a producer from the American Food Network. We have been following the famous Relais & Châteaux Gourmet Trail™ from Robert Feenie's lauded Lumière restaurant in Vancouver to The Aerie on the Malahat to Hastings House on Saltspring Island. Our final destination is The Wickaninnish Inn on Tofino's Chesterman Beach. It's been a delicious journey, with lots of good food and drink and excellent company at every stop.

We're heading north on the Trans-Canada Highway, the sun miraculously breaking through the clouds as we gaze across to the Sunshine Coast on the mainland. At Parksville, we turn left and begin to cross over to the wild west coast of Vancouver Island.

Coombs is the traditional stop to stock our picnic hamper. No kidding, there are goats on the roof at Coombs General Store, a novelty worth seeing. And inside, the selection of food amazes: Lavazza coffee, Italian pastas, Cadbury's chocolate, fruit, vegetables, cheese, breads, and no one leaves without a big ice cream cone — 25 flavours. There are also many small craft and souvenir kiosks surrounding the store.

After Coombs, the lakes, forests and snow-capped mountains begin to dominate. We're heading into the rainforest, where numerous turnoffs beckon for a leisurely hike and picnic. We choose Little Qualicum Falls, where the designated picnic area offers both outdoor and covered tables between the lower falls and the higher falls. Hike one or both first. There are excellent boardwalks and some wheelchair accessibility. Truly, some of the best British Columbia dining experiences are in nature. Once you've selected the right food and the perfect companions, a forest or lakeside setting is hard to beat.

Another good picnic spot is Cathedral Grove, which was donated to the people of British Columbia by forestry company MacMillan Bloedel. It is so named because standing under a canopy of ancient trees, one feels the majesty of a cathedral. Because the grove is located in a gully, the Douglas fir trees loom larger as they have had to reach farther for the light.

After a pit stop in the mill town of Port Alberni, we're on to our destination: Tofino. We tune into the local radio station that gives an ongoing weather report, essential in an area of high winds and big waves. Today, the waves are EXTREME, so we'll keep to the shore.

Originally there were only logging roads in the area, then gravel, and finally a paved road in 1959. In 1949, Tofino mayor Tom Gibson had persuaded a young doctor, Howard McDiarmid, to start his medical practice here when there were only 300 people in the little fishing village of Tofino. Over the years, McDiarmid bought the land where he and his family would eventually build The Wickaninnish Inn.

Beginning in the 1970s, an active green community developed from both local people and American pacifists. Clayoquot Sound is probably best known for the massive logging protest in the summer of 1993, when 12,000 people set up a peace camp near the Kennedy River Bridge.

The present population is around 1,500. In the last five years, the tourism and aquaculture industries have really grown. Whale watching, kayaking, sport fishing, hiking and surfing attract upwards of a million visitors a year. Luxury resorts with spas are plentiful.

Beyond the beach, the Pacific Rim National Park Reserve offers all kinds of hiking opportunities in bog, rainforest or cedar forest. If you want an in-depth experience, take a beachcombing hike with naturalist Bill McIntyre. When Bill retired as chief naturalist from the national parks service, he and his wife decided to follow their dream and open a bed and breakfast in Ucluelet. Bill offers a range of hikes that never fail to produce some new discovery, and he is often seen at The Wickaninnish Inn, meeting guests for guided forest walks or low-tide adventures.

UCLUELET/TOFINO

Clayoquot Organics

When Melanie MacLeod began farming 22 years ago, she first had to "beat back the rainforest." Japanese settlers had done intensive growing in the area in the 1940s, but farming on the wild west coast has never been easy. Melanie comes from a long line of Lower Mainland farmers, so she's been able to put her considerable knowledge to work on an acre of land close to Tofino and managed to carve out a thriving organic vegetable business that supplies the top local restaurants as well as Salals Co-op Grocery & Café. She grows in raised beds and greenhouses, and plans to expand to meet her customers' increasing demands.

Trish Muehlebach and Jenny Cohen, gardeners at Tofino's Clayoquot Organics.

Living in so remote an area, with little produce locally grown, residents are even more keenly aware of the food miles associated with importing fruit and vegetables. Melanie has filled a void in local food production, and happily, it is now difficult to eat out in Tofino without encountering her beautiful produce.

The Goat Lady

The Wickaninnish Inn's Nanoose Organic Greens and Ucluelet Goats' Cheese Salad with Sun-dried Blueberry and Sesame Vinaigrette led me to Jane Hunt. It was another once-in-a-lifetime foodie adventure, and I'll never forget her. Former Wickaninnish chef Jim Garraway had given me Jane's phone number with the instruction that, as this was a radiophone, I would need to say "over." Piece of cake. Jane and I had many successful conversations before I headed into the wild hills behind Ucluelet to meet her at Westerly Wynds Farm.

Jane graduated from the first veterinary class at Guelph University in 1964, and set up a clinic in Victoria's Vic West neighbourhood. Her husband, Don, says it got a bit crazy some nights when animals were being brought in from accidents. Twenty years later, seeking a more peaceful life, they bought 15 acres in the hills outside Ucluelet from a logging syndicate, and embarked on a journey toward self-sufficiency.

Besides the goats' milk, cheese and soap production, Jane is the only veterinarian for Port Alberni, Tofino and Ucluelet. It's a pretty rough drive over gravel and logging roads to reach her, so one hopes the pets and their owners don't have too many reasons to visit.

My trip to the farm is both breathtaking and poignant. Much of the area has been logged, and when I spot a black bear cub foraging for food in the middle of a clearcut, my heart stops. Jane's instructions are very specific, and once I've made two rights, a left and a very sharp right, the farm and a frisky welcoming committee of 27 goats are before me.

The goats are Saanen, brought from Alberta. The youngest, Summer, is six weeks old the day I visit. The eldest, Clinton, is a fearless buck who has a little smooch through the fence with every doe that passes by. Poor Clinton doesn't know yet that a new buck has arrived on the farm. Jane and Don drove to Abbotsford "in a raging snowstorm" to bring back Puddle Jumper, who is settling in nicely in his own pen. There are many other residents: peacocks, ducks, guinea fowl, pheasants, turkeys, chickens, French Angora rabbits, Great Pyrenees dogs and 13 cats.

One can only marvel at the extraordinary tableau vivant created by the many creatures,

Jane Hunt with a few of her 27 goats at Westerly Wynds Farm, Ucluelet.

organic gardens, the house and a dozen outbuildings ranging from a barn to a water tower. And even though everything seems to be in motion, there is a peace and stillness to the place that makes me see why the Hunts chose to settle here.

There is also a stunning view of Barkley Sound from the top of the cliffs. Jane says every kid has taken a plunge over the cliffs, and she's managed to coax each one up with a rope.

Jane started making the goat cheese nine years ago and "selling it to hippie friends." It was soon coveted by locals, including Rodney Butters, The Wickaninnish Inn's trailblazing chef. Rodney often visited Jane with his cat, and the sublime chèvre started to appear on the inn's dinner menu.

Out of a very small fromagerie in the back of her house, Jane pasteurizes 50 to 60 litres of goats' milk and produces 35 pounds of cheese a week. She always has chèvre and feta on hand for her regular customers, and, in the summertime, makes butter and ice cream, which the local children love, from the leftover milk.

I leave with chèvre, feta and a bar of the nourishing goats-milk soap, impressed as always by the passionate people behind these small cottage operations, and thrilled to have met the woman whose cheese sings on the plates at The Wickaninnish Inn.

Oyster Jim

It's 7:00 A.M. on a clear spring morning as Jim Martin slips his skiff into the still water of Grice Bay. We're heading for his famed oyster beds, scattered throughout the islands of Clayoquot Sound.

To understand the oysters, one first needs to understand their shepherd. Oyster Jim is a seriously rugged guy, a former boilermaker who emigrated from Colorado to the sleepy little fishing village of Ucluelet in 1985. He is a gentle giant, a man with great capacity for invention and work study, who is as eloquent describing his patented holistic exercise program as expressing his delight at the little acts of kindness from the boys in his scout troop. It's no overstatement to call him a legend in these parts. Whenever I mention his name, folks praise his local accomplishments and unwavering community spirit.

He recently brought a great dream to fruition when he and a battery of volunteers blazed and marked out the 2.5-km Wild Pacific Trail. Skirting the coastline around Ucluelet, it provides hikers with stunning vantage points of the ocean and islands below. I think

It doesn't get much better than this: breakfast served by Oyster Jim Martin.

of Jim each time I hike that trail, grateful for his determination to preserve the area's unique rugged beauty.

I'd heard about Oyster Jim long before our breakfast cruise. His large, succulent oysters are featured on the menu at The Wickaninnish Inn, where my fellow diners always rave about their meatiness and sublime flavour. One of the chef's recent takes on these amazing oysters was Three Oyster Jim's Clayoquot Sound Roasting Oysters with Basil Goats' Cheese Crust, Garlic and Pancetta, and Horseradish Root Ketchup.

I was determined to try my first Oyster Jim oyster with the man himself. Charles McDiarmid told me some of the best meals he's ever had were sitting on a log with Jim — a pile of oysters, a shucker and a few squeezes of lemon juice. It sounded like a hunter-gatherer's dream date.

Charles had explained to me: "A lot of places grow oysters on inflated drums that go up and down with the tide, but Jim grows his on the shore. The tide goes in and out. They take longer, but they turn out plumper, juicier, larger." As my experiences with oysters had more often than not been chewy, I was ready for something sensational.

Jim tells me to put away my notebook and pen just before he lets out the throttle, and we are skimming the water through Fortune Passage en route to Kershaw and Wood islands. This is indeed a fortunate passage, for we are not long out when a school of porpoises crosses the bow. Jim says they're used to his boat now, so our presence doesn't disturb their herring feast. Within seconds, Jim has spotted a black bear searching the shore for rock crabs, and he shuts off the motor so we can take a closer look. He has been keeping an eye on the bear for two years, and thinks it was orphaned early on.

Before my tour of the oyster beds, we head over to Wood Island, where Jim lights a small fire on the beach and fuels my anticipation of the feast to come. We scramble back over barnacled rocks, and I gladly accept a piggyback ride through shallow water to the skiff.

The cultivation process is simple. Jim starts the oysters at home from larvae and small barnacle chips. They next go into nursery trays that are laid out on the beach. The temperature in these waters is perfect for growing shellfish. As the oysters grow, Jim spreads them along the beach, separating out the single units from the clusters. At this stage, the oysters are susceptible to attack by rock crabs, so Jim has devised a special collapsing crab fence. It does a good job of keeping the crabs at bay, but collapses as necessary to allow spawning salmon through.

Once the oysters reach three inches in length, they are transported to trays that get stacked under water. There are up to 95 stacks at any given time, each containing 1,200 oysters. We cruise over the stacks, en route to the oysters' final resting beach, and Jim harvests a dozen specimens. He delights in the beautiful shell formations, and promises me a delicious breakfast.

Back on Wood Island, with the fire smouldering nicely, Jim roasts his prize oysters. He grows them specifically to be cooked in the shell, and within ten minutes, they're ready to shuck. Jim hands me what proves to be the biggest, juiciest, most flavourful oyster I have ever eaten. He shows me where to start, and how to spoon the flesh out. I'm sitting on a log with the oyster guru of Clayoquot Sound, enjoying the unsurpassed calm of early morning and thinking life can't get much better than this. Pass the seafood sauce, eh?

Raincoast Café

With memories of some extraordinary rice cakes served with a roasted cashew and ginger sauce I arrive back at the Raincoast Café to chat with owners Lisa Henderson and Larry Nicolay. It's mid-afternoon, one of the rare quiet times in their day. The restaurant is open for dinner only, so the prep work is mostly done and the flowers are arranged. Larry is taking time to check the evening's reservations, and Lisa draws me over to a corner table.

The couple first came to Tofino from Vancouver 11 years ago. They'd spent a summer looking around, and found themselves managing the Allyway Café, a charming little place tucked in behind shops in the centre of town. Their time at the Allyway was enjoyable, but, as Lisa says: "It didn't feel like ours."

Wild Rice Cakes with Roasted Cashew and Ginger Sauce

LISA HENDERSON, RAINCOAST CAFÉ

Serves 6. I once had a conversation with Satva Hall of Monsoon Coast Exotic World Spices about the huge range of interpretations of "vegetarian" on restaurant menus. We agreed that finding something exceptional is rare. These tasty rice cakes are exceptional.

4	medium russet potatoes	4
1 c	wild rice	240 ml

Boil potatoes in their skins until tender all the way through. Put aside. Meanwhile, boil wild rice with plenty of water until the rice pops and the inner whites are exposed (this is crucial to an edible rice cake). Strain and let cool. Peel and grate cooled potatoes and place in medium bowl. Add wild rice. Then add:

1 tbsp	salt	15 ml
2 tsp	pepper	10 ml
1 tbsp	cumin	15 ml
	good pinch of dried and crushed rosemary	
1/3 c	fresh basil, finely chopped	80 ml
4	green onions, thinly sliced	4

Mix together. Adjust flavours, if necessary. Form into 12 balls and then shape into patties. Shape sides so the patties look like little hockey pucks. Layer with wax paper between patties.

Roasted Cashew and Ginger Sauce

In a blender combine:

3/4 c	roasted cashews	180 ml
1 tbsp	fresh ginger	15 ml
2 tbsp	soy sauce	30 ml
	vegetable stock or water to desired consistency	
	Adjust flavours.	

Arrange seasonal vegetables on plate. Ladle the cashew sauce beside the vegetables and arrange two rice cakes in a stacked manner on top of sauce. The rice cakes can be served as a vegetarian main dish or as a starch for chicken or fish dishes.

Lisa Henderson and Larry Nicolay are the delightful owners of Tofino's Raincoast Café.

When the opportunity to be part of a brand-new building came up, they jumped at it. Larry's brother, who had previously designed restaurants in Vancouver, including Global and Crush, was their designer, and other family members pitched in too. The result is a small but functional prep room, and an open kitchen along one wall of the cleanly executed dining room. There are interesting flower arrangements, but generally the design is understated — a perfect foil for the food.

Lisa was a secretary who moonlighted in the front of house of various Vancouver restaurants. She is a self-trained chef, with no preconceived notions about what she should or should not be cooking. She and Larry agree that their goal is always "to challenge ourselves and other people."

They are inclined to Asian flavours, and allow me to label their style as "modern, with Asian influences," but really, anything goes. Lisa's Thai fish bowl includes local and exotic fish and shellfish, rice noodles, passion fruit, coriander and jalapeno with coconut cream. Fresh Sooke trout is stuffed with Dungeness crab and cilantro lime cream cheese and served with yam mash. Cowichan Bay Farm's chicken is matched with shiitake mushrooms, balsamic shallot cream and herb-roasted new potatoes. Lisa was excited about a dish served the previous night in which she had wrapped halibut in skunk cabbage leaves.

She says she is inspired by what comes in the door from her local suppliers: Clayoquot Organics, Trilogy Fish Company and the neighbouring fishers, shellfish growers and mushroom, fiddlehead and edible-flower pickers. Wines are mostly from British Columbia, with several organic choices; the coffee is Nicaraguan organic and the teas are Tazo.

When Larry excuses himself to collect their daughter, Emma, from school, Lisa asks him to remind her to hug her teachers. It's a sweet moment, and I can see they have found their idyllic lifestyle here in Tofino.

Dinner is served seven nights a week. Reservations are highly recommended, but people have been known to straggle in close to closing time, and Lisa makes sure they're fed. The restaurant seats 24 plus two high stools right in front of the kitchen (great for nosy foodies like me), and it regularly turns over three or four times a night. With recommendations from *USA Today*, *Travel and Leisure*, Frommer's and *Best Places in the Northwest* and, recently, a recipe in *Bon Appétit*, Raincoast Café is indelibly inked on the culinary map.

Ralph the Veggie Man

Ralph Parkhurst is a very congenial greengrocer who has long plied his trade on the island's west coast. Originally from Vancouver, he accepted a bread

This really is Ralph the Veggie Man in the store he founded in Ucluelet.

route in Port Alberni in 1989. His wife told him that if he had wheels, he would always make a living. That's turned out to be true, although he soon switched to produce as it was more profitable.

He opened a small store in Ucluelet, and also sold veggies out of his truck in Tofino. It was difficult to cover both towns, so he eventually focussed on Ucluelet, making weekly deliveries to Tofino. Recently, Ralph has moved on to Lasqueti Island to manage Ralph the Veggie Man II, and partner Shirley Banks has taken over in Ucluelet. The store has lots of organic dry goods, and buys organic produce when the value is there. It's a friendly spot, and I always enjoy stopping for picnic fixings en route to the Wild Pacific Trail or an afternoon at Terrace Beach.

Salals Co-op Grocery & Café

Organic Matters was a privately owned shop that long served Tofino folk seeking the organic alternative. When it had difficulty making ends meet, manager James Rodgers proposed the idea of a co-op that would be locally owned and controlled by its members.

Two years later, the co-op is thriving in a new building with a six-person board, a host of volunteers and one paid employee: manager Corinne Murray. There are 75 members and it's growing. Many shop the co-op exclusively; some also shop elsewhere. The good news is that anyone can shop there, so I dropped by at the start of a week's holiday in Tofino with my hungry family in tow.

The range of foodstuffs is impressive, this far from true farming country, and considering the effort it takes to bring products in. The co-op's policy is "as organic as possible, and as local as possible." Unlike some grocers, organic always takes precedence over local. I bought lots of veggies from Clayoquot Organics (Melanie MacLeod is also a board member); La Boulange bread from Qualicum Beach; very good Tofino Mist coffee; Saltspring's Soya Nova tofu; Clayoquot Sound Wild Blackberry Syrup; Barkley Sound kelp; and blackberries and chanterelles brought in by local pickers.

Corinne came to organics the way many people do — incrementally. She started with tomatoes. I've spoken to people who started with carrots or strawberries, the produce most sprayed and therefore, most hazardous to our health. Living in Tofino, Corinne bought her tomatoes at Organic Matters back in 1992, and it wasn't long before the whole concept of "eating food that didn't have chemicals" made sense to her. Now eating 100 percent organic, she feels she is giving her health an edge.

A life-long cook, Corinne switched from customer to brunch cook in 1993. A few years later, she did some travelling, ending up in Nelson where she took the vegetarian cooking program at Selkirk College. She then went on to cook for the Lifestyle Market deli in Victoria with local natural-foods caterer Laura Moore, and for private clients. Tofino lured her back. When we met, Corinne had been on the job at Salals for only three weeks, and was clearly enjoying the challenge. With her cooking background, she always has an idea for customers who ask: "What can I make for dinner?"

Sobo Global Cuisine

In a classic case of "I'll have what she's having," I order a large cup of thick white noodles in miso broth with chunks of tofu and salmon, topped with sliced wild green onions that a young native girl harvested just that morning. It is a simple, nourishing "best food" experience for which I thank Sushil Saini, Victoria food columnist and author, who happened to be in the lineup ahead of me at Sobo Global Cuisine. Her recommendation of anything is good enough for me.

The noodles were prepared by chef Lisa Ahier, formerly of Tofino's Long Beach Lodge Resort, who, with her husband, Arte, has launched "the purple people eater," a smart-looking steel catering truck, painted royal purple, that has attracted a loyal local clientele since it opened in April 2003. Says Lisa: "We've discovered that, with local support behind us, we could do whatever we want." Customers include cooks and wait staff from all the major restaurants in this beach community — always a good sign that the food is first rate.

Sobo is open from 11 A.M. to 7 P.M., six days a week, enabling Lisa and Arte to spend lots of time with their young son, Barkley. When Lisa worked in big hotel kitchens, she often said to her friends: "If I only had a little taco stand …." Here it is now, in all its glory, with a fabulous selection of seafood, noodle and salad dishes that represent the best kinds of healthy, fresh, fast food.

Lisa focusses on local, organic ingredients: vegetables from Clayoquot Organics, fish from Trilogy Fish Company and many wild ingredients, such as berries and mushrooms from local foragers. Alfons Obererlacher, of Cobble Hill's Engeler Farm, often brings fresh produce, as does Anthony Evans, a travelling producer from the Okanagan. Recent specials have included chilled melon soup with organic coconut milk, saki and mint and absolutely delicious tofu pockets with sushi rice, wasabi and peppery komatsuno leaves that Lisa snips from her garden to order.

The Ahiers plan to stay open until November, then switch to personal cheffing through the winter months, reopening their wildly popular "little taco stand" in the spring.

Tofino Brew House and Wild Fish Restaurant

Opening in August 2003, the Tofino Brew House promises to be a model of green engineering and organic cuisine. It will occupy the same building as Salals Co-op Grocery & Café and a lot of the same people are involved in its development.

James Rodgers, the project manager and primary shareholder, says the brew house will be a reflection of why he chose to live in Tofino in the first place. "The local community is receptive to new ideas and alternative lifestyles. It has the added bonus of receiving two million visitors a year. Here, you can put out your ideology and expose it to people from Germany and Japan," he enthuses. His state-of-the-art, environmentally friendly business is being built "in one of the only towns where you really have a hope of making a difference both on a local and a global level."

What all those locals and visitors will experience is a restaurant and lounge serving 80 percent organic and wild foods and beers (watch for Crannog from Salmon Arm and the Spinnakers' brews from Victoria); a precipi-thermal heating system based on the collection of rain and ground water and no-flush urinals. The building is being constructed from 90 percent recycled materials.

Chef Stephen Ashton will be on the line, that is after he's kayaked to work from his home on Wickaninnish Island. Formerly of Vancouver's Pan Pacific Hotel and Picasso's, he took this job because of the brew house's commitment to organics. Most ingredients will be sourced in and around Tofino from Clayoquot Organics and the local fishers.

Trilogy Fish Company

When I arrive at the Trilogy Fish Company, owner John Fraser is about to leave for North Sea Products, one of the few remaining plants that buys from the local commercial fishers. John buys all his fish locally, and he normally buys directly, too, but with the summer visitors already pouring through the door, he's run a bit low today. I seize the opportunity to ride with him, and we head down to the docks.

A couple of First Nations men are unloading a catch of sockeye salmon from their boat. John goes off to claim his order, and I chat with Rocky, one of the fishers. He says he loves to fish, loves to be out on the ocean. Fishers have been hurting badly from the recently depleted salmon stocks, but he feels the fish are starting to come back.

John returns with an iced haul of four- to seven-pound salmon, and loads them into the truck. When we return to Trilogy, his wife Donna is there to help carry them in. John gives my city shoes a horrified look, and passes me some Wellington boots and a hat. After I wade through a pan of clean water and wash my hands, he takes me into the processing area.

One of his employees, Drew, is filleting salmon, taking a lot of pride in his work. We first enter the cold-smoke room, where the curing temperature is set at 5°C. John grows his own alder at home and chips it to fuel the cold smoker. He never lets his cold-smoked fish get over 10°C, because "the cooler you keep it, the better it tastes." In the hot-smoke room, he also uses chipped alder. The

John's Favourite Salmon

DONNA FRASER, TRILOGY FISH COMPANY

Serves 4 to 6.
A perfect preparation for the buffet table — delicious served hot or cold.

1	2 1/2 lb (1 1/4 kg) side of salmon (preferably chinook)	1
1/4 c	butter, softened	60 ml
3-5	cloves (to taste) fresh garlic, chopped	3-5
1 heaping tbsp	Demerara-style sugar	15 ml
1 heaping tbsp	dry mustard	15 ml

Preheat oven to 350°F.
Place salmon fillet skin side down on a foil-lined cookie sheet. Mix all ingredients together, then spread evenly over the fillet. Bake for 20 to 25 minutes.
NOTE: To test for doneness, press your thumb down on the thickest part of the fillet. The flesh will part on the grain when done. Remove fish from the oven and serve with rice and your favourite vegetables or salad.

The little fish store that could: Trilogy Fish Company in "downtown" Tofino.

process takes about six hours. The finished product is immediately put into a 4°C blast cooler for two hours, then vacuum-packed before being transferred to the shop cooler out front.

John fished these waters for 30 years, mainly for crab. He used to love crabbing because "you could get around the inlets and see everything." When he turned to fish smoking, he thought he would be able to fish for six months, and smoke for six months, but the business has boomed and basically, he's needed on shore. For now, he's fine with that arrangement, as he and Donna still get out for a little sport fishing.

I know of a no more immaculate, well-stocked fish shop than that run by Donna at the front end of the Trilogy Fish Company. The iced displays of hot-smoked, cold-smoked, candied and fresh-off-the-boat salmon as well as halibut, tuna and cooked crab are impressive. The range of condiments and spices will inspire even the most reluctant cook. I was delighted to find fleur de sel, a wide variety of olives, tapenade, seafood sauces, vinegars, oils, salad dressings and all the fixings for sushi.

Donna originally came to Tofino to work as an X-ray technician. Like many here, she liked it so much that she did a variety of things to ensure she would be able to stay. A stint with a forest company and running her own art gallery came before the fish company. Now, she and John are building their dream home overlooking the inlet, and even through she swears she'll "never work another summer," she obviously enjoys her sun-drenched, happy shop.

It's June, and the summer visitors are wafting in. Donna and her sister are busy serving customers looking for something local and tasty for dinner. Out back, John is taking care of sport fishers who need their catches cleaned and vacuum-packed. Between customers, we compare food notes. Donna says she's looking for a new line of salad dressings, so I tell her about the wonderful golden sesame dressing from Occasional Occasions that I discovered at Nanoose Edibles, and she gives me one of the better tips I've had when she sends me off to meet "a superb organic chef," Lisa Ahier, who cooked for an all-too-brief a stint at the Long Beach Lodge.

The Wickaninnish Inn

I am seriously luxuriating in a south-facing double bathtub, looking out as far as the eye can see towards Hawaii. From somewhere out there come the airy notes of Vivaldi, and I pop my head out of the bubbles to see a lone flautist on the rocks below. A siren calling unsuspecting guests to venture forth into dangerous seas? No, merely a little pre-dinner music, Wickaninnish style.

The Wickaninnish Inn is a west-coast wonder, situated on the rugged and startlingly beautiful promontory that juts out between the North Chesterman and Mackenzie beaches. Manager Charles McDiarmid describes the inn's style as "rustic elegance." Certainly, one feels immersed in nature, yet no first-class amenity is spared. Any traveller, gourmet or otherwise, would be hard-pressed to find better.

As Chef de Cuisine Michael Bebault says: "It's about the unique destination here — jagged rocks, sandy beaches, the lively harbour." Against all that glorious nature and activity, he aims to "deliver the kind of menu and service each person wants." I'm dining this evening with a party of six women. Let's see if he can make us all happy!

The décor of bar and dining room is very powerful, very sympathetic to its natural surroundings. The first things one notices are the vast windows, and the sensation that there is no real boundary between room and beach, table and ocean. The overhead cedar beams and pillars have been adzed by local carvers Henry Nolan and his son. The adze, originally used by First Nations people, has been used here to create a pebbled texture that seems to bring the outside in. Henry was also responsible for carving the impressive front doors and many other features throughout the inn.

The bar has a modern feel that happily has not sacrificed comfort for looks. Big, inviting chairs and couches in different-sized groupings make the perfect stop before or after dinner. When someone in my party orders a Scotch, it

273

Seared Pacific Halibut and Steamed Vancouver Island Mussels with Saffron and Fresh Herb Spaetzle, Greens and Smoked Heirloom Tomato Broth

MICHAEL BEBAULT, THE WIICKANINNISH INN

Serves 4.

Halibut

| 4 | portions fresh line-caught halibut (6 oz/ 180 g) each | 4 |

Spaetzle

2	large eggs	2
1/2 c	milk	120 ml
1/3 lb	flour	152 g
	pinch salt	
	pinch freshly ground pepper	
0.016 oz	saffron	1/2 g
1 c	water	240 ml
2 tbsp	fresh chopped parsley, cilantro, thyme and basil	30 ml
1 tbsp	unsalted butter	15 ml

Broth

4	medium heirloom tomatoes	4
1	shallot, peeled and finely diced	1
1	clove garlic, peeled and minced	1
1 tbsp	white wine	15 ml
1 c	vegetable stock	240 ml
	apple wood smoking chips	
12	fresh Vancouver Island mussels (3 per person)	12

Greens

| 4 | small clusters mixed greens | 4 |

Spaetzle: Cook the saffron in one cup of water until it becomes a vibrant yellow liquid and has reduced by three-quarters. Remove from heat and cool. Whisk the eggs in a bowl. Add the milk, salt, pepper and saffron liquid. Add the flour while whisking until a thick batter is reached. If it is too thin, you may have to add a little more flour. Incorporate the herbs and allow the batter to rest for one hour before cooking to relax the gluten. Over a large pot of boiling water, place a colander and press the batter through the holes. When the dumplings rise to the surface, allow to simmer for one or two minutes, then remove and cool quickly in ice water and drain well.

Broth: In a smoker, smoke the tomatoes long enough so that they take on a rich smokey flavour (approximately ten minutes in heavy smoke). Sweat the shallot and garlic for two or three minutes and deglaze with the white wine. Add the tomatoes and vegetable stock and bring to the boil. Allow to simmer for 15-18 minutes. Remove from heat and pass through a fine chinois or sieve and keep warm. **To serve,** steam the mussels in the tomato broth until they open. Sear both sides of the halibut in a small amount of oil and place in a 350°F oven for approximately four minutes or until cooked but still tender and moist. Sauté the spaetzle in butter until hot. Place the spaetzle in a large soup plate and put a small cluster of the greens on top. Place one portion of halibut on top of the greens and three mussels in each dish. Pour the smoked tomato broth over top of the halibut. Garnish the halibut with a teaspoon of beluga (or other) caviar.

comes in one of Charles's father's heavy crystal gentleman's glasses. Even my New York City companions are impressed with the bartender's ability to pour every au courant cocktail they request.

A couple of steps down from the bar is The Pointe Restaurant, a semi-circular room set around a blazing open fire. The carpet has a rippled effect like the sea it seems to meet. Deep orange-coloured sconces on the walls become more noticeable as the sun sets. Eventually, the dining room is lit only by the sconces and candles set in rocks on the old-growth fir tables, and is it my imagination, or has someone opened a window? How could we now be hearing the surf? Actually, another magic wand has been waved behind the scenes: microphones strategically placed outside are allowing the crashing waves to be heard beneath the classical music. Such a brilliant score.

Our very beautiful waitress, Tara, sets the tone with a detailed discussion of the menus. Since it is April, the inn is still celebrating the Pacific Rim Whale Festival, so there's a special menu devoted to the fruits of the area: gooseneck barnacles, salmon, Dungeness crab, quail, asparagus. The whale festival celebrates the migration of the gray whale from late February to early March, or, this year, until mid-April. The resident whales stay until the fall. I've been in the dining room when a whale is spotted breaching close to shore, and discovered that the natural entertainment can, in fact, match the cooking here.

There is always a distinctive seafood menu, based on the local catch. These are enormously prolific waters, with high plankton content. Clams, crabs, scallops, mussels and oysters abound. The federal government regulates the fishery, opening and closing it as stocks allow. In recent years, there has been pressure on the salmon and halibut stocks, and the fishers have to catch their quotas or lose their licences. Sometimes an octopus is caught in a crab trap, and sometimes there are sea urchins on the menu.

Chef Bebault works with a kitchen brigade of 15. There are three to four cooks on the line at any one time and 600 brilliant plates a night come out of his kitchen. The restaurant now seats 85, but plans call for a bit more seating and a re-engineered kitchen. Dining at

> ## "I love working with the seasonal, close-to-home ingredients."
> — Chef Michael Bebault,
> The Wickaninnish Inn

The Pointe is a relaxed and friendly experience, yet service is 100 percent proper, with all dishes for each course arriving at the same time, borne by the requisite number of servers. The wait staff are not only nice, but highly knowledgeable, and not just about the food, but about the area and all aspects of the inn. I know Charles McDiarmid is a graduate of Cornell's hotel management school, and my impression is that everyone else is too!

This evening, our menu begins with the sexy Spiced Oyster Shooter (a big hit with the girls). The Carpaccio of Rock Scallops with Roast Grape Tomatoes, Tomato Oil, Smoked Salmon and Chervil Salad is so fresh and flavourful that many in our party order it two nights in a row. A silky Roasted Dungeness Crab and Brandy Bisque with Crab and Leek Dumpling follows; Lemon and Mint Sorbet is presented in an ice bowl with a feather of Lavender Fern from the forest; Pan Seared Steelhead is served with Octopus and Wild Mushroom in Puff Pastry with Snow Peas, Corn and Vanilla Emulsion. The seafood menu closes, as it opens, with something sensual: Caramelized Honey Parfait with Fresh Raspberries and a Peach Schnapps Sauce.

The Pointe's à la carte menu is actually a well-thought-out prix fixe, allowing guests to choose three, four or five courses. This fall, the choices fell under the evocative headings of autumn beginnings and late harvest continuation. I went straight to Wild Roasted Mushroom and Amaretto Purée with Toasted Walnut and Blue Cheese Strudel, and blissfully continued with the Seared Pheasant Breast with Braised Rutabaga, Cranberry Compote with Apple Cider Reduction and Aged Balsamic Syrup.

Vancouver Island's wild west coast area is not exactly a farming community, but here and there some exceptional food is being raised and produced — the best of which is regularly featured on The Wickaninnish Inn's menus. Charles McDiarmid generously introduced me to some of the remarkable local food producers, whose stories you've just read.

The Surfing Chef

Only in Tofino would one encounter a chef whose first career was surfing. Mike Bebault travelled the world chasing waves, spending most of his time in the famed Australian surf. At that time, he relished the freedom — "no clocks, no schedules."

Now that he is the main man in The Wickaninnish kitchen, one may wonder how his current career came about. "When I returned to Nanaimo from my travels, I began working in restaurants and received a lot of encouragement to go to school." Bebault mentions Bob Ingills in particular, fomer chef at Vancouver's Pan Pacific Hotel, who told him he had potential. Ten years ago, he took Bob's advice and enrolled in the culinary arts program at Nanaimo's Malaspina College. Part of the apprenticeship brought him in contact with another mentor, Gilbert Noussiteau of Victoria's Camosun College, who suggested he apply to The Wickaninnish.

"Basically, I called [then-chef] Rod Butters two or three times a day until he took me on," says Bebault. He began working seasonally at the inn, spending his winters in Costa Rica where he "cooked with great local ingredients like mangos that we'd just pick off the trees." Recently promoted to chef de cuisine at The Wickaninnish, which is now a wildly successful year-round operation, he says: "It's a big job, but I have an incredible team, and I love working with the seasonal, close-to-home ingredients."

Breakfast

I write this for my fellow peripatetic breakfast hounds, those

Chef Michael Bebault of The Wickaninnish Inn.

whose day is made by finding a sensational breakfast, and who are lost without it! Others may care little or not at all that The Wickaninnish Inn gets breakfast right every morning.

To begin, you will be greeted by one of several seriously healthy-looking waitresses, who has inevitably surfed before starting her shift. She proffers the daily juice special, which today is a combination of freshly squeezed apple, melon and blackberry. Its beautiful amber

The Wickaninnish Inn General Manager Charles McDiarmid.

colour and exotic flavour awaken the senses, and encourage one to take in the view.

Ah, so this is Chesterman Beach in the morning, a mile and a half of sand immaculately cleansed by the evening's rain, the sun illuminating a blue sky and calm ocean. The low tide has already invited strollers, joggers and surfers to venture forth, and two eagles, residents of a tree on the inn's north side, are soaring and seeking their own repast. All is quiet across at the Leonard Island Lighthouse, one of the last remaining manned lighthouses on the west coast. What's not to love, starting the day with this spectacular, peaceful, yet ever-changing vista and a promising breakfast menu at hand?

You can have breakfast any way you want it. Sometimes, I have a lovely bowl of oatmeal, served up with juicy raisins, steamed milk and crystals of deep brown sugar. At other times, I go for the Eggs Benedict with Ucluelet Goats' Cheese and Organic Spinach served on a homemade English muffin and accompanied by really good pan-fries. It is unspeakably rich and satisfying. My husband appreciates the man-sized British cooked breakfast that is made to his specifications: scrambled eggs; roast potatoes; smoked salmon; stone-ground toast and homemade preserves, all of which he chases with a skinny cappuccino.

As we tuck in, one of the eagles steals our attention by sweeping seaward for his own breakfast. A man sets his tripod up on the rocks. The elderly couple next to us finishes their breakfast. He walks around to pull out her chair, and they head out for a leisurely stroll along the beach. We are in no hurry, either. We finish our own breakfast in the lounge, sunk deep into armchairs with coffees and newspapers at hand, yet still glued to the view.

Photo Credits

The Aerie: pp. 135 bottom left and right, 136, 150.
Alderlea Vineyards: p. 112.
Blue Grouse Vineyards: pp. 114, 116.
Bold Point Farmstay: p. 243 top.
Brasserie L'École: pp. 4, 6.
Gordon Browne: p. 238 bottom.
Chateau Wolff: pp. 128, 129.
Cherry Point Vineyards: p. 117.
Creekmore Coffee: p. 208.
Adrian Dorst: p. 242 bottom.
Engeler Farm: p. 236 top.
Fairburn Farm: pp. 137 top, 163, 164, 235 bottom.
Andrei Fedorov: pp. 39, 45, 48, 49, 51, 52, 55, 58, 131, 132, 134 top, 167.
Gabriola Gourmet Garlic: p. 193.
Glow World Cuisine: p. 183 top.
Hastings House: pp. 63, 65 bottom right, 66, 133 top and middle.
Hollyhock: pp. 239 top, 249.
Rosheen Holland: pp. 196, 197.
House Piccolo: p. 70.
Gary Hynes: p. 20.
Kiwi Cove Lodge: p. 235 top.
La Boulange Organic Breads: pp. 236 bottom, 211.
Christophe Letard: p. 145.
Clive Levinson: p. 290.
Elizabeth Levinson: pp. 23, 29, 43, 61, 65 left and top right, 80, 84 bottom left, 87, 90 bottom, 92, 93, 94, 96, 98, 121, 153, 155, 156, 158, 172, 199, 201 bottom right and top, 204, 206, 220, 221, 228, 232, 233, 238 top and middle, 240, 243 bottom, 260, 261, 263, 266, 267, 272, 277.
Maclean's Speciality Foods: pp. 186, 187.
Rob Melnychuk: pp. 241, 242 top.
Monsoon Coast Exotic World Spices: pp. 77, 78.
Retta Moorman: pp. 7, 8, 9, 10, 12, 14, 15, 16, 17, 18, 24, 26, 27, 31, 33, 36, 41, 134 bottom.
Natural Pastures Cheese Company: p. 138.
Greg Osoba: p. 239 bottom.
Pender Island Bakery Café: p. 95.
Page Point Inn: p. 237 bottom.
Reef Point Farm: p. 252.
Salt Spring Flour Mill: p. 84 top and right.
Saskatoon Berry Farm: pp. 169, 170.
Steeples: pp. 135 top, 142.
TouchWood Editions: pp. 113, 115, 118, 119, 134 bottom, 137 bottom left and right, 141, 159, 162, 172, 175, 177, 179, 180, 183 bottom, 182, 185, 189, 190, 191, 201 bottom left, 213, 219, 225, 230, 237 top.
Vinoteca Restaurant: pp. 124, 126.
Wave Hill Farm: pp. 76, 90 top.
The Wickaninnish Inn: p. 278.
Wildfire Bakery: p. 37.

Contacts

SOUTH ISLAND

Victoria

Brasserie L'École
restaurant • dinner only
1715 Government Street
Victoria, V8W 1Z4
Tel: (250) 475-6260
www.lecole.ca
eat@lecole.ca
Sean Brennan, chef/owner
Marc Morrison, sommelier/owner

♣

Cafe Brio
restaurant • dinner year-round, lunch in summer
944 Fort Street
Victoria, V8V 3K2
Tel: (250) 383-0009
www.cafe-brio.com
reservations@cafe-brio.com
Sylvia Marcolini and Greg Hays, owners
Chris Dignan, chef

Caffé Fantastico
coffee shop
965 Kings Road
Victoria, V8T 1W7
Tel: (250) 385-BEAN (2326)
www.caffefantastico.com
ryan@caffefantastico.com
Ryan and Kristy Taylor

♣

Common Sense Café
restaurant • continental breakfast, lunch and takeout
1127 Fort Street
Victoria, V8V 3K9
Tel: (250) 475-0775
Jocelyne Therrien and Lisa Pennington

Cucina
restaurant/caterer • lunch Tuesday – Saturday • dinner and special events by appointment
Loft 10
532-1/2 Fisgard Street
Victoria, V8W 1R4
Tel: (250) 360-1348
Mirjana

Fourways Meat Market
butcher
3500 Quadra Street
Victoria, V8X 1G9
Tel: (250) 382-2431
Fax: (250) 382-2437
Dave Robinson

Italian Bakery
bakery, grocery and café
3197 Quadra Street
Victoria, V8X 1E9
Tel: (250) 388-4557
Alberto Pozzolo and Janet Cochrane

Moss Street Market
farmers' market Saturdays, 10 a.m. to 2 p.m., May to late October plus special Christmas market
corner of Moss Street and Fairfield Road (Sir James Douglas School)
Tel: (250) 361-1747
Marinie Smith

♣

Ottavio's Gastronomia
bakery, delicatessen and coffee bar
2278 Oak Bay Avenue
Victoria, V8R 1G7
Tel/Fax: (250) 592-4080
Monica Pozzolo and Andrew Moyer

The Personal Chef
caterer • by appointment
1330 Mt. Newton Cross Road
Saanichton, V8M 1S1
Tel: (250) 544-1780
Fax: (250) 544-1185
jennycameron@pacificcoast.net
Jenny Cameron

Planet Organic
organic grocery
3995 Quadra Street
Victoria, V8X 1J8
Tel: (250) 727-9888
www.planetorganic.ca
Diane Shaskin and Mark Craft

Pure Vanilla Bakery and Café
bakery and café
105-2590 Cadboro Bay Road
Victoria, V8R 5J2
Tel: (250) 592-2896
Audrey Alsterburg

Shady Creek Ice Cream Company
producer not open to public • product sold through Vancouver Island retailers
7268 Veyaness Road
Saanichton, V8M 1M2
Tel: (250) 652-8256
eng@islandnet.com
Christie Eng

Share Organics
home delivery • call to arrange
1885 St. Ann Street
Victoria, V8R 5V9
Tel: (250) 595-6729
Fax: (250) 595-6721
www.shareorganics.bc.ca
susan@shareorganics.bc.ca
Susan Tychie and Jason McQuarrie

Slater's First Class Meats
butcher
2577 Cadboro Bay Road
Victoria, V8R 5J1
Tel: (250) 592-0823
Rick Milburn

Spinnakers Brewpub
brewery, pub and restaurant
308 Catherine Street
Victoria, V9A 3S8
Tel: (250) 384-2739
www.spinnakers.com
Paul Hadfield

Travel with Taste Tours
culinary tours • call to reserve
#1 – 356 Simcoe Street
Victoria, V8V 1L1
Tel: (250) 385-1527
www.travelwithtaste.com
info@travelwithtaste.com
Kathy McAree

Wild Fire Bakery
bakery
1517 Quadra Street
Victoria, V8W 2L3
Tel: (250) 381-3473
Cliff Lier and Erica Heyerman

Zambri's
restaurant • lunch and dinner
#110-911 Yates Street
Victoria, V8V 4X3
Tel: (250) 360-1171
Fax: (250) 413-3231
www.zambris.com
zambris@shaw.ca
Jo and Peter Zambri

Metchosin

Happy Valley Lavender and Herb Farm
farm • open in season • call ahead for hours • annual Lavender Festival
3505 Happy Valley Road
Victoria, V9C 2Y2
Tel/Fax: (250) 474-5767
www.happyvalleylavender.com
lynda@happyvalleylavender.com
Lynda Dowling

Metchosin Farmers' Market
farmers' market Sundays, 11 a.m. to 2 p.m., mid-May to mid-October
Municipal Grounds, Happy Valley Road
Metchosin
Tel: (250) 474-3156
Bob Mitchell

Sooke

Ragley Farm
farmgate • open Saturday year-round, also Sunday in season
5717 East Sooke Road
Sooke, V0S 1N0
Tel: (250) 642-7349
Fax: (250) 642-1946
ragley@telus.net
Josephine Hill

The Seaweed Lady
producer • product available through Vancouver Island retailers • tours by appointment
Outer Coast Seaweeds
2018 Penang Road
Sooke, V0S 1N0
Tel: (250) 642-5328
www.outercoastseaweeds.com
outercoastseaweeds@shaw.ca
Diane Bernard

Sooke Country Market
farmers' market Saturdays, 10 a.m. to 2 p.m., mid-May to September
2047 Otter Point Road, behind the Petro Canada Station
Sooke
Tel: (250) 642-4687
Melanie Derksen

Sooke Harbour House
restaurant and inn
1528 Whiffen Spit Road
Sooke, V0S 1N0
Tel: (250) 642-3421
Fax: (250) 642-6988
www.sookeharbourhouse.com
info@sookeharbourhouse.com
Sinclair and Frédérique Philip, owners
Edward Tuson, chef

Tugwell Creek Honey Farm
farmgate • open Wednesday to Sunday, 11 a.m. to 4 p.m., April to August • tours by appointment
8750 West Coast Road
Sooke, V0S 1N0
Tel: (250) 642-1956
www.tugwellcreekfarm.com
dana-l@shaw.ca
Robert Liptrot and Dana Le Comte

Saltspring Island

The Bread Lady
bakery • not open to the public • bread sales at Market-in-the-Park (see listing)
251 Forest Ridge Road
Saltspring Island
V8K 1W4
Tel: (250) 653-4809
pvanhorn@saltspring.com
Heather Campbell

Bright Farm
not open to the public • produce available at Market-in-the-Park (see listing) and the Organic Market (see listing)
176 Tripp Road
Saltspring Island, V8K 1K5
Tel: (250) 537-4319
ceagle@saltspring.com
Charlie Eagle, Judy Horvath and Bree Eagle

☕

Hastings House
restaurant and inn • closed late November through mid-March
160 Upper Ganges Road
Saltspring Island, V8K 2S2
Tel: (250) 537-2362
800-661-9255 Canada and USA
Fax: (250) 537-5333
hasthouse@saltspring.com
www.hastingshouse.com
Shirley McLaughlin, manager
Marcel Kauer, executive chef
Thomas Render, chef de cuisine

House Piccolo
restaurant • dinner only
108 Hereford Avenue
Saltspring Island, V8K 2V9
Tel: (250) 537-1844
www.housepiccolo.com
piccolo@saltspring.com
Piccolo Lyytikainen, owner/chef

Madrona Valley Farm
farm and bed & breakfast • produce available at Market-in-the-Park (see listing)
171 Chu-An Drive
Saltspring Island, V8K 1H9
Tel: (250) 537-1989
www.madronavalleyfarm.com
info@madronavalleyfarm.com
Michael and Jeanne-Marie Ableman

Market-in-the-Park
farmers' market Saturdays, 8:30 a.m. to 3:30 p.m., first Saturday in April to last Saturday in October
Centennial Park, downtown
Ganges, Saltspring Island
Tel: (250) 537-4448
www.saltspringmarket.com
CRD Parks and Recreation

Monsoon Coast Exotic World Spices
producer • not open to the public • product available at Market-in-the-Park (see listing) and through Vancouver Island retailers
280 Robinson Road
Saltspring Island, V8K 1P7
Tel: (250) 537-9447
Fax: (250) 537-1311
www.monsooncoast.com
Satva and Chintan Hall

☕

Morningside Organic Bakery and Café
108 Morningside Road
Saltspring Island, V8K 1X1
Tel: (250) 653-4414
Alan Golding and Manon Darrette

Organic Market
Tuesday mornings year-round
112 Hereford Avenue
Saltspring Island
Tel: (250) 537-4319
Charlie Eagle

The Personal Chefs
caterers • by appointment
285 Meyer Road
Saltspring Island, V8K 1X4
Tel: (250) 537-1250
25mapleleaves@saltspring.com
Jacqueline Gengé and Brian Perry

Salt Spring Flour Mill
producer • not open to the public • product available at Market-in-the-Park (see listing)
169 Dogwood Lane
Saltspring Island, V8K 1A4
Tel: (250) 537-4282
dogwoodlane@saltspring.com
Pat Reichert

Saltspring Island Cheese Company
producer • not open to the public • product available at Market-in-the-Park (see listing) and through Vancouver Island retailers
285 Reynolds Road
Saltspring Island, V8K 1Y2
Tel: (250) 653-2304
David and Nancy Wood

Saltspring Island Garlic Festival
food festival held in August • call for date
Farmers' Institute Grounds
351 Rainbow Road
Saltspring Island
Tel: (250) 537-1219
Kristie

Soya Nova Tofu
producer • product available for purchase on site and through Vancouver Island retailers
1200 Beddis Road
Saltspring Island, V8K 2C8
Tel: (250) 537-9651
www.soyanova.ca
soyanova@saltspring.com
Deborah Lauzon

Wave Hill Farm
farm not open to the public • produce and flowers available at Market-in-the-Park (see listing) • meat and poultry by special order — call ahead
340 Bridgeman Road
Saltspring Island, V8K 1W7
Tel/Fax: (250) 653-4121
Mark Whitear and Rosalie Beach

Pender Islands

Iona Farm
farm not open to the public • produce available at Pender Island Farmers' Market (see listing)
3403 South Otter Bay Road
Pender Island, V0N 2M1
(250) 629-6700
iona@cablean.net
Rob and Ellen Willingham

Pacific Shoreline
fishers • seasonal • call for days and times of dockside sales
Pender Island
Tel: (250) 629-9950
Bonnie and Cal

Pender Island Bakery Café
bakery and café
1105 Stanley Point Drive
Pender Island, V0N 2M1
Tel: (250) 629-6453 or
(250) 629-3877
Fax: (250) 629-3879
dmurdoch@gulfislands.com
Dorothy Murdoch

Pender Island Farmers' Market
farmers' market Saturday, 9:30 a.m. to 1 p.m., Easter to Christmas
Pender Island Agricultural and Recreational Community Hall
on Bedwell Harbour Road at Otter Bay Road
Tel: (250) 629-6700
Ellen Willingham, President, Farmers' Institute

Saturna Island

Haggis Farm Bakery
bakery not open to the public • product available at Saturna General Store and through Vancouver Island retailers
110 Narvaez Bay Road
Saturna Island, V0N 2Y0
Tel: (250) 539-2591
Jon Guy and Priscilla Ewbank

Saturna General Store and Café
grocery, wine store and café
101 Narvaez Bay Road
Saturna Island, V0N 2Y0
Tel: (250) 539-2936
Fax: (250) 539-5136
Jon Guy, Priscilla Ewbank and Hubertus Surm

☙

Saturna Herbs
farm open to the public • no set times • product available at Saturna General Store and through online mail order
Breezy Bay Farm
131 Payne Road
Saturna Island, V0N 2Y0
Tel: (250) 539-5200
Fax: (250) 539-5201
www.saturnaherbs.com
saturnaherbs@canada.com
Flora House

☙

Saturna Island Vineyards
vineyard, winery, tasting room and café open to the public year-round
8 Quarry Trail
Saturna Island, V0N 2Y0
Toll free: 877-918-3388
Tel: (250) 539-5139
Fax: (250) 539-5157
www.saturnavineyards.com
wine@saturnavineyards.com
Rebecca Page, general manager
Eric von Krosigk, winemaker

☙

Saturna Island Farmers' Market
farmers' market Saturdays, 1 to 4 p.m., early July to end of August
Community Hall
steps from the ferry dock at Lyall Harbour

Mayne Island

Deacon Vale Farm
not open to the public • produce available at Mayne Island Farmers' Market (see listing) • sauces and preserves available through Vancouver Island retailers
380 Campbell Bay Road
Mayne Island, V0N 2J0
Tel/Fax: (250) 539-5456
www.deaconvalefarm.com
dvf@gulfislands.com
Don and Shanti McDougall

Mayne Island Farmers' Market
farmers' market Saturdays, 10 a.m. to 1 p.m., May long weekend to Thanksgiving
Agricultural Hall Grounds
Miners Bay
Mayne Island
Tel: (250) 539-5456
Shanti McDougall

Oceanwood Country Inn
restaurant and inn • closed November through February
630 Dinner Bay Road
Mayne Island, V0N 2J0
Tel: (250) 539-5074
www.oceanwood.com
oceanwood@gulfislands.com
Jonathan Chilvers, owner
David Kruse, chef de cuisine

☙

Galiano Island

Atrevida
restaurant in The Galiano Inn
134 Madrona Drive
Galiano Island, V0N 1P0
Toll free: 877-530-3939
Tel: (250) 539-3388
Fax: (250) 539-3338
www.galianoinn.com
info@galianoinn.com
Mel Gibb and Conny Nordin

WINE ROUTE

Alderlea Vineyards
vineyard, winery and tasting room open year-round • hours vary • call ahead
1751 Stamps Road
Duncan, V9L 5W2
Tel/Fax: (250) 746-7122
Roger and Nancy Dosman

Blue Grouse Vineyards
vineyard, winery and tasting room open Wednesday to Saturday, 11 a.m. to 5 p.m., October to March • Wednesday to Sunday, 11 a.m. to 5 p.m., April to September
4365 Blue Grouse Road
Cobble Hill, V9L 6M3
Tel: (250) 743-3834
Fax: (250) 743-9305
www.bluegrousevineyards.com
skiltz@islandnet.com
Dr. Hans Kiltz, Evangeline Kiltz and Sandrina Kiltz

Cherry Point Vineyards
vineyard, winery, tasting room, tours • picnic patio and gift shop open daily year-round • call for dates of summer outdoor concerts
840 Cherry Point Road
Cobble Hill, V0R 1L0
Tel: (250) 743-1272
Fax: (250) 743-1059
www.cherrypointvineyards.com
Wayne and Helena Ulrich

Glenterra Vineyards
vineyard, winery and tasting room open daily year-round, 11 a.m. to 6 p.m.
3897 Cobble Hill Road
Cobble Hill, V0R 1L0
Tel: (250) 743-2330
glenterravineyards@shaw.ca
John Kelly and Ruth Luxton

Venturi Schulze Vineyards
vineyard, winery, vinegary and tasting room open by appointment only
4235 Trans Canada Highway
Cobble Hill, V0R 1L0
Tel: (250) 743-5630
Fax: (250) 743-5638
www.venturischulze.com
info@venturischulze.com
Giordano Venturi, Marilyn and Michelle Schulze

Vigneti Zanatta and Vinoteca Restaurant
vineyard, winery, tasting room and restaurant open March to December
5039 Marshall Road
Duncan, V9L 6S3
Tel: vineyard: (250) 748-2338
restaurant: (250) 709-2279
Fax: (250) 748-2347
www.zanatta.ca
Loretta Zanatta and Jim Moody and family, owners
Fatima da Silva, chef

Château Wolff
vineyard, winery open daily year-round • tasting room open Saturday and Sunday year-round
2534 Maxey Road
Nanaimo, V9S 5V6
Tel: (250) 753-4613
Fax: (250) 753-0614
Harry von Wolff

MID-ISLAND
Shawnigan Lake
Steeples
restaurant • daily dinner and weekend brunch
2744 East Shawnigan Lake Road
Shawnigan Lake, V0R 2W0
Tel: (250) 743-1887
www.steeplesrestaurant.ca
darren@steeplesrestaurant.ca
Darren Cole, chef/co-owner

The Malahat

The Aerie
restaurant and inn • seasonal tours of local farms
600 Ebadora Lane
The Malahat, V0R 2L0
Tel: (250) 743-7115
Fax: (250) 743-4766
www.aerie.bc.ca
resort@aerie.bc.ca
Markus Griesser, general manager
Christophe Letard, chef de cuisine

Cowichan Valley
The Asparagus Farm
farmgate open to the public in season • call ahead for dates and times
1550 Robson Lane, Cobble Hill
Tel/Fax: (250) 743-5073
www.islandnet.com/~cford/
Charles and Carole Ford

Black Coffee and Other Delights
café
4705 E Trans-Canada Highway
Whippletree Junction,
Duncan, V9L 6E1
(250) 746-9973
cleveland@cvnet.net
Corrine Wilson, Andrew Simonson and Morris Cleveland

Broken Briar Fallow Deer Farm
farm/restaurant supplier • some venison sales on site
2692 Mt. Siker Road
Chemainus, V0R 1K0
Tel: (250) 246-9749
tdgroves@island.net
David Groves

Cowichan Bay Farm
*farm store open daily year-round
• products also available through
Vancouver Island retailers*
1560 Cowichan Bay Road,
RR #1
Cowichan Bay, VOR 1N0
Tel/Fax: (250) 746-7884
farmer@cowichanbayfarm.com
www.cowichanbayfarm.com
Lyle and Fiona Young

Engeler Farm
*farm and cooking school • produce
available at New Duncan Farmers' Market
• call ahead for farmgate sales*
4255 Trans-Canada Highway
Cobble Hill, VOR 1L0
Tel: (250) 743-4267
Fax: (250) 743-8367
www.engelerfarm.com
engelerfarm@telus.net
Mara Jernigan and Alfons
Obererlacher

Fairburn Farm
*farm and bed & breakfast • call ahead for
meat orders*
3310 Jackson Road
Duncan, V9L 6N7
Tel/Fax: (250) 746-4637
www.fairburnfarm.bc.ca
info@fairburnfarm.bc.ca
Darrel and Anthea Archer

Feast of Fields
*food festival held at a different farm every
September • call for date and venue*
Tel: (250) 743-4267
Mara Jernigan

The Mushroom Guy
*mushroom foraging tours and dinners
• call to reserve*
Magnetic North Cuisine
4830 Stelfox Road
Duncan
Tel: (250) 748-7450
www.magnorth.bc.ca
bill@magnorth.bc.ca
Bill Jones

Saskatoon Berry Farm
*orchard u-pick and farm store open in
season • call for dates and times*
1245 Fisher Road
Cobble Hill, VOR 1L0
Tel: (250) 743-1189
toonfarm@yahoo.com
Alwin and Connie Dyrland

Cedar

Cedar Farmers' Market
*farmers' market Sundays, 10 a.m. to 1
p.m., mid-May to early October*
Crow and Gate Pub, off Cedar
Road
Tel/Fax: (250) 722-3526
George Benson

Mahle House Restaurant
*dinner Wednesday to Sunday
year-round*
2104 Hemer Road
Nanaimo, V9X 1L8
Tel: (250) 722-3621
Fax (250) 722-3302
www.mahlehouse.com
info@mahlehouse.com
Maureen Loucks, chef/owner
Delbert Horrocks, sommelier/
owner

Ladysmith

Barton Leier Gallery*
*gallery of cover artist Grant Leier and his
wife, artist Nixie Barton • open to the public*
3140 Decourcey Road
Ladysmith, V9G 1E2
Tel: (250) 722-7140
bartonleiergallery@shaw.ca
Grant Leier and Nixie Barton
*Their paintings are food for the
soul!

Hazelwood Herb Farm
*farm • herb plants, gift shop and self-
guided tours daily, 11 a.m. to 5 p.m., April
to September • 11 a.m. to 5 p.m. Friday
to Sunday, October to Christmas Eve • call
for dates of annual festivals*
13576 Adshead Road
Ladysmith, V9G 1H6
Tel: (250) 245-8007
www.hazelwoodherbfarm.com
info@hazelwoodherbfarm.com
Richard Wright and Jacynthe
Dugas

Herb Wise
*not open to the public • online orders
through website*
649 Delcourt Avenue
Ladysmith, V9G 1N9
(250) 245-3311
www.herbwise.ca
herbwise@telus.net
Delaine and Bruce Burnett

Kiwi Cove Lodge
farm and bed & breakfast
5130 Brenton Page Road
Ladysmith, V9G 1L6
Tel: (250) 245-8051
Fax: (250) 245-8010
www.kiwicovelodge.com
kiwicove@shaw.ca
Peggy and Doug Kolosoff

Page Point Inn
restaurant and inn
4760 Brenton-Page Road
Ladysmith, V9G 1L7
Tel: (250) 245-2312
Toll free: 1-877-860-6866
Fax: (250) 245-7546
www.pagepointinn.com
info@pagepointinn.com
Lawrence and Lexie Lambert,
owners
Steven Mugridge, chef

Nanaimo
Glow World Cuisine
restaurant • lunch and dinner daily • weekend brunch
7 Victoria Road
Nanaimo, V9R 4N9
Tel: (250) 741-8858
Eric and Larry Lim, owners
Gert Voigt, owner/chef

Island Natural Markets
grocery store
6560 Metral Drive
Nanaimo, V9T 2L9
Tel: (250) 390-1955
islandnatural@shaw.ca
Rhonda Lambert and Casey
Mitchell

McLean's Specialty Foods
specialty food store, delicatessen and café
426 Fitzwilliam Street
Nanaimo, V9R 3B1
Tel: (250) 754-0100
Fax: (250) 754-0161
www.mcleansfoods.com
mcleans@nisa.net
Eric and Sandy McLean

Shady Mile Farm Market
grocery store and café
3452 Jingle Pot Road
Nanaimo, V9R 6W9
Tel: (250) 729-3801
Bill and Sharon Earthy

The Wesley Street
restaurant • lunch and dinner
1 – 321 Wesley Street
Nanaimo, V9R 2T5
Tel: (250) 753-6057
Gaetan and Linda Brousseau

Gabriola Island
Gabriola Gourmet Garlic
studio open daily year-round
1025 Horseshoe Road
Gabriola Island, VOR 1X0
Tel/Fax: (250) 247-0132
www.gabriolagourmetgarlic.com
gabriolagourmetgarlic@shaw.ca
Ken Stefanson and Llie
Brotherton

Gabriola Agricultural Association
Farmers' Market
farmers' market Saturdays, 10 a.m. to 2 p.m., beginning of May to Thanksgiving
Agi Hall
465 South Road (top of the hill
from the ferry)
Gabriola Island
Tel: (250) 247-8216
ebus87@island.net
Tannie Meyer

Heavenly Flowers & Good Earth
Vegetables
farm not open to the public • farmgate open in season • call for dates and times
600 South Road
Gabriola Island, VOR 1X0
Tel: (250) 668-0670
Rosheen Holland and Bob
Shields

Lantzville/Nanoose Bay
The Book Worm Café
café • breakfast and lunch
7221 Lantzville Road
Lantzville, VOR 2H0
Tel: (250) 390-4541
Chris Thomas and Vicky Adamson

Harvest Bounty Festival
food festival held at a different farm every August • call for date and venue
Tel: (250) 248-8207
Debbie Schug

The Landing at Pacific Shores
resort restaurant
1600 Strougler Road
Nanoose Bay, V9P 9B7
Tel: (250) 468-2400
Andy and Susan Pearson, owners
Christine Lilyholm, chef

Nanoose Edibles
farm • farmgate hours vary • call for dates and hours
1960A Stewart Road
Nanoose Bay, V9P 9E7
Tel: (250) 468-2332
Fax: (250) 468-2324
Barbara and Lorne Ebell

Parksville
The Earthshake Café
café • breakfast and lunch
487b East Island Highway
Parksville, V9P 2G7
Tel: (250) 951-2030
Carol Mann

Qualicum Beach

Creekmore Coffee
*coffee roastery • not open to the public
• coffee available through Vancouver
Island retailers*
P.O. Box 555
Qualicum Beach, V9K 1T1
Tel: (250) 752-0158
Fax: (250) 752-0138
coffeecreek@shaw.ca
David and Elaine Creekmore

Fore & Aft Foods
*caterers • by appointment • condiments
sold through Vancouver Island retailers*
5390 Island Highway
Qualicum Beach, V9K 2E8
Tel: (250) 757-8682
Beverley Child and Patrick
Brownrigg

La Boulange Organic Breads
*bakery • retail sales on site • product
also sold through Vancouver Island retailers*
692 Bennett Road
Qualicum Beach
Tel: (250) 752-0077
Fax: (250) 752-0078
laboulange@home.com
John Taraynor and Jean Wilson

Qualicum Beach Farmers' Market
*farmers' market Saturdays, 9 a.m. to noon,
mid-May to September*
Fir Street at Memorial Avenue
Qualicum Beach
Tel: (250) 752-2857
Bea

RainBarrel Farm
*farm • not open to the public • produce
and flowers available at Qualicum Beach
Farmers' Market (see listing) and Qualicum
Beach Thrifty Foods*
599 Garden Road East
Qualicum Beach, V9K 1M5
Tel: (250) 752-0424
lmant@shaw.ca
Marilyn Mant and Tami Treit

Fanny Bay

Ships Point Inn
bed & breakfast
7584 Ships Point Road
Fanny Bay, V0R 1W0
Toll free: 1-877-742-1004
Tel: (250) 335-1004
www.shipspointinn.com
shipspointinn@aol.com

☕

Denman Island

**Bien Tostado Custom Coffee
Roasting**
*coffee roastery • not open to the public
• online orders through website*
3711 East Road
Denman Island, V0R 1T0
Toll free: 1-877-334-4433
Tel: (250) 335-1864
www.bientostado.ca
coffee@island.net
Elaine Head and Steven
Carballeira

Cowppuccino Café
*café • open in summer only • call for
dates and times*
5590 East Road
Denman Island, V0R 1T0
Tel: (250) 335-2195
Evelyn Martins

☕

Denman Island Chocolate
*factory not open to the public • chocolate
available though Vancouver Island retailers*
Site 136, C5
Denman Island, V0R 1T0
Tel: (250) 335-2418
Fax: (250) 335-0112
www.denmanislandchocolate.com
info@denmanislandchocolate.com
Ruth and Daniel Terry

East Cider Orchard
*orchard • apple and cider sales on site in
season and through Granville Island, East
Vancouver and Courtenay Farmers' Markets*
2831 East Road
Denman Island, V0R 1T0
Tel: (250) 335-2294
decosson@mars.ark.com
Anne de Cosson and Larry Berg

Jacquie's Ices
*ice-cream stand • open in summer only
• call for dates and times*
Gravelly Bay
Denman Island
Tel: (250) 335-2199
Jacquie Barnett

Windy Marsh Farm
*farm not open to the public • farmstand
open daily in season*
8700 Owl Crescent
Denman Island, V0R 1T0
Tel: (250) 335-1252
Bob and Velda Parsons

☕

Hornby Island

The Flower Lady
*flowers and produce available at the
Hornby Island Farmers' Market (see listing)*
Hornby Island
Tel: (250) 335-0987
Anna MacKay

Hornby Island Co-op
grocery store
Central Road
Hornby Island, V0R 1Z0
Tel: (250) 335-1121
Phoebe Long, manager

Hornby Island Farmers' Market
*farmers' market Wednesdays and
Saturdays in season, 11 a.m. to 2 p.m.*
behind the Community Hall
Hornby Island

Savoie Farm
farm not open to the public • flowers and produce available at the Hornby Island Farmers' Market (see listing) • flowers also sold from a stand across from the Cardboard House Bakery
2-7 Carmichael Road
Hornby Island, V0R 1Z0
Tel: (250) 335-0276
Elaine and Mary Savoie

The Sushi Lady
sushi available at the Hornby Island Farmers' Market (see listing)
Hornby Island
Tel: (250) 335-0399
Tania Hale

☕

NORTH ISLAND
Cumberland
Auchterlonie's Bakery
2747 Dunsmuir Avenue
Cumberland, V0R 1S0
Tel: (250) 336-2551
Roberta and John Auchterlonie

☕

Chez Cuisine Kitchen
cooking school • call to reserve
2552 Dunsmuir Avenue
Cumberland, V0R 1S0
Tel: (250) 336-8830
Connie Papin

Hazelmere Farms
farm • farmgate open in season • call ahead for dates and directions
3222 Grant Road
Cumberland, V0R 1S0
Tel: (250) 336-2308
Fax: (250) 339-6676
huawongs@telus.net
Lijen and Sherlene Hua

Courtenay/Black Creek Campbell River
Campbell River Downtown Market
farmers' market Sundays, 10 a.m. to 1 p.m., beginning of June to end of October
Tyee Plaza, Campbell River

Comox Valley Farmers' Market
farmers' market Saturdays, 9 a.m. to noon, mid-April to mid-October
Exhibition Grounds, Headquarters Road, Courtenay
Wednesdays, 9 a.m. to noon, mid-April to mid-October
4th and Duncan, Courtenay

Edible Island Whole Foods Market
grocery store
477 6th Street
Courtenay, V9N 1M4
Tel: (250) 334-3116
Fax: (250) 334-0575
edible@island.net
Sue Tupper, Sue Clark and Jackie Somerville

Natural Pastures Cheese Company
cheese factory not open to the public • on-site retail shop open weekday afternoons
635 McPhee Avenue
Courtenay, V9N 2Z7
Toll free tel: 1-866-244-4422
Tel: (250) 334-4422
Fax: (250) 334-2922
www.naturalpastures.com
naturalpasturescheese@telus.net
Mary Ann Hyndman Smith, Edgar Smith and Rick Adams

On Line Farms
farm stand open in season • call ahead for dates and times • produce sold at the Saturday Comox Valley Farmers' Market (see listing)
5660 Island Highway North
Black Creek, V9J 1T2
Tel: (250) 338-8342
Price Lang and Marjan de Jong

Seaview Game Farm
farm tours and farm shop open daily year-round • call for cooking class schedule
1392 Seaview Road
Black Creek, V9J 1J7
Tel: (250) 337-5182
Cell: (250) 287-6334
www.seaviewgamefarm.com
Michel Rabu, chef/manager

☕

Quadra Island
Bold Point Farmstay
end of Bold Point Road
Quadra Island, V0P 1H0
www.farmstay-ca.com
info@farmstay-ca.com
Tel: (250) 285-2272
Rod Burns and Geraldine Kenny

☕

Quadra Island Farmers' Market
farmers' market Saturdays, 10 a.m. to 2 p.m., first Saturday in May to last Saturday in September
behind the credit union on West Road

☕

Topcliff Farm
farmgate in season • call for dates and times
1181 Topcliff Road
Quadra Island, V0P 1N0
Tel: (250) 285-2343
sitkasil@connected.bc.ca
Linda Lessard and John Kragen

Cortes Island
Cortes Café
café open during Cortes Island Farmers' Market (see listing)
Manson's Hall
corner of Sutil Point Road and Beasley Road

Cortes Island Farmers' Market
farmers' market Fridays, 12:30 to 3:30 p.m., year-round
Manson's Hall
corner of Sutil Point Road and Beasley Road

Hollyhock
educational retreat and restaurant
end of Highfield Road
Cortes Island
Box 127, Manson's Landing
Cortes Island, V0P 1K0
www.hollyhock.ca
Tel: 1-800-933-6339
Debra Fontaine, head chef

L.J.'s Kitchen
caterer • products available at the Cortes Island Farmers' Market (see listing)
Tel: (250) 935-6838
Lisa Jo Osland

Reef Point Farm
bed & breakfast
end of Sutil Point Road
Cortes Island, V0P 1K0
Tel: (250) 935-6797
Ginnie and Bruce Ellingsen

Ruby's Homemade Ice Cream
producer • product available on site and at the Cortes Island Farmers' Market (see listing)
482 Smelt Bay Road
Smelt Bay
Cortes Island, V0P 1K0
Tel: (250) 935-6404
Ruby and John Gordon

The Tak
café
800 Sutil Point Road
Cortes, V0P 1K0
Tel: (250) 935-8555
scottkennedymercs@hotmail.com
Scott Mercs

WEST COAST
Ucluelet/Tofino
Clayoquot Organics
farm not open to the public • produce available at Salal's Co-op Grocery, Tofino
Tofino
Tel: (250) 725-3967
mmacleod@island.net
Melanie MacLeod

The Goat Lady
farm not open to the public • visit by prior appointment only
Westerly Wynds Farm
P.O. Box 1029
Ucluelet, V0R 3A0
Tel: (250) 726-2682
Jane Hunt

Oyster Jim
producer • oyster sales on site
P.O. Box 947
2480 Pacific Rim Highway
Ucluelet, V0R 3A0
Tel: (250) 726-7350
Jim Martin

Raincoast Café
restaurant • dinner year-round
101-120 Fourth Street
Tofino, V0R 2Z0
Tel: (250) 725-2215
www.raincoastcafe.com
raincafe@island.net
Lisa Henderson and Larry Nicolay

Ralph the Veggie Man
grocery store
1701 Peninsula Road
Ucluelet, V0R 3A0
Tel: (250) 726-7425
Shirley Banks

Salals Co-op Grocery & Café
grocery store
150 4th Street
Tofino, V0R 2Z0
Tel: (250) 725-2728
Corinne Murray, manager

Sobo Global Cuisine
behind Beaches Grocery
1184 Pacific Rim Highway
Tofino
Tel: (250) 725-2341
Arte and Lisa Ahier

Tofino Brew House and Wild Fish Restaurant
brew house and restaurant
150 4th Street
Tofino, V0R 2Z0
tbp@island.net
Tel: (250) 725-1254
James Rodgers, manager

Trilogy Fish Company
fish store
Box 327, 630 Campbell Street
Tofino, V0R 2Z0
Tel: (250) 725-2233
Fax: (250) 725-2234
www.trilogyfish.com
info@trilogyfish.com
John and Donna Fraser

The Wickaninnish Inn
restaurant and inn
Osprey Lane at Chesterman Beach
Tofino, V0R 2Z0
Tel: (250) 725-3100
Fax: (250) 725-3110
www.wickinn.com
info@wickinn.com
Charles McDiarmid, manager
Michael Bebault, chef de cuisine

The inexhaustible hunter-gatherer Elizabeth Levinson writes the column "At My Table" in *Focus on Women* magazine and is the author of *Getting Fresh In and Around Victoria: The Guide to Going Organic.*